Through the Eyes of a Fisherman

A Journey of Faith, Fishing and Friendship

Dennis Blue

Through the Eyes
of a Fisherman

A Journey of Faith
Fishing and Friendship

"Come follow me," Jesus said, "and I will make you fishers of men."
— Mark 1:17

Dedication

To the people I have come to know and the friendships I have made through fishing. "If you wish to know a person's true character, take them fishing," Dennis Blue.

Acknowledgements

To my family and friends who encouraged and supported my efforts to write *Through the Eyes of a Fisherman*. Special thanks to my editor and publisher, Denis Ledoux, who brought my recollections to life through his editing skills, patience and insight and for bringing my book to publication. Thanks to Sally Lunt who did an amazing job with the book cover, layout, and photos. Finally, to Chris Madsen who provided her expertise in proofreading. Without the help of these amazing people at The Memoir Network, this book would not have been possible.

Contents

Chapter 1
From Ford to Fishing

It had only been two-weeks since my retirement from Ford on March 1, 1988, not long enough for me to fully realize that I was now embarking on a career as owner and operator of my own business, True Blue Charters. My wife, Dorothy, and I were busy packing again, not the entire household with furniture and all, as with our former relocations around the world for Ford, but only what we would need to be comfortable for a six-month stay at our condo across Michigan in Onekama as I launched myself in business. It was time-consuming work nonetheless as just enough seasonal clothes and personal items that would assure our comfort had to be sorted to take from our home in Northville. Our daughter, Luanne, and son, Dennis, ages twenty-one and nineteen respectively, were now in college and working part time and would continue to use our house in Northville as their residence during the summer when not visiting Onekama.

We had bought the Onekama condo in 1984 while I was still at Ford and had kept our base in Northville. Now Onekama, two-hundred miles and a four-hour drive to the north, would be our residence from April through October, during the charter fishing season. After four years of recreational fishing out of Onekama, I was about to launch a sports fishing company.

During the year leading up to this move, Dorothy and I had spent much time in prayer as we contem-

Dennis and Dorothy, 1988

plated my taking an early retirement from Ford— my leaving was completely voluntary—and stepping out on faith to pursue a dream of starting a charter fishing business. While the charter business would be mine alone, it did involve Dorothy as it would affect her life in a big way. It didn't seem logical to many of my peers at Ford that I would give up potential career advancement and increased compensation and retirement benefits and embark on an uncertain future—albeit one financed by my retirement income. A few close friends in management confided that they admired me for my decision and wished me luck. For Dorothy and me there was no uncertainty. As had happened many times in the past, we saw God open doors that created the opportunity for me to retire early with full benefits.[1]

As Dorothy and I were packing, the phone rang. It was Hunter Pickens, my friend and former boss at Ford-Asia Pacific in Melbourne, Australia, who was now working for Ford in Dearborn. "I want to be the first to officially book a charter," he insisted, and we decided on a May 28 trip. Hunter said he had to hurry to a meeting and we would talk more on the charter. Then he hung up. I turned to Dorothy, who was standing nearby listening to my brief conversation and gave her a big hug.

"We are on our way, sweetheart," I exclaimed. "This is the first of many charters."

Dorothy, who was also close friends with Hunter, was as excited as I. She said, as she continued sorting through our things and putting them in the "stay" or "go" piles, "Hunter's phone call seems to make the work of packing so much easier!"

We both laughed as I recorded the date in my charter log. Who would have predicted, I mused as Dorothy and I continued packing, that in six years from when my overseas time had come to an end in 1982, I would be retired and chartering would become the course of our lives. God, of course, already knew where He wanted me to be in March 1988 and now only God knew how the venture would proceed.

You might say that I had been preparing to launch True Blue Charters all my life. My passion for fishing began during my early years in the muddy ponds, creeks and rivers around Flat Rock, Michigan, where I grew up on a farm. After graduating

---

[1] See my previous book, *Running the Good Race*, Chapter 15, page 403.

from Michigan State University, I moved in with my parents who were living on Grosse Ile, an island in the Detroit River near Lake Erie. There my passion for fishing and boating continued to grow. During the next twenty-five years, working as an ex-pat for Ford Motor Company, I got to fish in waters around the world—Venezuela, Brazil, Australia, New Zealand.

By nature, I think fisherman have an affinity for God's creation, a love for the outdoors and the creatures that inhabit it. Fishing at dawn with the sun rising, I was so often taken with the beauty of the world, a truly religious experience for me. "For since the creation of the world, God's power and invisible qualities—his eternal power and divine nature—have been clearly seen, being understood from what has been made so that people are without excuse" Ro 1:20. Over the years, I had found many opportunities to use fishing as a means to witness to those around me about Christ, either by word or deed. I have always been inspired that the first four disciples chosen by Christ, Peter, Andrew, James and John, were fishermen. Christ invited them, "Come, follow me, and I will make you fishers of men." Mk 1:17

Following our return to the US from Brazil in June 1982, Dorothy and I had bought a home in Northville, Michigan, about twenty-five miles north of Ford World Headquarters, in Dearborn, where I would continue working until February 26, 1988. Upon returning, we had also purchased a new 31-foot Tiara sport fisherman, which we named, of course, *True Blue*. I chose to dock our new boat at a marina in Gibraltar, a small village on Lake Erie about two miles from Grosse Ile, where I had lived with my parents during the late 1950s and 1960s. While Gibraltar was forty miles from our home in Northville, docking there was worth the drive. I had many memories of duck hunting in the marshes around Gibraltar and Rockwood, where my dad taught school before I was born, in the early 1920s, and of my early years working with Ford at the Monroe plant. In addition, friends told me boating and fishing the Detroit River and Lake Erie were even better now than when I lived on Grosse Ile thirty odd years earlier.

Dorothy, Luanne and Dennis enjoyed boating around my old haunts around Grosse Ile and cruising Lake Erie and Lake Huron that first summer of 1982. The fishing was what I was after, and what I found was sufficient, but then the salmon bug bit us—bit me, that is. Dorothy and the kids were content with an occasional weekend cruise on *True Blue* and catching perch and walleye in Lake Erie, but as much as I enjoyed fishing on Lake Erie, I was also aware that I was missing something. I was hearing there was world-class salmon fishing in Lake Michigan on the west side of the state, and this did not exist in Lake Erie. In the summer of 1982, I made a few fishing trips with friends to Lake Michigan and was smitten with salmon fishing. In 1983, Dorothy agreed with me to make the switch to the western shore of Michigan, and we had *True Blue* transported over the highway to Frankfort, two hundred miles north of our home in Northville. Frankfort was one of the premier salmon-fishing ports on Lake Michigan.

Salmon were not indigenous to Lake Michigan.

They were introduced in 1959 from the Pacific coast to control the alewife population. This was nine years prior to my leaving for Venezuela. Until my return from overseas in 1982, I had never fished for salmon, but that summer, I began to enjoy the sport. Consequently, in 1983, we travelled to Frankfort from Northville every summer weekend and used *True Blue* as our "condo on the water." Dennis, Luanne and I were catching salmon on every outing, but Dorothy fished only occasionally. She preferred steering the boat, making lunch and enjoying the experience.

The salmon fishing out of Frankfort was even better than I had expected, but there was one negative—the boat traffic was heavy on the weekends. We didn't care much for dodging other fishermen while fighting a large salmon. Since the weekend was the only time we could be there, the congestion was a big negative. One Saturday in August, Dorothy and I counted over two-hundred fishing boats within our sight! When I complained to a dock mate about this, he recommended we move on to Onekama, a small Lake-Michigan port thirty-five miles south of Frankfort. The fishing there, he told us, was excellent, and the boat traffic was much lighter than in Frankfort.

In the fall, Dorothy and I visited Onekama, a village of about four-hundred residents located on Portage Lake with easy access to Lake Michigan. We fell in love with the town and the general area. But, could we find good docking and storage facilities? After talking to the owner of Onekama Marine, Jim Mrozinski, I knew we had a hit and we booked both winter storage for *True Blue* and a boat slip for the summer of 1984. That winter, Dorothy and Luanne were clear that they had had enough of our "condo on the water" accommodations, and it was time to find some land-based home. When we next returned to Onekama in the spring, Dorothy and I bought a chalet in the Pirates Cove Condo Association. Our new summer residence was right next to Onekama Marine,

Onekama Marine and Pirates Cove Condos

where we were docking our boat. Now the non-fishermen—or should I say non-fisherwoman—could sleep in while the anglers—Dennis, Luanne and myself—went about having our fun.

During the six years between returning to the US and my retirement, I had taken many friends and family fishing for walleye, perch and now salmon. Taking people out was not a new experience, and I thought the big difference between then and now that I was launching True Blue Charters was that I would be paid for my effort. I was soon to learn there were many differences between having fun taking friends fishing and having a customer pay you for your expertise in order to have you produce results. When fun fishing with friends, if they were not catching fish, I could always fall back on "you should have been here yesterday." This quip no longer worked. A paying customer wants to know, "What are you going to do today so that I land a good catch?" Fishing for fun and fishing as a business are akin to cooking hotdogs on a grill and serving as an executive chef at the Waldorf Astoria.

True Blue, my thirty-one-foot Tiara which I had purchased in 1982 without any thought of establish-

ing a fishing company, was a l r e a d y equipped with e l e c t r o n i c s, d o w n r i g g e r s and fishing tackle for salmon. Be-yond this equipment, I still had a lot

True Blue, a 31-ft. Tiara, Onekama, 1988

missing for a viable company— and right up there was learning to establish and run a charter busi-ness. Apart from the fishing, there are marketing, ob-taining commercial insurance and licenses and preparing for and passing safety inspections from the United States Coast Guard and State of Michigan— just to name a few of the tasks I now had to master. I was soon to realize the transition from a corporate background with its vast resources at my disposal to being a sole proprietor where the buck would stop with me was a daunting change. For the first time in years, I was out of my comfort zone. I was twenty-four years old, when I joined Ford, and I had thirty years to hone my skills and build my reputation. I was now fifty-five as I embarked on a new career which I thought I understood, but now I know I really didn't.

In short order, it struck me that, at my age, I had a steep learning curve if I was going to survive as a profitable business. Charter fishing is hard work, physically and mentally. You could say it called for age-appropriate responses. And as with professional athletes, whose careers are determined by the physical demands of their profession, so too did I understand that my success would be limited by my ability to execute physical responses. At the "young" age of fifty-five, many charter captains are thinking retirement and not starting a new business. While I was physically fit for my age— "for my age" being an operative concept! —and had no doubt about being able to perform the duties of a charter captain for the foreseeable future, nevertheless, I decided to established a short trial period of two to three years to prove to myself that I was up to the task physically and that I could establish a fiscally sound business within my self-imposed deadline.

If I could not succeed in that time, then what?

I was about to find out.

My biggest challenge was defining my business goals and aligning it with my ministry. As for "defining my business goals," I took inventory of the skills I had acquired over thirty years in the corporate world: making quick and complex decisions, planning business processes and growth, reading a balance sheet, evaluating return on investment and wielding people skills. I determined many of the skills I had acquired at Ford were valuable, but I was still not sure how to apply them to a one-man operation.

21

There were no corporate policies, audit requirements or higher-level approvals to guide my decisions; my opinion was the only one to direct action. Learning from my mistakes instead of applying company policy was now how I would learn to operate—and I hoped to learn fast enough not to "sink the boat."

There were some even less tangible but crucial skills—perhaps you could call it attitude—that I had picked up: having a passion for what I did, giving one-hundred and ten percent to every effort, conducting myself always with honesty and integrity. I knew these attributes would be essential in running my own, or any other, business.

Using my existing skills, I developed a balance sheet and business plan for True Blue Charters. I calculated I needed around twenty charters to break even and cover my expenses with my income. I knew from my own experience as a boat owner and talking to other captains that the fixed cost of a charter business—dockage, storage, insurance, boat payments and licenses—was high. Variable costs—fuel, wages on a per-trip basis, fishing gear and maintenance—varied by number of charters and even by charter. Income was determined using my charter rates for a one-half day (five-hour) and a full-day (eight-hour) and multiplying that rate by the number of each charter I ran. With a relatively short season of four to five months, knowing that I needed a minimum of twenty to break even, I set as my goal to run thirty charters to ensure an operating profit: income from charters less fixed and variable costs. In addition to profit, thirty charters would assure a steady cash flow. The established charter businesses were running forty to sixty charters per season. I hoped I could eventually achieve these numbers, but for the first season, thirty seemed a realistic goal. Having my Ford pension to fall back on provided a financial cushion, but I had decided, if I couldn't cover my expenses and pay myself a nominal wage after two to three years, I was in the wrong business and God didn't want me there. If a large income was my goal, I could have stayed at Ford where I would make more in a few months than I could chartering all year!

My goals certainly included being solvent with True Blue Charters as it was important to achieving a larger purpose—to align with my life ministry. I wanted to use my fishing business as a ministry to witness to those around me just as I had done during my thirty years at Ford. I had long known that my passion for fishing was much like my erstwhile passion for flying which had enabled me to serve as a mission pilot for New Tribes Mission in Venezuela. The plane was only a means to an end. My passion for fishing was also the same. I intended to use my boat, *True Blue*, as a means to be God's ambassador and to witness to those around me about Christ.

Since that first summer of 1984, when we first docked the boat at Onekama Marine, it had been my home port where I had a boat slip and stored my boat and from which I now proposed to operate my business. By 1988, I had established myself as a reliable and respectful customer, so I felt I had some basis to approaching Jim Mrozinski with a proposal to use the dock as a business landing. Portage Lake Marina, directly across Portage Lake from Onekama Marine, had already established itself as the charter-boat marina on Portage Lake and already had nine charter boats docked there. I could, of course, join the "charter fleet" at Portage Lake Marina, but I didn't want to leave Onekama Marine. Walking the one-hundred yards from our chalet at Pirates Cove to where my boat was docked was too good to give up. In addition, I liked the marina and had friends there.

I understood from a dock mate that, during the early years of Onekama Marine's more than twenty-five years of operation, there were charter boats docked there. After a year or two, they were asked to leave due to the complaints of the other boat owners. When I broached the subject of basing my business at his dock, Jim, not wanting the marina to depart from its family orientation, was hesitant to agree. He was concerned, as had happened in the past, that a charter business would create issues with extra parking, noisy day customers and congestion at the fish-cleaning station. I assured Jim I would be mindful of complaints and rectify them as necessary. I also pointed out seventy percent of the boats in the marina were those of fishermen. There was already noise from boats starting their engines at five a.m. and a crowded fish-cleaning station. I would be returning from a half-day charter between ten and eleven a.m. before the recreational fisherman returned at mid-day and so would not be adding to the crowd at the fish cleaning station or changing the prevailing ambiance in the marina. Jim ultimately agreed to let me run my charters from Onekama Marine. It was a decision that would benefit both of us. When I told Dorothy about how Jim acquiesced, I winked at her and said, "Actually, what choice did

Jim have? God had already decided this was where I was going to run my charter business."

Both because I needed to know the other nine captains on Portage Lake and because I wanted to support the Portage Lake Charter Boat Association, I became a member of the organization in June 1988. The other member captains welcomed me from day one and freely shared information on fishing the area. These charter captains came from a wide range of backgrounds: a jewelry store owner, two motel owners, a grocery store owner, a union chairman, a university professor, an insurance broker, a school teacher and a full-time fisherman. Even though I was still learning to fish salmon, my exploits as an international fisherman helped give me creditability with my new peers. I was also able to use some of my Ford experience to help organize and plan events for the association. It is important to note that all but two of the charter captains in our association—me and Jim Bennett, the full-time fisherman—had other occupations. The high overhead costs and short season made it difficult to earn enough income to live on and raise a family. Jim had already expanded his business to Florida to provide a year-round income, which I did not need to do as I had my Ford pension to fall back on.

Both Jim Bennett and Kevin Hughes, two of the first captains I met in 1988 after joining the Portage Lake Charter Boat Association, helped me immensely in growing my charter business, and I valued their opinions then and now.

My first tutor, Jim Bennett, in his mid-fifties, tall and athletic and always tanned, was one of the pioneers of salmon fishing in Lake Michigan and the Manistee River. He was already a legend when I met him in 1988. In 1996, he was inducted into the Freshwater Fishing Hall of Fame located in Minneapolis, Minnesota. During the winter of 1986, Jim had started a fishing business in Islamorada, Florida, in addition to his salmon charter business in Onekama. That summer of 1988, as I was launching my business, he encouraged me to consider charter fishing in Florida, especially because of my saltwater fishing experience overseas.

"One thing at a time," I told Jim. "I'm still learning to catch salmon." Maybe in the future, I thought, not realizing how fast the future would be upon me.

My second tutor, Kevin Hughes, was a school teacher in Flint when I first met him in 1988. I found him to be a pleasant young man in his mid-twenties who loved to fish. His dad had a vacation home in Onekama where Kevin had spent his summers with his family and had "learned the ropes" by working as a first mate on a charter boat. He was an experienced salmon fisherman by the time we met and was always willing to share information on salmon fishing with me. Our friendship was more of a father/son relationship due to our twenty -five-year difference in age but from an experience standpoint I was the apprentice. Over time, he moved to Onekama where he became superintendent of the Onekama Public School system and ran charters in the summer from his own charter boat. As coincidence would have it, Kevin's dad, Howard, and I played baseball against each other in college—he at University of Detroit and I at Michigan State University.

As mentioned earlier, salmon had been introduced into Lake Michigan in 1959 to control the alewife population. The alewife, a herring native to the Atlantic Ocean, had entered the Great Lakes through the Welland Canal, a key section of the St. Lawrence Seaway. They did so during the 1950s and, later in the decade, without natural predators, had surged in population. Summer die-offs would produce millions of dead alewives polluting the beaches of the Great Lakes. At its worst in the mid-1950s, rotten fish were bulldozed into dump trucks and carried off. Salmon are a natural predator of the alewives and so numerous hatcheries were built around the Great Lakes in the ensuing years to increase the salmon population. This eventually balanced the predator/prey ratio necessary to maintain a healthy fishery. Today hatchery production is down by more than fifty percent as natural reproduction of salmon in the Great Lakes has increased significantly. Born-in-the wild salmon now account for approximately seventy percent of the population. Based on 2016 data, the charter industry for all species of fish contributed seventeen-million dollars to the Michigan economy.

In April 1988, as soon as the ice was out on Portage Lake, I put *True Blue* in the water so as to have plenty of time to ready the boat and the fishing gear for my first salmon season as a charter captain. During the time before the season opened, I booked several more charters for later. I also fished several times a week with friends and my new first mate, a high school senior in Onekama, to ensure I was ready for my first paid charter on May 28, 1988, with

Hunter Pickens. His trip was "for real." Despite fishing several years with friends, this would be my first paid charter. I didn't want anything to go wrong. My first mate and I were excited as we had prepared well and were ready for the beginning of my new career.

When the big day finally arrived, my first mate and I were at the boat by five a.m. to ensure everything was ready for our five-thirty a.m. departure. At five-fifteen. I saw Hunter and his two-sons walking down the dock where I greeted them with a big hug. I would occasionally see Hunter at Ford before I retired but hadn't seen him in about a year. After chatting a minute, but not wanting to lose time on the water, we shoved off on the beginning of a new adventure in my life. Hunter and I had a great time together as we knew we would. We reminisced about Australia and how blessed we had been over the

Dennis, on right, with customer, 1988

years. The kids caught a half-dozen salmon and were thrilled. What a great way to kick off my new career!

Overall, my first summer as a charter captain went well. I ran a total of twenty-eight charters, most of them with people I knew. A small number of customers came by referrals from friends or other charter captains. I also added a few trips, gratis, for family or as fund raisers for local organizations such as the Lion's Club and our Portage Lake Charter Boat Association. I had not yet been able to do the kind of marketing and advertising of my business to see much result beyond these bookings. I hoped more charters would come the following season from mailing brochures, word of mouth and winter boat shows.

The most important lesson I learned during that first season was paying attention to detail. Much as when I was flying I had performed essential pre-flight checks to ensure a safe flight, I needed a checklist to follow before starting *True Blue*'s engine. On one occasion, when my customers arrived at dock at five a.m. ready to depart, I realized I had failed to have enough fuel to run the charter. Fortunately, Jim, the owner of the marina, showed up at six a.m. and personally fueled my boat. (Not a good way to impress the marina owner after he reluctantly agreed to let me base my charter business at his marina!) Another time, my first mate forgot to check fishing lines following a trip and the next morning three big salmon broke free because of frayed fishing lines. Unfortunately, they were the only three fish my anglers had a shot at reeling in on that day. It was more than embarrassing as it showed a lack of professionalism on my part. As captain, the buck stops with me. It would have been easy to blame the first mate, but after all, I was the one who had trained him. When the second fish broke off, I told the unhappy angler that I suspected a frayed line and immediately checked and replaced other lines that were frayed. Unfortunately, a third fish broke off after I had checked the lines. Perhaps it was one I had missed?

Fortunately, these customers were understanding and they semi-accepted my apology for lack of attention to detail. They felt much better after we arrived back at the dock and I said there was no charge for the trip. A little good will goes a long way as this group became regular customers. The list of mishaps is longer, but you get the idea. While I never had a written checklist for the boat as I did for the plane, I learned to follow an exact routine immediately after each charter (check fuel, holding tank, and fishing tackle, and then clean the boat) and the following morning (check for ice, running lights, electronics, proper lures). I also continually reminded my first mate to ensure everything was in order without my having to ask. On the plus side, we also had a few great catches with customers. Sometimes, I even surprised myself and my fellow charter captains, but of course, I never let on.

Dorothy was the consummate wife, mother and manager of our household. We both knew, without her strong will and independence, we couldn't have pursued the life we had with Ford overseas. However, she was now content to let me do my own thing with the fishing business. Throughout our married life, we have experienced answer to prayer. God had never let us down, and we were confident this change in careers would be no different. Dorothy and I consulted with one another often, and I valued her input, but truth be told, she did not enjoy fishing. Dorothy's main interest was that, in our new life, we were doing God's will, and in that, she was confident. In our previous moves when overseas with Ford,

Dorothy and I were in unfamiliar territory, new cultures, languages and few friends. Our dependence on each other was essential to function as a family. Now it was different, this was the good old USA and Onekama was home, I could survive on my own as Dorothy pursued her own interests. While at times I could have used her help with scheduling charters, following up on inquires and running to the bank or post office, I preferred she be free to pursue her own activities. Not that she didn't help out, which she did on occasion, but this was my baby. She could take care of hers on the golf course.

Another carry over from my Ford days was keeping good records. From the day of my first charter, I began taking notes. I recorded information—name, address, phone number, email address, names of children—and anything else that would make our relationship more personal. I also took photos on each charter and group pictures of the family and their catch. In December, I sent out my first newsletter to each customer with photos included, being sure to mention names of customers and notable incidents such as first or biggest fish. Several customers wrote back to thank me for the newsletter, while others mentioned it when booking their next charter. I didn't recognize it at the time but this first step to personalize my business would become the foundation of my success.

After my first season ended in October and the boat was placed in storage, I made an assessment of my progress toward my self-imposed two-year goal. If my first year was any indication, I was ahead of schedule. I had run enough charters to make a small profit, my customers were pleased with the fishing experience and some had already booked for the coming year. Apart from small glitches, there were no major problems that caused me to re-evaluate my business plan. Listening to some of the problems other captains had to deal with, I concluded I was either very lucky or very good at what I was doing.

During the fall and winter, Dorothy and I split our time between Onekama and Northville. We still maintained our contacts at church and with friends in Northville. Dorothy commuted to Northville every week or so during the summer to see the Luanne and Dennis, play golf at Washtenaw Country Club, where we had joined upon our return from Brazil in 1982 and to visit with her brother and sister-in-law, Ron and Ina Hacker, who lived just a few blocks from us in Northville.

At the same time, our social circle and interests

Ina and Ron Hacker, 1988

were expanding in Onekama. Dorothy and I had attended the Covenant Church in Manistee when we could in the summer. Dorothy was making new friends on the local golf courses around the area, and I was busy with the charter boat association on projects such as expanding our customer base and helping out as a board member at Onekama Marine. Luanne and Dennis, while still living at home in Northville, were pretty much on their own with work and social activities. They had also liked joining us in Onekama whenever they could. With Ron and Ina living close by and Dorothy's short trips back to Northville, Luanne and Dennis—now young adults— had help and oversight when they needed it.

Dorothy and I discussed the possibility of one day selling our home in Northville and moving to a bigger house in Onekama. The condo was basically a summer home. It had approximately one-thousand square feet on two floors with a kitchen, two baths and three small bedrooms—all the rooms too small to make the condo a year-round residence. We had upgraded the insulation and had installed a new fuel oil furnace to make the condo comfortable for visits during the winter. Staying there was okay for a few days, but the house was definitely not a year-round residence given our cold Michigan climate, when the temperature occasionally drops to near zero degrees Fahrenheit. Little did we realize at the time that having a smaller summer place in Onekama would work out just fine in the not too distant future.

Looking back, I realize my first charter season was more like fishing with family and friends. With only this experience to draw from, chartering was going to be a piece of cake, I thought. I had yet to experience the difficulties that come from some of the less desirable customers whose rowdy behavior and excessive drinking would prove to be a challenge.

After a successful and enjoyable 1988 charter season, I concluded, "What could go wrong?" I was about to find out. "Pride cometh before destruction." Pro. 16:18

Through the Eyes of a Fisherman

Chapter 2
Learning to be a
Charter Captain

It was a snowy evening in December 1988. Dorothy and I had just finished dinner at our home when I received a call from a Ford executive. The company was negotiating the sale of Philco-Ford Brazil and my expertise in the negotiations were much needed. Since I had worked at Philco-Ford Brazil prior to my retirement in March 1988, the on-site managing director had specifically requested me to come to Brazil to help with the compensation and benefit negotiations.

I was at a loss for words. The thought of returning to Brazil—and to Ford as an independent —had never entered my mind. Ford offered a six-to-nine-month contract at my previous salary with all expenses paid. This was generous. I would only travel to Brazil as necessary and would maintain an office at the Ford World Headquarters in Dearborn using Ford staff for administrative assistance.

My first thought was, "Thanks for thinking of me, but no thanks." Having worked on Ford staff before I retired, I felt comfortable saying, "It is the furthest thing from my mind, but let me talk it over with Dorothy and I'll call you in the morning." Dorothy was as surprised as I when I told her. Apart from the fishing shows I was exhibiting at to attract new charter clients, winter was a slow time of the year. The money would be good, and six to nine months of occasional travel with office work in Dearborn was not a long-term commitment. I had to admit talking about Philco-Ford Brazil and my time working in Brazil rekindled my enthusiasm for the corporate life I once lived so successfully and for the upcoming negotiations which would place me once again in the midst of a fray. If I accepted, this work would be like old times. I also was flattered that my expertise as a troubleshooter and negotiator was still in demand at Ford.

"Why don't you go? I know you would enjoy it," Dorothy said, after we talked this a bit.

That was all I needed to hear. The next day, I signed a six-month contract in Dearborn and was on my way back to Brazil by the end of the week. The trip rekindled a spark in me that I thought had been extinguished. I wondered, "Had I retired too soon? Was this the life I still wanted?" I was about to find out!

In the coming months, I made three trips of about ten days each to Sao Paulo. During the last trip, in June 1989, an agreement was reached with Itautec, a Brazilian banking and investment firm and following government approval, it was signed the following October.

Negotiating the sale of Philco-Ford Brazil was bittersweet. Seeing old friends I had worked with and reliving the past brought back fond memories of my time there—and the family's—from 1978 until we returned to the US in 1982. I drove by our former house in Morumbi, the soccer stadium where Dennis and I saw many games and Calvary International Church where our friend, Bill Fawcett, had been pastor. Mario, the son of our former maid, Maria, was still working at Philco-Ford Brazil where I had gotten him a job, but Maria had retired and I wasn't able to contact her due to my short stays.

Participating in the negotiations reminded me of the sale of Ford Tractor in 1986 and Ford Aerospace in 1987. I had represented Ford interests and, at the same time, had advocated for Ford employees to receive the best compensation and benefits possible from the new owners. The 1988–89 Brazil negotiation posed a particular concern as Philco-Ford Brazil was the company that I helped to grow by launching a new plant in Manaus. Because of that involvement, I knew and worked with many of the Philco-Ford Brazil employees in Manaus. For the most part, employee interests were protected during the sale and I felt comfortable with the compensation and benefits we had negotiated with Itautec.

When I returned home after my first trip to Sao Paulo, I thanked Dorothy for encouraging me to go. I was glad I had taken the assignment. By the time of my third and last trip to Sao Paulo in June, however, I told Dorothy I now knew this was my last assignment with Ford. I didn't want to give up the freedom of running my own fishing business and being out of doors for a return to the corporate life. I had needed that one last negotiation to know for sure it was time to cut my ties with the past. I had the same feeling and assurance I experienced when I stepped outside of my comfort zone and left Ford to pursue my passion as a charter captain. An assurance that I was fulfilling God's purpose. Any doubt I had about retirement was gone. God had never been wrong before and He wasn't this time. My transformation from the corporate man to the charter captain had received a big boost, and I was now focused on the future and what God had in store for me in the fishing business.

Between trips to Brazil, in the winter of 1989, I travelled to fishing shows at Detroit, Cincinnati,

Dennis at fishing show, 1989

South Bend, Toledo and Fort Wayne to market True Blue Charters. The Cincinnati Show at the five-hundred thousand square foot Albert B. Sabin Convention Center was the largest out-door-sportsman show in the Midwest. The shows provided an opportunity for me to book as many charters as I could, given the time allotted, and to meet fishing tackle manufacturers and other captains. One of the big advantages of the shows was to meet prospective customers face to face. Exchanging information and getting to know each other made the selection process for both me and the customer so much easier than over the phone. Based upon US Coast Guard regulations, charter boats can take up to a maximum of six passengers. When customers were booking, I encouraged them to limit the size of their group to four people as there would be more room on the boat and more turns catching fish. On occasion, especially with families, I would agree to take the maximum of six passengers.

These outdoor-sportsman shows were also a great way to network among businesses. Several of the fishing tackle companies became sponsors of *True Blue* to promote their products. Two charter boat captains, Frank English, owner of a small grocery store near Onekama, and Bill Browne, a professor at Central Michigan University, and I did fishing shows and charters together in those early years. Bill had contacts with the University that led to several group charters with faculty. Frank eventually went on to become president of the Michigan Charter Boat Association in 2003, and we still serve together on the Portage Lake Harbor Commission. Tragically, Bill died from leukemia in 1995 after a long illness. We fished together several times, just the two of us, during his illness talking about friends and family and our faith in Christ. He was a great fishing buddy, and I miss him.

Winters in Onekama can be filled with fun and excitement. Average temperatures in the mid-twenties Fahrenheit and average snowfall of two to four inches are perfect for skiing, snowmobiling and ice fishing. With fishing shanties scattered around the ice, Portage Lake can resemble a small village.

In an effort to market member charter businesses to a larger audience, The Portage Lake Charter Boat Association started a first of its kind spoon manufacturer's tournament in May 1989. Dating back to the early 1800s, spoons are oval metal stampings, concave on one side to produce a wobble when pulled through the water. A spoon is designed to imitate a fleeing bait fish, one to eight inches in length and painted in a variety of colors. They are by far the most popular artificial bait used by fishermen. Each charter boat in The Portage Lake Charter Boat Association was assigned a manufacturer and that charter boat had to use only the spoons of the manufacturer assigned to it. The motive behind this, of course, was the publicity we hoped the manufacturers and the association would generate and which would bring us more business.

The first year was a big success with seventeen spoon manufacturers from around the Great Lakes participating. We even had to bring seven charter boats from nearby Manistee and Frankfort to fish the tournament with us as we only had ten charter boat members in the Portage Lake Charter Boat Association. Media coverage leading up to and following the tournament was excellent with articles in the Detroit News and other newspapers in Michigan. Winning the tournament and the Golden Spoon Award proved to be a valuable marketing tool both for the manufacturers and for the charter boats. The tournament as a whole also proved the Association could pull the charter companies along with it and so proved the value of membership.

Now for the story behind the story. The charter boat association had received a tournament registration form and several spoon samples from a company called Tyson Lures, located in Minneapolis, Minnesota. None of the charter captains had heard of Tyson Lures nor seen the strange looking Sudden Ambush spoon that resembled a tie clip. After discussion, none of the captains wanted to fish the strange looking "tie clip" they had never seen or heard of before. Not wanting to leave any willing company out and since I had the lowest seniority of the resident captains, I saw this as my chance to pay my dues and I volunteered to fish

Sudden Ambush spoon

with Larry Tyson, the owner and manufacturer of the Sudden Ambush spoon.

Much to everyone's surprise, Larry flew to the tournament from his home in Minneapolis to the Manistee Blacker Airport—in his private jet! That surprise created a positive impression among many of the captains but didn't lessen the disdain for this strange looking spoon.

The day of the tournament was the first time I

fished the Sudden Ambush spoon. I was resigned to the fact that it would be a difficult day trying to catch a salmon on a tie clip. The day proved not so distressing as we had two big fish that I would guess were in the fifteen- to twenty-pound range, which was a good weight for spring chinook salmon. By fall, these fish would have weighted in the twenty- to thirty-pound range after another summer of feeding on alewives before returning to the rivers to spawn and die. Of course, I did not know what total poundage others had caught. A crowd of about sixty spectators, mostly family and friends, milled about the post-fishing weigh-in station. Dave Barron, a television personality from Traverse City, was also there to tape the weigh-in for the local news that evening. When people asked how we had done, Larry and I shrugged and said "OK." Some of the other captains snickered, but I paid no attention. Before our turn came to weigh in, we could see there were a few nice catches by other boats.

When it came to us to weigh our catch, our first seven fish were nothing special, averaging twelve pounds. As we placed our eighth fish on the scale, however, an appreciative murmur rose from the crowd and this placed a smile on Larry's face. The ninth and tenth fish were even better and brought applause as both salmon tipped the scale at over fifteen pounds—just as I had surmised! The Sudden Ambush spoon missed first place by less than a pound, and we won biggest fish of the tournament. I looked over at Kevin Hughes and winked.

"Great job, guys," he congratulated us.

As it turned out, Larry owned several successful

businesses and making spoons was just a hobby. Larry and I continued to fish the spoon tournament and several other tournaments on Lake Michigan during the next three years. We never won but were always competitive with the Sudden Ambush spoon. Larry and I became good friends, and he was very generous paying me a retainer to represent this strange looking spoon in tournaments. My standing with my fellow charter boat captains also took a boost because they saw I was more interested in doing what was right for the association rather than for myself. (This approach had also served me well throughout my corporate life.)

Attending the fishing shows the previous winter had paid off: I had forty charters booked for the summer of 1989. Many of these had been booked at the shows. The nature of my clientele was different from that of my previous season when I knew most of my customers personally. Over half of my 1989 charters, however, were first-time customers whom I did not know. How quickly things can change! The first two charters of the season were with new customers, and these proved more or less a disaster. Based on the previous season, I had been lulled into a false sense that all customers are easy to please. I was in for a rude awakening.

The first group of the new customers, consisting of four buddies in their mid-twenties from Ohio, showed up late and hung over from drinking too much alcohol the previous night. To make matters worse, they carried on board a large cooler filled with beer. I hesitated about letting them bring the cooler on the boat but decided not to make it an issue. After all, they were paying customers. We had hardly left the dock when they began opening beers and soon were loud and rowdy. Soon after setting the fishing lines, they wanted to know when the fish were going to start biting, to which I laughed and told them to be patient.

"That's why we call it fishing, not catching," I said.

From the looks on their faces, they didn't think it was funny. Within ten-minutes, they began complaining that the first mate was not putting the right lures on the fishing lines. I politely asked them to be patient; we would find the fish soon. After another ten minutes and another beer, one of the customers became belligerent and rude to both the first mate and myself. I asked him again to behave. Two of his friends asked him to be quiet. He was quiet for a few minutes, but then started complaining again. I stepped out from behind steering wheel and politely, but very firmly said, "If you just want to drink beer, it's a lot cheaper to go to a bar than on a charter. You fellows decide, but if you stay, I expect you to behave in a civil manner."

"You've got to be kidding!" the unruly customer replied. With that, I asked the first-mate to pull the lines.

"We're going in!"

That set the customer into another tirade.

"If you don't stop, I am calling the sheriff to meet us at the dock."

Under maritime law, a ship's captain has the ultimate authority for the safe passage of his vessel and the persons on board. I never had to follow up on such a threat, but I know several captains who did.

Immediately, he quieted down. No one said another word during the forty-minute ride back to the dock. As unhappy as I was with their behavior, I prorated the charter fee and told the group if they ever wanted to come back without the beer, they were welcome. I don't know if they had learned a lesson, but I believe I had.

The issue of when to pro-rate a charter fee was left to the discretion of the captain. This incident was my first with an unruly customer, and my inclination was to charge the normal rate, as most captains would have correctly done. My decision to pro-rate the fee was perhaps foolish, but I never doubted it was the right decision for me at the time. Something about "turning the other cheek" and "do unto others…"

Three days later, my next charter didn't turn out any better. Again, these were four new customers referred by another charter captain. The weather was questionable, three- to four-foot seas with light rain. I offered to reschedule the trip or give them a refund of their deposit, but they insisted we proceed as planned. They assured me they had been out in rough seas before and enjoyed the experience. As we were going through the pier heads from Portage Lake into Lake Michigan, I could sense by the look on their faces this was not going to be a fun trip. Joking and laughter turned to silence as the first wave crashed over the bow of the boat. Again, I offered to go back and try again another day, to which they all declined. The apparent leader of the group said, "We paid for a motel last night and don't want to waste the money." The first-mate had just set the first line when one of the customers ran to the side of the boat and threw up. The wind blew vomit back on the boat and the customer. While I was busy helping the sick customer to a seat, one of the other customers had gone below and threw up! I instructed everyone to stay on deck because it was safer and more comfortable than being in the cabin.

Just then a fish bit, and we had a salmon on. The mate set the hook and handed the rod to the only one of the group who was not sick. I went to the back of the boat to help the struggling angler stand up while the mate netted a nice twenty-pound salmon. There were a few high-fives from the group as the mate hurriedly reset the line, and I went back to the wheel to keep the boat on track in the rough seas. By then, all four customers were sick.

"Guys, it's too rough to fish," I decided and spoke in a voice that indicated I was not open to discussion. "We are going back to the marina."

This time, no one disagreed. Back at the dock, none of the men said much as I took a group photo with their catch and the mate cleaned the fish. Fortunately, because they had caught a twenty-pound chinook, there were plenty of filets for everyone to take home. I pro-rated the cost of the charter for coming in early and thanked them for their business. They replied they would be back next year. (By the way, the group never came back.)

As my first-mate and I were cleaning up the mess in the cabin, an uneasy feeling came over me. If this was what chartering was about, did I really want to do this the rest of my life? Had I missed an excellent opportunity to return to Ford as a consultant

Two things became readily apparent: first impressions are generally correct, and all customers are not created equal. In both of these early instances, I allowed my desire to run a charter to cloud my better judgement to the detriment of both the customers and myself.

Sorting through customers—separating the wheat from the chaff, as the Bible would have it—was something I had not ever had to do. It requires the business owner to walk a fine line: all businesses need to stay profitable and for that they need customers, but at what cost? From my perspective, I wanted to welcome anyone to the boat as I believed they were there for a reason. However, as I had just experienced, there are times when turning down a charter is best for everyone. As captain, I had the responsibility for the safety of my customers. If something went wrong, I was the one responsible to take care of it.

Those first two charters of the 1989 season were a wake-up call. No longer was I to be guided by the unexamined principle that "a charter is a charter." I began to rethink both my marketing strategy and my booking. If a charter isn't fun for the customers, why should they come back? Catching fish is important, but so is the experience. As captain, I knew I had to determine, from now on, that prospective customers, when they booked the charter, understood what I considered acceptable conduct. It was not when they were boarding *True Blue* that they needed to learn this. Little did I realize how significant that shaky beginning to the 1989 season would be in growing my charter business.

Being a small port, Onekama hosted only ten charter boats in comparison to Ludington and Manistee to the south and Frankfort to the north where fifty to sixty charter boats docked at each port. The charter business at the larger ports depended more on "walk on" customers who were visiting the area as tourists. Charter businesses in Onekama, due to the port's small size and lesser amount of tourism, depended on booking charters and bringing people to Onekama specifically to fish. Over time, several of the other charter boat captains and I jointly and successfully marketed Onekama as the "best kept secret on Lake Michigan." We insistently spread the message that Onekama was a destination to recreate and fish as we touted its quiet, pristine beaches, its excellent fishing and its first-class charter boats and captains.

Each captain set his own rates based on the size of his boat, his experience and the competition from other charter boats. For the larger ports such as Manistee, Frankfort and Ludington which boasted significant tourism that allowed for a large number of "walk on" customers, the rate was generally set based on four anglers with a surcharge for the fifth and sixth angler. As previously mentioned, Onekama captains, including myself, generally booked charters before the season and used a flat rate up to the US Coast Guard maximum of six passengers. I found it worked particularly well for me with my emphasis on family charters. There was no extra charge for bringing a fifth or sixth non-fishing spouse or child. This proved to be popular, and the check writer was always appreciative.

My son, Dennis, and several of his friends helped as first mates on *True Blue* that summer of 1989. The wages and tips were good, but getting up at four-thirty a.m., seven days a week, was a bit of a challenge for them and they soon were less interested in first-mating. It was difficult to find first-mate replacements who were willing to stick with the job. Being that Onekama was a small port, most first mates were local high school or college students looking for summer work. I was fortunate to find excellent young men and women to work for me. Yes, I had two young ladies as first mates, and they did an excellent job. Michelle Bates and Marcie Cruise, both in their late teens, loved to fish and didn't mind the early hours and the hard work. Marcie even painted lures that proved effective for catching salmon. Both had fathers with boats at Onekama Marine. Michelle and Marcie have turned into fine ladies with successful careers of their own. I paid my first mates a fixed daily rate plus tips. The word on the docks was that *True Blue* was a good boat to work on. I offered good pay; the boat went fishing almost every day; and I let the first mate do his/her job. In all my years chartering, I never had a first-mate not show up without prior notice. I could run a charter without a first mate but preferred not to for the safety of the customers.

The highlight of that fishing season was not about fishing. On August 25, 1989, our daughter Luanne was married to Pat Letarte, a fine young man from Northville who was now working in California in the real-estate business. Their wedding was at the Methodist Church in Northville with the reception at the Washtenaw Golf and Country Club, of which Dorothy and I had been members since 1982. I will never forget reading 1 Corinthians 13 at her wedding with tears in my eyes. My little girl was now a beautiful bride! How had the years passed so quickly! Following their honeymoon, Pat and Luanne headed to California to make their home.

As my knowledge and experience of salmon fishing increased so did my catch rates, but not without some trials along the way. Having to catch fish each day separates the captains that want to be good fishermen from those who already are good fishermen. Several times during those first two years, I made the mistake of imitating what other captains were doing, instead of initiating my own plans. I spent several charter trips moving from one spot to another based on where other captains were fishing and employing whatever baits they were using. The results were often that we did not catch many fish and even got "skunked" once or twice. You learn humility in a hurry when you only have one or two fish to clean for your customers while the other captains at the fish cleaning table have six or eight fish each.

One day after a charter that was not particularly successful, my friend and fellow captain, Kevin Hughes, set me straight when he said, "Quit trying to copy what others are doing. You are a good fisherman! Just do what you think is best and the results will follow."

What Kevin was saying is that each captain has his own "secrets" as to how fast he runs his boat with different lures, how deep and how far behind the boat he trolls lures and the list goes on. In other words, each captain and boat crew have to develop their own technique of what works best for them rather than for someone else. There are so many variables in fishing you truly never learn them all. Just when you think you have fishing all figured out, you get surprised with something new. I learned to keep detailed daily records of my fish catch to identify some of the variables and adopt what worked best for me under given conditions. This was another instance when fishing as a hobby with friends was so different from leading paid fishing charters.

We averaged five fish per trip in the early years, and as my skills improved in subsequent years, the catch increased to eight fish per trip. Chinook salmon up to thirty pounds were our primary target. They were good to eat and abundant in Lake Michigan. Since they are hard fighters, they were also fun to catch. Coho, steelhead, brown trout and lake trout made up the rest of the catch.

A typical day for me during that summer's busy charter season went something like this: I'd be up at four a.m. for breakfast—my favorite meal of the day—and then check the marine forecast. Arriving at the boat by four forty-five a.m., I'd checked that my first mate had ice in the cooler, had placed lures on the rods and was ready for the arrival of customers. We'd leave dock at five a.m. for a five-hour charter. I'd chat with customers, catch fish with or for them, help my first mate when necessary, catch more fish, take pictures of customers, catch more fish again. The boat would arrive back at the dock by eleven a.m. and it was time to take group pictures of the customers with their catch on the fish rack and clean their fish while the first mate cleaned the boat. Before the customer departed, I would be sure to ask if they wanted to book a trip the following year or minimally be sure I had current contact information to be in touch with the customer. At twelve noon it was time to check that boat and the toilet and the fish cooler are clean, put rods away, pay first mate (first-mates were paid a small flat fee per trip and all tips) and confirm time of our departure the following morning. At one p.m., I'd have lunch, check my telephone for messages, book new charters and relax. In addition to the daily routine, there were oil changes, unexpected repairs on the boat, replacing damaged fishing gear, helping customers find and book accommodations, arranging for box lunches and the list goes on. I kept meticulous records on each customer and sent a year-end newsletter to past and present customers, often with photos of their catch. In those days I didn't have a cell phone with a camera. All photos were taken with my camera, and then the film had to be developed later. Sometimes, with as many clients as I had over a summer, it was hard for me to keep track of who was who in the photos. It was, however, a great marketing tool to build a loyal customer base and repeat business.

By the end of my second season, I had run forty-five charters and was beginning to see myself as a successful charter captain. I had suffered some setbacks and difficult learning experiences such as those of my first two trips of the season, but I also had some successes like that of the spoon tournament. I was more selective in my bookings, more confident in my own ability as a captain and I had achieved my two-year goal of establishing a profitable charter business. Most importantly, I knew without a doubt this was my new ministry.

The fall of 1989 brought a respite from chartering, but unfortunately, we had to have our black lab Abby put to sleep. I had bought her in Sao Paulo in 1979 and remember fondly sneaking her into the Maksoud Hotel which didn't allow pets. How excited the kids had been when they first saw Abby and when, two years later, Abby had her nine puppies. Abby had traveled several thousand miles with us and we missed her. We still had Abby's pup, Buffy, who was born in Brazil, to remind us of Abby, but Buffy herself was now eight-years old and having difficulty with arthritis. I didn't even want to think about how long we would still have Buffy with us.

The fall also brought opportunities to fish with friends. One of these was Joe Semester. Joe and Nancy Semester, our good friends from Venezuela, were now living in Ohio. Dorothy and I will forever be grateful for their support when Dorothy's folks were killed in a horrific plane crash in

Joe Semester and Dennis,
Onekama, 1990

Venezuela in 1969. They came to Onekama to fish with me numerous times dating back to when I first bought my boat in 1982. Joe, who worked for Goodyear, Nancy and their two daughters attended the Fellowship Church in Valencia, Venezuela where we first met and became close friends. Joe frequently accompanied me fishing peacock bass and on my flights in the Amazon for New Tribes Mission. Joe and Nancy were now retired and busy with grand-kids and church activities at home in Akron. Joe was an artist working with wood or metal. On one of his visits, he gave me a filet knife he had made from tool steel. It has a hand-carved bone handle and a wooden case. It was so nice I never used it and kept it as a remembrance of a good friend. I never charged Joe for our fishing trips together. He would offer to pay, and I always said, "I get more enjoyment from our time together than you do! Why should you pay for my good time"?

As I prepared for the 1990 season, there were many things to pay attention to. For starters, I realized the historic Portage Point Inn on Portage Lake might prove to be an excellent source of customers for the charter boats in Onekama by distributing our brochures and referring their guests to us. This turned out to be so. Built in the early 1900s, the hotel catered to customers brought by steam ship from Chicago and other ports from around Lake Michigan. The boats docked in front of the Inn, a beautiful, three-story, white building with a dark green gambrel roof. A three-story portico supported by Tuscan columns extending seventy feet along the front of the building overlooking Portage Lake. A covered porch covered the main entrance and was buffered by well-groomed shrubs and flowers.

Another thing I had to pay attention to as I prepared for the 1990 season was technology. The 1980s brought significant technological changes to the charter fishing industry. Navigation, fish-finders and communication systems were improving at a rapid pace. LORAN, the land-based navigation system introduced during WW II, was being replaced by the satellite Global Positioning System (GPS). Fish finders, devices used to locate fish underwater, and radar were now solid-state electronics and VHF radios, while still required by the US Coast Guard, were replaced with cell phones. These new devices delivered greatly improved performance at lower cost. Technology and how to use it was becoming a major part of a charter captain's success. I had installed radar, auto-pilot, chart plotter and fish finder on *True Blue* in 1982. By the time I started chartering in 1988, my "new" electronics were obsolete and had to be replaced with newer state of the art equipment.

I was noticing another subtler change also taking place. In the 1960s and 1970s, charter captains with much experience but little customer focus had provided salmon charters. In those early

Portage Point Inn, Onekama

days, customers would tolerate almost anything: bad equipment, a poorly maintained boat or a rude captain and crew—if they were catching fish. By the late

1980s, a new segment of the market was emerging: parents who wanted a quality family-recreation experience. After several charters with rowdy behavior and drinking, I welcomed my realization that the growth of this new market segment would permit me to attract a different clientele. Being new and without a backlog of experience holding me back, I was one of the first charter captains in our area to focus on family recreation.

Being a family man, I was already thinking and feeling the change as evident by the number of family charters I was already booking. These customers still wanted to catch fish, of course, but other criteria such as enjoying the environment, time with family and the quality of the charter were becoming equally important. Consequently, the cleanliness of the boat, the courtesy of the captain and crew, the safety equipment, the privacy of enclosed toilet facilities and a willingness to teach Mom and Dad and the kids how to catch a fish, all added to the desirability of the charter. It was no longer strictly a fishing business; it was a recreation business competing with other forms of recreation for consumer dollars. My customers wanted to catch fish, but they also wanted to enjoy the entire experience on the water. I credit my early focus on families as my target market to be the single most important commitment I did to build a successful charter business. In fact, the motto on my brochure and business card was, "A Quality Recreation Experience." I knew I had found my target market when a first-time charter, consisting of a dad, a mom and two children, told me after an enjoyable day on the water that I had been highly recommended to them as a captain who was fun to be with and enjoyed showing kids how to fish. I didn't fully recognize it at the time, but my inclination for sharing knowledge with others as I had at Ford would serve me well in the future. God already had a plan for growing my business, but I just didn't know what it was yet.

In that winter of 1989–1990, I also identified two new markets with the potential to expand my charter business—fly fishing and women anglers. Both market segments had previously been overlooked by the charter industry, but they offered growth for new customers. Fly fishing has historically been viewed as a freshwater sport but catches of salt-water fish on a fly were gaining attention. Also, the perception that women were not interested in fishing was beginning to change. With increased media coverage and female fishing organizations, more women were coming into the sport each year. The problem I had to overcome was taking into account the growth in these markets segments was occurring in states that bordered on salt water, not on Lake Michigan. Was this a nudge by the Holy Spirit that Dorothy and I were heading south? With Luanne now married and living in California with her husband Pat and Dennis working full time and going to school, Dorothy and I found ourselves with freedom from parenting and time to move about.

I had a busy boat show schedule the winter of 1989–1990. I was exhibiting at Ft. Wayne, Toledo, Cincinnati, Cleveland and Detroit. The shows were great fun, and I met new prospective customers, traded "shop talk" with other charter captains and familiarized myself with fishing tackle manufacturers. The shows were certainly productive as I booked over thirty trips that winter. One of my biggest enjoyments at these shows was when a family I had fished with the previous summer came up to my booth with their kids in tow and booked a charter for the following season. With some families, it was the beginning of a long and very personal relationship I would have with them. Although I continued to send out a newsletter to all my customers encouraging them to book early, by the spring of 1990, I was calling the previous year's customers to make sure I reserved a date for them to fish before they missed the season. Besides show bookings, word of mouth and repeat sign-ups were also accounting for a large percent of my business that third season. This was what I had been working hard to achieve.

I could feel my charter business was taking roots and now I had data to prove it; my reputation for quality service and providing a family-oriented atmosphere was now about to pay dividends. I ran almost sixty charters the summer of 1990 with over half being families and repeat business. For the first time as a charter captain, it occurred to me that my physical well-being was a key to my livelihood. How fortunate I was to be able to have the physical stamina to meet the demands of chartering! In future years, my reliance on a young and strong first mate increased as my physical prowess declined but that was too far in the future to be on my mind in 1990.

I also realized that as the number of charters increased so did the difficulty of scheduling in my regular customers. Running two charters a day is not recommended for the long haul as it means eighteen-hour days: up at four a.m. for the five-a.m. morning charter and to bed at ten p.m. following the four-p.m. afternoon charter. I tried to avoid two-charter days as often as possible, but as the core of my repeat business continued to grow, so did the likelihood of squeezing in a customer who forgot to book early or one I had had to reschedule due to weather. Despite my reluctance to do an afternoon charter to avoid those long days, I made every effort to get a regular customer booked, even at the expense of a little sleep.

One of the toughest decisions I continued to have to make as a charter captain that summer of 1990 was when to cancel a charter due to weather. Two major factors had to be considered, 1) was it safe to fish? and 2) how seaworthy were your customers? Lake Michigan can get extremely rough, as waves reach fifteen-feet or higher. As a general rule, waves one to three feet were acceptable for eighty percent of customers, waves two to four feet are still safe but uncomfortable. At five feet and above, it is better to reschedule. Getting customers sick is not a way to get repeat business. Over time, I developed a feel for when I should cancel or reschedule as I had many repeat customers and knew their tolerance for mal de mer. The presence of kids, of course, made a difference, and I didn't want to ruin their fishing experience with rough seas. When customers had motel reservations and a bad weather forecast for the dates of their charter, that was a serious complication factor. Light rain and fog could be tolerated but not thunderstorms and high waves. I generally would call people several days ahead of their scheduled charter and give them an update on the forecast. I would also call with a final scheduling decision the day before they left home. Even then, sometimes I cancelled and wished I hadn't, and other times I didn't cancel and wished I had.

As I had already observed, the market was growing in the salt-water sphere and the idea of winter fishing was drawing my thoughts to Florida. With ocean fishing in mind, in November 1990, Dorothy and I went to Mazatlán, Mexico, where I participated in a week-long fly-fishing school put on by Billy Pate and Jack Samson. Dorothy and I agreed the overall cost of the trip and of the school was an investment in learning saltwater fly fishing. An added incentive may have been the beautiful area we were to visit. Mazatlán, a city of over two-hundred and fifty thousand in the 1990s, was a rapidly growing tourist destination located on the Pacific coast of Mexico. Mazatlán, as we were to find, reminded us of the coastal cities of Venezuela with its white sand beaches, tropical climate and great fishing. I called Luanne and Pat who were still in California and asked them to join Dorothy and me for a few days, and they jumped at the chance. Seeing Pat and Luanne would be an added benefit of our trip that we hadn't counted on and that saved us the cost of another trip to California later that year.

Billy Pate was one of the foremost big-game fly fishermen in the world. He was one of the pioneers of fly fishing for tarpon and sailfish in the 1980s and held the world record with a one-hundred and eighty-eight-pound tarpon on the fly. Jack Samson was equally well known as a writer, a World War II war correspondent, an editor and a fisherman. During his tenure as managing editor of Field and Stream, it became the foremost sportsman's magazine in the world.

I had caught big marlin and tuna in Australia and New Zealand but never on a fly rod. The opportunity to learn from the best was too good to pass up.

Billy Pate and I hit it off from the start. He was easy going, a true southern gentleman—he was from South Carolina and profoundly knowledgeable about fly fishing. The previous year, he had caught several sailfish on the fly in Quepos, Costa Rica,

l-r Laurie Woodbridge and mate, Dennis and mate, 719 lb., black marlin on *Sea Baby II*, Cairns, Australia, 1973

and had received accolades from the fishing world.

On the first day, Billy and Jack taught students knots, casting and rod handling technique. All equipment was provided by the school: fourteen-weight fly rods, flies and large reels, capable of holding four hundred yards of line and a quality drag system. The braking pressure applied to the revolving spool by the drag mechanism produces extreme heat that will lock up on all but the highest quality reels. Naturally this equipment is expensive and not practical for other than this type of fly fishing. The last two days were spent on the water fishing for sailfish and putting into practice what we had learned. There were eight students, four per boat, and we would each fish one day with Billy Pate and one with Jack Samson. Participants were encouraged to ask questions and there were plenty of those from all of us. As I observed and listened during the classes, I couldn't help but think how I might apply these techniques to a new business in Florida someday. For now, I would just learn and enjoy my time with Billy Pate and Jack Sampson.

The technique, "Bait and Switch," perfected by Billy Pate, is to troll four hook-less baits, usually mullet, ballyhoo or other smaller bait fish, behind the boat. When the sailfish bites one of the baits, it gets a taste of the fish but without a hook the first mate can pull the bait away from the fish and slowly reel the bait to the boat "teasing" the fish to follow. With the fish at the back of the boat, the mate quickly reels the bait into the boat as the captain puts the boat in neutral, the sailfish excited and ready to strike, looks frantically for the bait as the angler casts his fly to the fish. If all goes well, the sailfish will take the fly and the battle is on. Many times, the fish is within ten to fifteen feet from the back of the boat when it bites the fly. I thought light-heartedly, "I wish I could figure out how to coax salmon to the boat!" Unfortunately, I never figured that one out.

My first day fishing with Jack Samson was exciting but there were no hook ups. We saw sailfish come up to our bait but turned away without taking the bait and we had no opportunity to cast to them. Just watching the sailfish with their large dorsal fin out of the water come in behind one of the hook-less baits was exciting. Jack was a pleasure to be with as he related stories of his extraordinary life experiences. In a way, I was glad we didn't get any bites as it provided us time to talk. I also enjoyed watching the captain and crew and how they worked as a team on the boat. I hadn't spoken Spanish since I left Venezuela in 1972, so I was pleased I could still converse with the captain and the crew in Spanish. Having fished Australia with some of the best captains in the world, it was interesting to see the differences between them and the Mexicans. No disrespect intended to the captain or crew of our charter boat in Mazatlan, they were very good, but the Australian captains and crews are better when it comes to sportfishing for big game fish.

The second day, when I was switched to Billy, we were just the two of us on board as the two other anglers had had to leave to catch a flight home. It was a slow morning with only one fish seen. Billy and I chatted about his career in fishing and how blessed he had been over the years to lead such an interesting life. Just after lunch, Billy and I were relaxing. It was a beautiful day, calm and sunny with the low rumble of the diesel engine lulling us to sleep. Suddenly, the mate shouted in Spanish, "Pez vela!" (Sail fish!) I jumped to my feet and picked up the fly rod. Even with sunglasses, the reflecting sun made it difficult to see the dorsal fin of the sailfish piercing the sparkling blue water at sixty-feet behind the boat. The sailfish came in behind the bait, striking at the bait with its bill, as the mate slowly retrieved (teased) the sailfish to the boat.

My heart pounded with excitement.

The mate lifted the bait from the water as the captain put the boat into neutral. I cast several feet in front of the sailfish—one, two, three strips, retrieving the fly, when suddenly the sailfish turned on the fly, its bill protruding a foot out of the water. The line came tight and I set the hook with an aggressive strip strike, pulling hard on the fly line in my left hand and immediately the sailfish leaped clear out of the water twenty feet behind the boat.

"*Que hermosa vista*," (What a beautiful sight), the first mate shouted. The sun reflected off the water droplets and the iridescent colors of the sailfish. After twenty minutes, several more jumps and coaching from Billy, we had the sailfish to the boat. The mate took the fish by the bill, removed the hook and carefully lifted the fish on board for a picture. Different than the marlin and yellow fin tuna that I caught in Australia, the sailfish are not as big and powerful, so they can be handled safely with care.

Billy and I would have put the fish back in the water, but the local practice was to keep the catch for food. As it was my first sail fish on a fly, we agreed to keep the fish, take pictures and give it to a market for local consumption. Normally, both Billy and I, left to our own practices, would release everything except for potential records or for special occasions such as this one. For my part, releasing is a practice I started in Australia in 1973 after catching a seven hundred and nineteen-pound black marlin which I took to shore for a picture. The next day, there was nothing to be done, given that the meat of the black marlin is not tasty, but to tow the carcass out to sea for the sharks. What a shame to kill a beautiful creature like that black marlin just for a few pictures, I thought then, and I resolved not to repeat this.

Dennis and Billy Pate,
Mazatlan, 1990

One of my prize possessions is a picture of Billy Pate and me with my first sailfish. Mine was the only sailfish caught by anyone in our group in the two days of fishing. Since that day, I have caught over forty sailfish on a fly, and not restrained by local custom, I have released all of them, but none of these catches were as memorable as that first one with Billy Pate.

That evening Dorothy, Pat and Luanne joined me and the other school attendees for dinner at Senor Frog's. With Billy and Jack, we were celebrating completing the class. Dorothy and Pat danced the "frog dance" (dancing with swim flippers on your feet); Luanne and I didn't dance but laughed until our sides hurt. I should mention that Dorothy, "a teetotaler," has never had an alcoholic beverage in her life. Doing the "frog dance" is her innate personality, not the result of imbibing too much!

The next day, Dorothy and I took Luanne and Pat charter fishing and they each caught their first sailfish on conventional tackle. As neither Dorothy, Luanne nor Pat had participated in the fishing school, they had not yet fished and this was a treat for them to catch their first sailfish. I enjoyed talking to the captain and first-mates, not only to practice my Spanish, but to learn from them. The techniques they used were much like those we employed in Australia.

On the way back to port, Dorothy said, "Why don't you wear a large brimmed hat like Billy Pate does?"

"I guess I should," I replied. I had a few spots on my face and arms from too many days in the sun before I started using sunscreen, but nothing serious. "I'll try one next summer," I added, but never did.

A month later, in December 1990, Billy Pate called me about partnering with him to buy a boat for fly fishing in Quepos, Costa Rica, and starting a fishing business. Billy had an American friend, now a resident of Costa Rica and living in Quepos, who could register our business there. This was important as only a resident of Costa Rica could own a business. Billy proposed that I would stay in Quepos on a tourist visa during the peak season from January to May, to oversee the operation. My Spanish was a little rusty, but as I experienced during our time in Mexico, a little practice would soon bring it back. My biggest problem was mixing Spanish and Portuguese, which I had learned during my three years in Brazil. *Habla Espanol* or *Falha Portuguese*? Do you speak Spanish or do you speak Portuguese?

When I talked to Dorothy about my conversation with Billy, she was hesitant. "What about your mom, Ron and Ina, and what about grandchildren?"

"What grandchildren?" I asked.

Dorothy confessed Luanne was expecting her first child in August or September. As this was a mother-daughter discussion, I obviously had been kept out of the loop. Being that far away would make it difficult to stay in contact. We had been down this road before and had always decided to wait to see if God would open or close doors. While waiting, Dorothy and I decided I would go to Costa Rica in February 1991 to see what it was like before reaching a final decision.

I asked Doug West, my buddy from Onekama, if he would like to accompany me to Costa Rica to check out the area and do some fishing. Doug had never fly fished before but was eager to accompany me.

As most charters did not provide fly fishing tackle, Doug and I flew to Miami a few days before our trip to Costa Rica and bought fourteen weight fly rods and Billy Pate reels from Worldwide Sportsman, a tackle shop in Islamorada, Florida, owned by Billy Pate. Billy had developed the fly reels in partnership with a tool and die company and Pate reels soon set the industry standard for fly reels around the world. Billy, the consummate southern gentleman, took time away from his busy schedule to spend a day with Doug and me getting the tackle rigged up for our trip. As we talked, I mentioned to Billy I had been thinking of starting a fishing business in Florida some day in the future.

Billy hesitated and then said, "Why don't you and Doug buy twelve-weight rods and reels instead of the fourteen-weight? You could then use them for tarpon here in Florida. We use fourteen-weight equipment as there is the possibility of catching a marlin, as well as sailfish, and we need the heavier rod and reel just in case."

Doug and I thought it was a great idea, possibly saving us having to buy the twelve-weight fly rods and reels at a later date for use in Florida.

Doug and I flew from Miami to San Jose, Costa Rica on February 17, 1991. Doug was fun to be with as nothing ever seemed to bother him. A kind and generous person, Doug always carried a large amount of cash in his pocket. "Just in case," he said. Recalling my encounter with a pick pocket in Sao Paulo in 1982, I was nervous and helped Doug find a place to hide his cash.

Costa Rica, a country of approximately 4 million people, has the most stable political and economic system and highest literacy rate in Central America. San Jose, the capital, a city of approximately two hundred and eighty thousand with the lowest crime rate in Central America, is regarded as safe. The city has a European flavor and is noted for its public art and beautiful parks. The main source of revenue for the country is tourism.

After settling in at our hotel, Doug and I took a taxi into San Jose to do some sightseeing and have dinner. The city was clean. The locals who are referred to as *"Ticos"* proved to be friendly, and I was pleased to realize my communication in Spanish came back quickly. The next morning, we took a thirty-minute charter flight from San Jose to Quepos, a town of twenty-two thousand residents, located on the Pacific Ocean. While Quepos is only fifty air miles west of San Jose, the trip by road adds up to one-hundred and forty miles, due to the circuitous mountain route. Costa Rica is a beautiful country, its mountainous terrain covered with green foliage and its rivers cascading down the mountains to the Caribbean Sea on the east and Pacific Ocean to the west. Flying into Quepos, Doug and I could see white sand beaches skirting the deep blue water of the Pacific for miles.

We checked into the Wet Dolphin Hotel, *Dorado Mojado* in Spanish. The hotel was new, its two-story cement blocks painted a bright yellow. A hand painted sign of a large dolphin hung over the front entrance. After settling in our nicely appointed rooms, we contacted our charter captain and spent the afternoon sightseeing. In the center of town was a large three-hundred-foot wooden wharf, in need of repair. In the 1950s, the wharf was used to load bananas onto cargo ships destined for the US but eventually the banana company moved elsewhere, and the port closed. Moored next to the wharf were several boats, including our charter boat.

The next morning a shuttle from the hotel took us to the wharf. It was a beautiful morning, the sun peaking over the hills behind us and a blue cloudless sky arching over the Pacific to the west. We arrived promptly at seven a.m., ready to board, but this would prove to be a difficult and dangerous boarding. Three-foot swells prevented tying the boat to the wharf. The boat pitched up and down in the swells and it also moved left and right and front and back. Seeing a wooden ladder attached to the wharf, we climbed on to the ladder, and as the boat came to its closest, hopped from the ladder to the boat. We learned there had been several accidents, but this precarious access was the only way to board.

Over the next three days, we caught and released six sailfish ranging from seventy to one-hundred pounds each. On our last day, Doug hooked a blue marlin that he fought for over an hour. I poured buckets of seawater on him to keep him cool in eighty-degree tropical heat. We had the fish close to the boat when the reel locked up and Doug lost the fish. He was exhausted and disappointed as was everyone else on board. The captain estimated the fish at over two hundred pounds.

Back in Islamorada, Doug and I wondered out-loud to Billy that maybe we should have purchased the fourteen-weight rods and reels, to which he laughed and apologized to Doug about the reel. It had just been introduced and apparently needed a design change. Although he recognized it would not bring the blue marlin back, he gave Doug a new reel and lifetime-replacement warranty—just in case it happened again. As we were leaving, the world-wide sportsman Billy grinned as he commented to Doug, "A two-hundred-pound blue marlin on a twelve-weight rod would have been a great catch!"

I recommended Quepos to Billy and thought it worthwhile to start a business there. However, based on my previous conversation with Dorothy, I told Billy that I didn't have the time nor the inclination to spend several months a year overseeing a business in Costa Rica. Billy understood and said he still might send a boat to Quepos for his personal use. A year later, he had a boat in Quepos just like the one we had talked about. I had some misgivings about not partnering with Billy, but Dorothy and I didn't feel comfortable with the move. Call it what you will—intuition or common sense—but we knew it was the gentle hand of God shutting the door and telling us not to go. We have experienced the Holy Spirit's guiding hand in our lives many times over the years, and this nudge was no different. I made two additional trips to Costa Rica in 1992 and 1993 with friends, but neither was as memorable as that first trip I made with Doug.

We had another big event in 1991, the birth of our first granddaughter, Emilee Ann Letarte, on September 3, 1991. Little did we realize how much joy a grandchild would bring to our lives. Pat and Luanne were still in San Bernardino, California, where Pat was buying older homes, fixing them up and renting or re-selling them. Dorothy and I took a trip to California in March to see little Emilee. She was so small and cute.

In 1992, the following year, Billy Pate had serious problems with the diesel engine on his boat in Quepos. After a year of repairs and many Costa Rican *colons*, the local currency, Billy decided to cut his losses and sold the boat to a local buyer. When I saw Billy later back in Florida, he smiled and told me how lucky I was not to get involved in that costly venture.

"Thank you, Lord!" I prayed in gratitude. I knew it wasn't luck.

During those first five years—1988 to 1993—I felt like I had thirty-five years earlier when I started at Ford. I was learning new skills, earning the respect of my peers and meeting new people, and it was exciting and satisfying. On top of it all, I loved the business that I was growing. The same traits that I learned at Ford applied to my charter business: hard work, integrity and respect for people. My transformation from a corporate executive to charter captain was more than well on its way—it had happened!

There had been some mistakes along the way, but I like to call them learning experiences. Overall, the progress in growing my fishing business was evident.

l-r Luanne, Dennis and son Dennis, 1992

The one constant throughout the five years was that God was in control, closing the door on returning to Ford as a consultant and on moving to Quepos, redirecting my salmon charters to a family-oriented business and opening the door wider to Florida. No matter the change in circumstances, I knew the Lord was directing our path. "Jesus Christ is the same yesterday and today and forever." Heb 13:8.

Life was good, and it often seemed like a long vacation, but I needed something more to focus on during the winter. It also caused me to reflect on retirement which, to quote the Webster's Dictionary, is a time "to leave one's job and cease to work." That's not what I wanted to do. Initially I enjoyed the free time, but all the free time in the winter was now becoming an impediment, time I could be using to build my business and ministry. A better definition of retirement is "changing careers or goals," not "ceasing work." We only have so much time on this earth and it goes by faster than we think it will when we are young. We need to use each day to its fullest. By 1993, having so much free time from October to March didn't fit my definition of what I wanted.

Through the Eyes of a Fisherman

Chapter 3
Moving to Florida

The thought of developing a winter fishing business in Florida had been intriguing me for a few years, but I had always put off doing anything about growing a branch of my business. I was still consolidating my Lake Michigan company. The idea however would not leave me. When Jim Bennett, who was a member with me of the Portage Lake Charter Boat Association, had suggested four years earlier in 1988 that I do so, I was launching my salmon-fishing business. He had reminded me of the potential of a Florida company over the intervening years but the idea of adding salt water fishing to my list of undertakings had seemed a diffusion of my energy.

I had not abandoned thinking about a second fishing business in Florida. I was just biding my time. When I had gone to Mexico in 1990 so that I could participate in Billy Pate's fly-fishing school in Mazatlán, I had seen the possibilities of a Florida business, but I had still not been ready to split my energy over two businesses and make a move. I had signed up for Billy's training believing that it would be a preparation for taking part in the growing fly fishing sector of the fishing industry—if ever I wanted to do that, but I had held off taking any action. I was simply not ready.

By Christmas time 1992, I recognized I had gained the confidence that comes from running a successful business. My salmon fishing enterprise in Onekama had done fifty-plus charters during the summer of 1992. The season had kept me busy and happy. It was obvious that I had consolidated my efforts and had created a successful business. Now, it was winter and I was resting, but the truth be told I was also restless and bored. I had too much free time during the winter when I was not fishing.

I was now ready to explore actively the possibility of a Florida endeavor. As always, any new move involved speaking to Dorothy. In the days after Christmas, as I spoke to Dorothy, I could see that she was listening to my ideas seriously. When I suggested a trip to Florida to explore what I might do there as a charter captain, as she has done many times before, Dorothy said, "Whatever you think. It won't hurt to look, and it will be fun to spend a few days in a warm climate. If God wants us in Florida, doors will open."

That's how, in January 1993, Dorothy and I found ourselves driving to Florida to just "look around" for two-weeks. We travelled the west coast from Tampa to Islamorada in the Keys, where Jim Bennett had his winter fishing business. On the way down to the Keys, we explored many areas and liked

Charlotte Harbor. Charlotte Harbor, located about sixty-miles south of Tampa had an open water estuary, populated with numerous mangrove islands and covering over one hundred square miles. This area was not yet overly developed and had excellent fishing waters protected from the wind by mangrove islands. Boca Grande, on Gasparilla Island, bordered the Gulf of Mexico and was located at the entrance to Charlotte Harbor. Gasparilla Island is connected by bridge to the mainland. Boca Grande is known for its historic downtown, its white sand beaches and its excellent fishing. Boca Grande Pass and the surrounding beaches are known as the "Tarpon Capital of the World," due to the large migration of tarpon to the area in the spring and the summer. We talked to many people during our travels and these conversations confirmed what I had discerned in 1989: fly fishing and the participation by women in fishing were expanding markets. This growth was clearly evident in Florida. As a result, the opportunities for fly-fishing guides and certified casting instructors were unlimited.

Dorothy and I continued down to the Keys where we met up with Jim Bennett in Islamorada. We liked the area around Islamorada and I knew Jim would help me settle into the fishing business there, but when Dorothy grasped that the closest golf course was a forty-five-minute drive, Islamorada slipped off the radar. We decided to continue exploring the west coast. A legitimate question would be: why didn't we also explore the east side of Florida? The answer is we did—or, rather, had. During our eight years in Venezuela and Brazil, I had made about twenty round trips to the US, about a fifth of them with Dorothy and the kids as we took our annual home leave, and the rest by myself on business trips to Dearborn. Without exception, when the family was with me, we would stop for a few days in Miami, Palm Beach or Ft. Lauderdale to relax, fish and sightsee. While I was more familiar with this east coast, it was not a good choice for a charter business. During the winter months—December through April, the prevailing northeast winds make it difficult to fish offshore without a large seaworthy boat. This would have made setting up a business more expensive. In addition, there were few protected estuaries as in the areas around Charlotte Harbor on the West Coast. The deciding factor for a west coast business, however, was that I preferred to fly fish the shallow backcountry waters rather than for big game fish in the Atlantic.

The Gulf of Mexico side of Florida offered hundreds of square miles of mangrove islands surrounded by shallow water that provided excellent back-country fishing. Before the January 1993 trip, Dorothy and I had never visited this coast of Florida and we had been impressed on our way down. Land development and tourism, so prevalent on the east coast of Florida, had not yet overcome the west coast and we liked the laid-back old Florida life style. Our big question after one week in Florida was: where could Dorothy and I find a conjuncture of both a good fishing port and a good golf course?

The second week we were in Florida, as Dorothy and I were driving back north along the Gulf coast from the Keys, we were comparing notes on what we had seen and decided to stop again in Port Charlotte. With about sixty thousand people, the town is located on the northeast end of Charlotte Harbor and twenty miles by road northeast of Boca Grande. We liked what we had seen of the area the previous week as we headed south to the Florida Keys and now we wanted a second look. After breakfast the following morning, we visited a real estate office in Port Charlotte to inquire about golf courses in the area and were told about Riverwood, a golf course development, ten miles north of Port Charlotte where the Myakka River enters into Charlotte Harbor.

Riverwood was just breaking ground. Only a few holes of the course had been completed and there were no houses except for the models. Plans were for an eighteen-hole golf course surrounded by homes sites, all with a view of the golf course. The first phase of the development, named Stonebridge, would contain sixty houses. Dorothy and I liked what we saw of Riverwood. That night at dinner, we discussed the advisability of making a decision so soon. We had intended to take our time to evaluate the pros and cons of the different areas we had visited and perhaps rent a place for a few weeks the following winter before reaching a final decision. At that point, Dorothy and I had only been in Florida for ten days, and here we were deciding to purchase a home and move to Florida.

As we talked, Dorothy, always the insightful one, conjectured that waiting for another year to decide would add little to what we already knew and not address the more immediate issue of my desire to be busy during the winter months. What she said made sense to me. If Riverwood met our every expectation for a place to live, to play golf and with Charlotte Harbor so close to fish, what were we waiting for? Dorothy reminded me of what she had said before we left Michigan, "If the Lord wants us there, he will open the doors." She then concluded, "I can't imagine us finding such an ideal location unless the Lord was involved." Following our "Open Door Policy," we gently nudged the door by putting a deposit on a beautiful lot, overlooking a lake and the golf course, contingent on the sale of our home in Northville prior to the completion of our new house in October.

Our son, Dennis, was still living at home in Northville while working and pursing his education. We enjoyed having Dennis around, but we had also encouraged him to think about one day having a place of his own. Not that I blamed Dennis for not moving out—living in a comfortable home without paying rent was hard to beat! He also liked his mother's cooking whenever she was in town. Two years previously, as an incentive for him to pursue his education, I had told Dennis that, as long as he continued his college education, he didn't have to pay rent. Dennis now had a good job with a tool and die company and his employer was helping him pay for his after-hours schooling at a local college. Every time I brought up the subject of paying rent, he would reply, "I am still in school, am I not?"

When Dorothy called Dennis from Florida, she let him know we had made a deposit on a house in Port Charlotte and asked what he thought of selling our home in Northville. Dennis was surprised by the suddenness of our decision to move and a little apprehensive as to what this meant for him, but he was still happy for us. Dorothy explained there would be several months before we moved, and we would have time to help get him settled to his own place before we departed for Florida.

Mom was living in a senior citizen's apartment in Riverview and her health was good for a ninety-two-year-old. Dorothy and I agreed we wouldn't mention the potential move to her until we knew more details, but we intended for her to come to Florida to live with us. Meanwhile, we would continue to wait for the Lord to direct us.

When Dorothy and I got back to Northville, we listed our house with a real estate broker who was also a friend from church. If our house didn't sell prior to the completion of our Riverwood home in October, we would cancel our plans to move and accept that God wanted us to stay in Michigan.

Together with Dorothy and me, Dennis decided it would be best for him to move as soon as possible to allow time for a smooth transition while we were still in Michigan, and within two weeks, Dennis found a nice apartment not far from Northville. Dorothy and I helped him get settled into his modest apartment which consisted of one bedroom, bath, kitchen and living room. Dennis was actually looking forward to his new life as a bachelor and to future visits to Florida, but for Dorothy and me, moving Dennis to an apartment was a bittersweet experience. Both Dennis and Luanne were mature for their age. Moving so often during our fourteen years overseas with Ford, they were accustomed to adapting to new surroundings but that didn't make it any easier for

Dorothy and me to see our remaining child leave the nest. On the other hand, we agreed it was the right thing to do, and we were excited as to what God had in store for Dennis in the future.

When we told Ron and Ina of our plan to move to Florida, they were not surprised given all our prior moves with Ford. "At least, we will have a place to visit in the winter," they joked. Dorothy and I explained we would keep the condo in Onekama and my salmon charter business so we would still be close enough to visit during the summer. Our final call was to Tom, who was also not surprised to hear we were planning another move, and he was pleased that we could take Mom with us. Having a home for Mom would address a longer-term issue of how Tom and I would take care of her when she could no longer live alone.

That winter of 1993, I exhibited at fishing shows in Cincinnati, Toledo and Detroit and booked more than thirty charters. The show in Detroit was packed with over one hundred thousand attendees over four days. During a lull in the crowd, I was counting the few open dates I had remaining for the upcoming fishing season when it occurred to me that two-thirds of my bookings at the show were repeat customers! I had booked only ten new customers. Many of my previous customers had come to see the show, and at the same time, had booked a charter for the following summer. The cost of travel, renting booth space and designing and printing brochures to do a show was not cheap. Was it worth the cost just to add ten or twelve new customers? On the other hand, would I risk losing existing customers by not having a presence at the shows, particularly the Detroit one, which drew from my base of Michigan customers? These families obviously enjoyed coming to the show to visit with THEIR captain and talk excitedly about last summer's catch. I would have to give this some thought over the summer, maybe asking customers to see what they thought—as if I didn't have enough to occupy me.

Dorothy and I had planned a skiing trip to Red Lodge, Montana, on March 27 with Chuck and Nancy May. We had just started packing our bags two days prior to our trip, when Mom's neighbor called to advise us Mom was on her way by ambulance to the Wyandotte Hospital with an irregular heartbeat. Dorothy and I arrived at the hospital within an hour and were relieved to see Mom sitting up in bed having a bite of lunch. The doctor said, after initial tests, that her condition didn't appear to be serious and that she should be able to go home in a day or two after her medication had been adjusted. At first, Dorothy and I decided not to go on the trip to Montana, but with the doctor's assurance that Mom's condition was not critical and weighing in that we had already paid for the trip, we decided I would stay home with Mom and Dorothy would go on the trip with the Mays.

After the third day in the hospital, Mom was doing much better and was to be released from the hospital on March 29. At two a.m. the day of her release, I was awakened by a phone call. Generally, phone calls at that time of the morning are not good news and this one wasn't. A nurse told me Mom had fallen getting out of bed during the night and had broken her hip. She was at that moment in surgery to re-place her hip and I should come as soon as possible. I dressed hurriedly and prayed for Mom as I made the one-hour drive to the hospital.

By the time I arrived about three a.m. Mom was back in her room following the surgery and still se-dated. The nurse in charge told me the surgery went well and Mom was doing as good as expected consid-ering the trauma of the fall and of the surgery. As I sat by her bed, I felt tired and drained emotionally. I knew God would sustain us as He has done so many times in the past but that doesn't take away the sad-ness and hurt of seeing a loved one suffer. The ex-citement of moving to Florida and starting a new business no longer seemed important. It is God's way of putting things back in perspective that really mat-ter.

I stayed with Mom in her room, nurses coming by periodically to check on her, and by six a.m., she was alert and asking when she could go home. I felt so bad for her, as she was anticipating going home and being in her own apartment again. I explained to her that she had fallen and had just had an operation to replace her broken hip and now needed therapy to gain more strength before going home. Mom was dis-appointed and began to cry as I held her hand to comfort her. I assured Mom the Lord was there with us and would sustain her as He has always done, to which she managed a weak smile and nodded affir-matively. I then called Dorothy and Tom to bring them up to date. Dorothy wanted to catch the next flight home, but I encouraged her to stay the two extra days and return as planned, which she did.

Tom also wanted to fly to Michigan to see Mom, but I suggested he wait until we knew more about her condition. Dorothy and I had planned to talk to Mom about moving to Florida when we got back from our skiing trip, and I am glad we waited as we had more important things to deal with now.

A few days after surgery, Mom reluctantly started physical therapy at the hospital, but despite daily encouragement from the nurses and Dorothy and me, she just didn't have the strength nor the will to continue. She kept asking to go home. After a week of therapy, the doctor recommended Mom continue therapy at home where she might feel more comfortable in her own surroundings. He suggested she go to her apartment rather than to our house as the apartment was designed to be handicapped accessible and she could have meals delivered. Dorothy and I picked up Mom at the hospital, and when we pushed Mom in a wheel chair into her apartment, she was welcomed with a bouquet of flowers and balloons on the table. We had let Mom's friends know when she was coming home, and this was their greeting. Mom looked and acted ten years younger being in her own apartment surrounded by her friends who soon came by.

We had a visiting nurse come to care for Mom each day, and Dorothy and I would also call daily or make the one-hour drive to see how she was doing. While this seemed a workable solution, it became obvious that Mom could not stay alone. Dorothy and I decided to delay moving to Florida until we knew more about how to care for Mom. Apartment rules required that residents be able to care for themselves independently. We didn't want to put Mom in an assisted living facility or a nursing home. After discussion with Tom and his wife Joann, they suggested I bring Mom to their home in Frederick, Maryland. Joann had worked as a nurse in Frederick and had numerous contacts with doctors and hospitals in the area. Tom and Joann had a large four-bedroom ranch house with room for Mom and with easy access to the outside. Our home in Northville had no downstairs bedrooms and Mom was unable to walk upstairs. She would have preferred to stay in her apartment, but she realized that was no longer possible.

As there were no direct flights from Detroit to Frederick, on May 21, Mom and I flew from Detroit to Washington DC, sixty miles from Frederick, where Tom was to meet us. During the flight, Mom and I talked about the farm and what great times we had there. Times were tough—no running water in the house, living on what we raised on the farm, little in the way of material possessions but rich in family values and love for one another. Dad, Grandma, Grandpa and Lawrence, our hired hand, were all gone now! How times have changed! I sensed Mom knew we didn't have much longer together.

Tom met Mom and me at the airport where we talked over lunch for an hour. Mom was tired and her hip was bothering her from the trip, so Tom suggested they get started on the one-hour drive back to Frederick. I hugged Mom for a long time, trying to hold back the tears, before saying goodbye. I didn't know if I would ever see my mother again. My return flight to Detroit was for later that afternoon, and it seemed a long wait as I pondered what would happen to my mother.

Tom and I kept in touch, and I was pleased to hear Mom was adjusting to her new surroundings. Mom continued with physical therapy, but it was difficult for her to walk even with a walker. Tom felt it was unlikely Mom would ever walk again.

The summer salmon season in Onekama was busy with over fifty charters booked. I was settling into the charter business. My customer base was good and my knowledge of the salmon fishery had greatly increased since 1988. My corporate background helped in promoting fishing charters with larger businesses as I "spoke their language." One of my corporate customers booked the entire Portage Point Inn and eight charter boats to accommodate their three-day annual business meeting with over one hundred in attendance.

In June, Dorothy and I flew to Florida and everything was right on schedule for completion of our house by October. We had three months to sell our house in Northville or exercise our contingency to opt out of the Riverwood contract. I called Tom from Florida to update him on the purchase of our new house, Mom was not doing well, and he and Joann were concerned how much longer they could care for her at home. Tom, however, encouraged us to continue with the purchase of the house as it had no bearing on Mom's care, whether Dorothy and I were in Michigan or Florida.

The next day, while Dorothy and I were still in Florida, our real estate broker In Michigan called to advise us that she had a buyer for our home in

Northville with a closing in September. What great timing, we thought, another indication the Lord was directing us to Florida. The Northville realtor faxed the closing documents to us at the motel in Port Charlotte where we were staying. Before signing the documents, Dorothy and I talked. Who would have thought we would be moving again? We had been happy in Northville since moving there in 1982 after fourteen years overseas. We had established friendships and had been close to Mom and Ron and Ina. We were actively involved with the Methodist Church and our friends there. I had a successful salmon charter business and time to enjoy the winter activities in Onekama. Yet here we were in the process of moving to Florida.

We recalled the numerous times moving around overseas and depending on God to open doors when He had other plans for us—otherwise we stayed put. We knew commonsense and faith were often not compatible and knew God was in control, but we didn't have a clear vision about a ministry in Florida. Our reservation about moving was partially the concern for Mom as we wanted her to come with us but knew that was no longer possible. The Lord has never let us down, and we had no reason to believe this would be any different. We signed the contract and returned the documents to our realtor. There was no turning back now.

Upon our return to Northville, I contacted Palmer Moving and made plans for shipping our household belongings to Florida in October. Some of the employees that Dorothy and I knew from our previous travels with Ford twenty some years earlier were still working for Palmer and said they would take good care of us.

As if we weren't busy enough, Dennis called to tell us he didn't care for apartment living and would prefer to own his home. He had been in his apartment since the previous January and said he didn't like being cooped up inside all the time. Dorothy and I agreed and helped him buy a small two bed-room-house in Walled Lake, Michigan, nine miles from Northville. It was the best thing we could have done for him. Dennis enjoyed having a home to call his own. He liked working on the house; Dorothy and I spent time helping him fix things and paint the house. We knew Dennis would be fine when he bought a chocolate Labrador puppy he named Fred to keep him company.

l-r, Dennis and Rick Hagelthorn, F-4 Phantom, Selfridge AFB, 2-17-1988

The highlight of the 1993 salmon season occurred in July when Rick Hagelthorn, a friend who also worked for me at Ford Aerospace and Communications Corporation, came to fish with me. I hadn't seen Rick since my retirement five years earlier and it was great catching up with events in his life and reliving memories at Ford Aerospace together. While fighting a big salmon, Rick looked over his shoulder and shouted, "This is almost as exciting as our flight together in the F-4 Phantom."

"Are you kidding?" I replied. "Nothing compares with that. It seems like it was only yesterday."

Rick, who was also a pilot in the Michigan Air National Guard, had planned an orientation flight for the two of us as part of our work for the Department of Defense. Ford Aerospace, a subsidiary of Ford where I was working with Rick at the time, was manufacturing the Aim-9 Sidewinder missile and several other secret classified missiles for the Department of Defense. After formal clearances from the Air National Guard and Department of Defense in Washington, D.C., permission was granted and a date set for our flight in February 1988, just prior to my retirement. I went with Rick to Selfridge Air Force Base in Mt. Clemens, Michigan, for a full-day orientation on flying in a F-4 Phantom. Using a flight simulator, an instructor guided me through an emergency ejection from the aircraft and how to use an oxygen mask and a G-Suit with pressure applied.

On February 17, 1988, four F-4 Phantom jet aircraft "scrambled", a military term used during the Battle of Britain to quickly get flight crews in the air. Rick, with me as his co-pilot, was squadron leader of the four planes in our attack group. Our mission was to repel a simulated attack on Selfridge Air Base by two B-52 bombers that had taken off from Wurtsmith Air Force Base in Oscoda, Michigan. We split into two groups with Rick and me and another F-4 immediately climbing to fifteen thousand feet. Rick was in the front seat and I in the rear. What a thrill to look out the window and see another plane just feet off your wing tip. The other two F-4's engaged the B-52's at seven-thousand feet from below while we descended on the B-52's from above. I was breathing through the oxygen mask and uncomfortable from the pressure of the G- Suit. The power and speed of the F-4 is overwhelming. Everything is three dimensional with no up or down. Picture a three -dimensional movie or space-walk at Disney World in real time. Everything is coming at you from all directions. As we descended, the radio was alive with chatter among the pilots. Rick zeroed in on the first B-52 and fired. We scored a hit! (These were not live missiles! A simulator records the trajectory of the missile). Before I could catch my breath, we were in a tight ninety-degree bank and climbing. A second B-52 was silhouetted against the sky slightly above us. Rick fired a second missile and recorded another hit. From my vantage point in the rear seat, I could see the other F-4's turning for a second pass at the B-52's. What might have appeared to be chaos to the uninitiated was a well-executed plan to destroy the "enemy." The encounter took no more than ten minutes.

As centrifugal force increases in a tight turn, the pressure in the G-Suit increases to retain blood in the upper body and brain to prevent loss of consciousness, tightening your core body muscles also helps. On two occasions that day, I experienced tunnel vision, the first sign of losing consciousness, and I tightened my body muscles. As I did, I slowly regained my vision. Heading home to Selfridge, Rick let me take the controls. I had much previous experience piloting propeller driven aircraft but could not have imagined the performance of a jet aircraft without having experienced it personally. After landing and high-fives, we returned to the debriefing room and reported on the mission.

I was exhausted but thrilled. This was an experience I would never forget. I thought at the time, "What a way to end thirty years with Ford and embark on a new chapter in my life!"

Rick and his family chartered with me numerous times over the next several years in Onekama, and we still keep in touch.

Between charters, keeping in touch with Mom and building a new house in Florida, 1993 was busy on all fronts. Dorothy and I called every week to talk to Mom and encourage her. At the end of August, Tom and Joann moved Mom to a nursing home twenty minutes from their house as they no longer could meet her medical needs at home. I talked to Mom by phone and tried to encourage her. I told her we had kept the apartment in Riverview for when she was ready to come home, she replied, "No, Son, it's time for me to be home with the Lord." Tom, Joann and their family visited Mom almost every day, I told Mom Dorothy and I would come to visit after Labor Day as soon as the charters slowed down.

Tom called on September 13, saying Mom had taken a turn for the worst and we should come to say goodbye. The following morning Dorothy and I made the twelve-hour drive to Frederick, not saying much, praying for Mom and reliving our memories. We arrived in Frederick around seven p.m. and drove straight to the nursing home to see Mom. She was not able to talk but acknowledged Dorothy and me with a weak smile, I held Mom's hand as I prayed with her for about an hour. Around eight p.m., the nurse suggested we let Mom rest and come back in the morning, so Dorothy and I kissed her goodbye and headed back to the house. Tom and Joann hadn't come with us to the hospital as they wanted to allow us time with Mom. We had just arrived back at Tom's house when the phone rang; Joann and Tom were shopping for groceries and not at home, so I answered the phone. The nurse said Mom passed away just after we left the nursing home and offered her condolences. I hung up and hugged Dorothy, and we both cried. We were so glad we had been there to say goodbye. Tom and Joann were disappointed they had not been with Mom, but we all knew Mom was just waiting to say goodbye to Dorothy and me before she went to be with the Lord.

The next morning, I called Bobcean Funeral Home in Flat Rock and arranged to bring Mom to Michigan where she would be buried by my dad at the Flat Rock Huron Valley Cemetery. Bobcean had handled the arrangements for my Dad's funeral in 1963. It didn't seem possible that was thirty years earlier. Realizing this, I felt older. A generation had passed, my mom was the last of our parents, Dorothy and I and Tom and Joann were now the patriarchs and matriarchs of the Blue family. The funeral was small, maybe forty family and friends in attendance. I can remember Mom saying she didn't have many friends anymore as most had died. It is always hard to say good bye to someone you love, but as Christians we know that we still have an eternity together.

Tom and Joann stayed a few days with us in Northville after the funeral, and we all went to Mom's apartment to pack her belongings in a rental trailer for Tom to take back with him to Maryland. Mom didn't have much in the way of personal belongings and furniture living in a one-bedroom apartment. With Dorothy and I moving to Florida, it didn't make sense for us to take anything other than a few mementos. Luanne was married and living in California and Dennis settled into his own house, so Tom and I agreed his children could make better use of the furniture. Before we parted, I reiterated to Tom and Joann that Dorothy and I would never forget their heart-felt commitment to take care of Mom during those difficult last days.

As Dorothy and I were driving home from Mom's apartment, I felt so blessed to have a mother like her. Much of who I am today is because of her and my dad. As with my dad, I wished I would have spent more time with Mom as she grew older. She was so proud of Tom and me, as we were of her. I'll tell both Mom and Dad so when I see them again in heaven.

Dorothy and I returned to Florida at the end of September. The house was right on schedule for completion. I wished Mom could have come to stay with us as she would have enjoyed it, just as she had enjoyed her trips to Venezuela and Australia when we were living there.

Over the past several weeks, I had been researching flats boats and decided on a twenty-foot Action Craft, a quality flats boat made in Cape Coral, Florida, not far from Port Charlotte. Paul Gard, owner of Action Craft, advised me that Gulf Wind Marine, located near Boca Grande, was a dealer and looking for a fishing guide to promote Action Craft in the Charlotte Harbor area.

The next morning, I stopped by Gulf Wind Marine and met with the sales manager. Gulf Wind Marine, a large Sea Ray dealer with a sixty-boat marina, took the Action Craft franchise to expand their market to fisherman. The sales manager was a natural born salesman, a southern boy, tall and lean with a big smile and easy disposition. He said Paul Gard had called to advise him that Action Craft would give me a guide discount on the boat.

It was common practice for guides to trailer their boat and launch at public ramps to keep costs down. Not wanting to launch and retrieve the boat every day at crowded public ramps, I asked the sales manager if he knew a place I could keep the boat on a boat lift. He knew of none. but said I could keep the boat at a dock in the marina. I didn't like that idea due to the rapid growth of algae and barnacles on the bottom of the hull.

"Let's go talk to Terry," he then said.

Terry Lynch, owner of Gulf Wind Marine, was outgoing, short and stocky, slightly bald and in his fifties. He had purchased the Gulf Wind location twelve months previously and was determined to grow the business. We chatted for a while, and I could tell by Terry's "can do" attitude that this was a man I could do business with.

I related my concern about leaving the boat in the water, and Terry agreed. "No problem," he said, "we can install a boat lift in the marina to keep your boat on." Terry then led me outside behind the single-story office building, overlooking the marina, and showed me a perfect location for my boat lift. It was right next to a popular seafood restaurant and the water taxi to luxurious Palm Island Resort. Customers and guests would have to walk by my boat to get to the restaurant and the water taxi.

"I'll pay to put in the boat lift," Terry said, "and lease it back to you for a fair price."

I thought of my docking experience in Onekama and elsewhere for a minute, and based on this familiarity, said, "Two-hundred dollars a month."

Terry countered with two-hundred and fifty, and I immediately replied, "Two-hundred and twenty-five".

Without hesitation, Terry said, "It's a deal," and we shook hands.

I was a little taken back as the agreement and the convenience was almost too good to be true. I wanted to sign a lease agreement, but Terry said, "No problem, we have a hand shake. That's good enough for me."

I was thinking for my own protection but didn't have the nerve to discuss it further. That handshake was the only contract Terry and I had until I left Florida fourteen years later. Terry and I went back to his office- and I ordered my new Action Craft with a two-hundred horse power Mercury outboard. With Terry's help, I was placed on the Mercury Pro Staff

Program with a discount on the motor. As I drove back to the motel we were staying at, I thought, with a discount both on the boat and the motor, God must really want us here!

Dorothy and I returned to Onekama in early October 1993 to prepare for our move to Florida. I had several more salmon charters before storing *True Blue* in a large building at Onekama Marine for the winter. Normally I didn't fish salmon that late in the season. However, with the trips we had made to Florida and Maryland and then Mom's funeral, I had to reschedule several charters into October to accommodate all my customers. As it turned out, we had great fishing right up until I took *True Blue* out of the water for storage. It took a few days to put the boat "to sleep" for the winter: winterizing the engines, cleaning the boat and fishing gear and making it ready for next spring.

During that 1993 summer in Onekama, I had talked to numerous customers about my not attending the boat shows. I asked if it would influence their decision to book another charter with me. Without exception, all of the customers I talked to replied that it wouldn't influence them at all. They liked going to the show and seeing me there, but the reason they booked with me was the quality of the charter, not because I was at the show. What better endorsement could you ask for than that! It also confirmed what I already knew: as the number of repeat customers increased, the need for new customers decreased. In addition, as my base of repeat customers grew so did the number of referrals from satisfied customers. The cost of the shows now outweighed the value of the few new bookings I needed each year. Based on the feedback from my customers and the knowledge that I would be spending the winter in Florida, I decided not to book any shows for the winter of 1994. As it turned out, I didn't ever again do any fishing shows in Michigan after moving to Florida.

Once again, as she had experienced so many times before during our moves around the world, the responsibility of moving fell primarily on Dorothy. By now, she was an old hand at it, but moving was still hard work. I was still busy with charters in Onekama and would lend a hand when time permitted, but for the most part, it was Dorothy's responsibility. I made a trip to Northville just before we moved out of the house in September to join Dorothy at a farewell party hosted by our neighbors and friends. We knew by experience, having moved so many times in the past, that saying goodbye to family and friends is the hardest part of moving. This time however, it wasn't quite the same as we would remain close enough to see each other occasionally during our summers in Onekama. We did get together with these folks over the coming years.

After the house in Northville was vacated, it took two more weeks for Dorothy and me to pack our personal items and close the condo in Onekama before leaving for Florida. We also took Buffy, our yellow Labrador born in Brazil. It was her first trip to Florida. Buffy was 12 years old, and it was hard for her to get around. She had travelled everywhere with us, and I wasn't sure how many more trips she could make. After leaving Onekama, Dorothy and I made one last stop at the Huron Valley Cemetery in Flat

Rock to say goodbye to Mom and Dad before departing to Florida the next day.

Dorothy and I arrived back in Riverwood on October 23. The house was beautiful! The view overlooking the lake and golf course and the smell of fresh paint and carpet confirmed we had made the right decision. I then hurried to Gulf Wind Marine to check on my new boat and boat lift, and sure enough, there was my Action Craft setting on a new boat lift in the ma-

Dorothy and Dennis at
new house in Florida, 1993

rina just as promised by Terry Lynch. My first impression was right: this was going to be a good place to do business!

Palmer Moving delivered our household belongings to Riverwood three days later on October 26, and Luanne and Emilee came to Florida to help us unpack. It was great having them with us if only for a week. Pat was busy with his real estate business and couldn't get away from work to join us.

Our house, overlooking a lake and the golf course, was cement block covered with stucco, painted a light beige with white trim and a tan tile roof. A covered main entrance led into the vaulted great room which had a panoramic view of the lake and golf course and connected to an open kitchen and dining area. The three bedrooms had their own baths and two opened onto the covered lanai extending across the back of the house. An attached two-car garage with laundry room completed the layout. We had met our neighbors on previous visits and considered ourselves the original homesteaders of Riverwood. Our community, Stonebridge, was a tight-knit "village" of sixty homes, and it stayed that way until we left fourteen years later. A big plus was the Riverwood community center directly across the street from the entrance to Stonebridge, four blocks from our house. The community center, designed to accommodate several hundred residents of Riverwood, was built around an Olympic-sized swimming pool with weight room, jacuzzi, shower room, library, conference room and office with computers and printers. Outside were tennis courts and a dog park. For the first couple of years, while Riverwood was still growing, it was like having our own recreation center where Stonebridge residents could get together and socialize. Over-time Riverwood grew to over thirteen hundred homes, condos and villas and is recognized as one of the premier golf course communities in Florida.

Dorothy and I joined the golf club at Riverwood, and Dorothy played golf every day. She was the ladies club champion nine of the fourteen years we were in Riverwood, and her performance earned her a status bordering on celebrity. She even had her own parking space at the golf club reserved for her. We also bought a golf cart for Dorothy to play golf and get around Riverwood. Seeing how content

Dorothy was with her new friends and playing golf confirmed once again the move was right for us.

Dorothy and I visited several churches and found an Assembly of God Church that became our church home until we left Florida. We were involved in numerous functions at the church as well as a weekly bible study with several other neighbors in Riverwood.

Dorothy - Second place, Michigan Seniors, 1989

By Thanksgiving, there were approximately twenty Stonebridge residents that had occupied their new residences. We gathered at the Riverwood community center for Thanksgiving dinner and to thank God for bringing us all together in Florida.

Through the Eyes of a Fisherman

Chapter 4
First Four Years
in Florida

We were settled into our home in Riverwood—settling in was something that Dorothy could do well! There remained the challenge of establishing my fishing business in Florida. Would setting up my new charter business in the Sunshine State be like starting over again?

Well, not really, as I had already succeeded at the major transformation from corporate executive to charter captain and had established a successful salmon charter business in Michigan. Instead of asking myself how to go about transferring skills learned in my corporate life and learning new ones necessary to become a charter captain, I was now just shifting gears—a different boat, new fishing techniques and a different variety of fish as well as different rules and regulations and the different task of finding saltwater customers.

I could build on the similarity with my days at Ford: letting the passion for my work guide me, knowing how to learn new skills, being adept at meeting new friends, and—yes—being aware of making a few mistakes along the way and having the presence of mind to analyze a problem and work my way to a best—or at least viable—solution.

It was evident to me that the same skills that had directed me to success at Ford—and salmon fishing—could be applied, with some tweaking, to different situations and venues anywhere in the world. While innate and learned skills are important in reaching our goals, I was reminded as I devoted the next months to adapting to salt-water charter-fishing, that each of us, no matter our position or status, have unique gifts bestowed on us by the Holy Spirit according to God's Grace. We are to use these to achieve God's purpose here on earth and, in doing so, arrive at success in our enterprises.

Don't get me wrong: there was still a lot to learn! But, this time around, as I set up my second charter business, the essential skills required for the success of my enterprise were already in place—and honed. Earlier, in 1989, I was learning how to establish a budget, run a charter and select customers. Now, I was just adapting these skills to the Florida charter-business environment

So, I set about to learn to be a salt-water captain. Among the first tasks to master was that I had to become acquainted with the waters where I would bring my customers. Charlotte Harbor and Pine Island Sound are separated from the Gulf by a series of barrier islands. The waterway covers miles of shallow grass flats interspersed with mangrove islands. The first few months I was in Florida, wanting to learn the area, I fished everyday by myself. It did not take me long to learn that getting lost in the myriad of islands and coves is not difficult if you are not paying attention!

Tides are a critical part of fishing the back country. In the Charlotte Harbor area—as everywhere there is salt water, of course, there are two high tides and two low tides each twenty-four-hour period. Some days at low tide, there is not enough water to float your boat, a few hours later at high tide, the water could be two to three feet deep in the same area. During my learning period, I occasionally misread the tides and had to get out and push the boat across the mud until the water was deep enough to float it again.

Apart from the tide charts which tell the time and range in feet of the high and low tides each day, there are a number of other variables, such as wind velocity and direction and the distance you are from the entrance of the harbor, that affect the tides in Charlotte Harbor. The tide flows from the west through the Boca Grande Pass into Charlotte Harbor from the Gulf of Mexico. The further the distance to the east from Boca Grande Pass, the longer it takes for the tide to change. There is approximately a three-hour difference in the timing of high and low tide from Boca Grande Pass to the Myakka River at the east end of Charlotte Harbor, a distance of approximately twenty miles by boat. Learning how tides ebb and flow in Charlotte Harbor results as much from the captain's experience as from the tide charts. After a while, an experienced captain "knows" and can make good decisions.

I learned to love the back country, and back-country fishing would become my favorite way to fish. I thrilled at sighting a fish and casting to it with a fly or artificial lure. I learned to throw a cast net (sixteen feet in diameter) to catch live menhaden, a small bait fish, four to six inches long, that I provided to customers who had trouble casting a fly. I stopped using live menhaden when I found out it was sometimes harder to catch the bait and keep it alive in my bait-well than catching the fish. When I had customers who couldn't cast an artificial lure or fly, I would buy shrimp from a local bait shop, anchor on a favorite fishing hole in the back country and wait for the fish to come to us. As must be evident from this paragraph, the guide is almost totally dependent on the skill of the angler to spot the fish and cast a lure to it with accuracy. At its best, back-country fishing can become great team work between the guide and the customer. And at its worse...we use shrimp!

Stealth is essential when fishing in one to five feet of water of the back country. The noise of the boat, loud talking and even the shadow of a bird or of the angler would spook the fish. To limit the boat's own noise, I would cut the engine. Then, I would stand on a poling platform mounted on the back of the boat above the outboard engine and pole the boat using a twenty-two-foot graphite push pole. Learning to maintain balance and maneuver a tippy boat with wind and anglers moving around is an essential skill.

The increase in my range of sight as I stood four-feet above the deck on the poling platform gave me the ability to spot fish at a greater distance from the boat and alert the angler. When the water got too deep to pole, which happens at about the five-foot depth, I would use my twelve-volt trolling motor which was mounted on the front of the boat. It would quietly move the boat over the shallow flats. One way for an angler not to endear himself to his guide after the guide had done all of this was to make noise when approaching a fish in shallow water. After I had quietly polled to within casting distance of a tailing redfish, sometimes the angler would be inattentive or careless and drop a rod, pliers or anything else that landed with a thud on the boat bottom. The noise spooked the edgy fish which immediately scuttled away. This was a learning moment for me when I really understood the meaning of forgiveness.

In November, while I was still learning the backcountry waters, Terry Lynch introduced me to Dean Beckstead, owner/developer of the exclusive Palm Island Resort and of island home-sites. Palm Island, a barrier island bordering the Gulf and directly across the Intercoastal Waterway from Gulf Wind Marine, is accessible only by water. Palm Island Resort provides water taxi service between Palm Island Marina and the mainland to accommodate resort guests and home owners. Some Palm Island residents had their own boat and used Gulf Wind and Palm Island marinas as docking when they commuted back and forth. There is also a large barge, pushed by a tug, that runs every half-hour transporting vehicles and supplies from the mainland to Palm Island. Dean Beckstead, pleasant and soft spoken, in his late forties, introduced me to many residents on Palm Island who became good customers. The following year, Dean asked me to oversee Palm Island Resort's fishing program, arranging charters for Palm Island residents and guests.

That same fall, in November 1993, I attended Captain Pete Greenan's three-day fly-fishing school at Uncle Henry's Marina on Boca Grande. Since fly fishing was going to be important to my charter business, I knew I had to increase my knowledge of fly fishing the area and really nail it down. Captain Pete, in his thirties and a full-time fishing guide, was an excellent instructor and fly fisherman. We subsequently took group charters out together and remained friends until I left Florida. Captain Pete was impressed with my casting the heavier twelve-weight fly rod. My skill was another instance of the entrepreneur being well served by receiving as much instruction as possible before launching himself. It was Billy Pate who had taught me to cast during his school in Mazatlán, Mexico. Time and money well spent!

The following month, on December 2 and 3, the Federation of Fly Fishers, an international organization dedicated to the advancement, conservation and education of all things fly fishing, sponsored a first-of-its-kind, casting-instructor certification program. Of course, I signed up. This program produced another seemingly unexpected relationship when I met Captain Sandy Melvin, owner of Gasparilla Outfitters, on Boca Grande—but, as always, I know whose hand was involved in making this happen. Captain

Sandy, as you will learn later, had a significant role in expanding my fly fishing career.

The instructor of the casting-certification program, Steve Rajeff, was a legend in fly casting and had won the American Casting Association World Fly Casting competition numerous times. He also held the world record fly casting distance with a cast of an astonishing two-hundred and forty-three feet! We six students in the class learned casting mechanics and techniques on how to teach casting to our customers. The second day, we practiced casting and critiquing each other on our casting stroke. Much like golf, if you don't learn the proper techniques initially, you continue to practice your mistakes.

I was intimidated by the knowledge and skill required to be a good fly caster yet impressed with how much Steve Rajeff knew and how confident I was he could teach me much. To pass the course, we had to demonstrate the numerous types of casts: overhead, side arm and roll cast to a minimum standard under the watchful eye of Steve Rajeff. Three of the six students passed, Sandy and I among them. The students who didn't pass had little prior knowledge of fly casting and were not prepared for the rigorous performance required to pass the course. To my knowledge, Sandy and I were the first to be certified as casting instructors by the Federation of Fly Fishers in Florida and were proud to be certified by none other than Steve Rajeff himself.

The following year, Sandy's Gasparilla Outfitters became a certified Orvis Outfitter. Orvis, a high-end retailer of fly fishing equipment, was highly respected in the fly fishing industry for its world-wide certification of outfitters and guides. Sandy invited me to be part of the Orvis guide program to help with fly casting instruction and charters. I was pleased to do so as teaching fly casting was also a great way to improve my own fly casting skills.

Pat, Luanne and Emilee plus my son, Dennis, came to Florida over the holidays that Christmas of 1993. It had been a year of sadness and joy. I couldn't help but think of Mom and how I missed her not being there to celebrate with us—she had passed only a few months earlier—but I was also thankful for my family and for the new opportunities that lay ahead. It was comforting to be together as a family in our new home. Getting together like this in Florida for the holidays became a tradition. I don't recall a Christmas or Easter while we were there that one, if not all the family, including Ron and Ina and their kids, didn't come to Florida. I enjoyed taking them fishing and seeing the dolphins and manatees.

My Holiday 1993 newsletter to my customers in Michigan proved to be a big hit. I highlighted that my absence from the forthcoming winter fishing shows was not an indication of a shrinking business but rather of expanding my business to Florida. I invited each customer to come experience salt-water fishing with me. I related how salmon-fishing customers would benefit from my knowledge of new lures and techniques. While I had learned these for Florida conditions, I assured them I could apply much of it to salmon fishing in Michigan. At the same time, I encouraged each customer both to come fish with me in Florida and to book early in Michigan for the prime salmon fishing months of June, July and August. Within the next few weeks, I had four charter bookings for Florida and over thirty charters for the following summer in Michigan. All of this without having to attend a fishing show! Not much wrong with that, I concluded.

As the year turned into 1994, Dorothy and I reflected on the past three years: the training at Billy Pate's fly fishing school in Mazatlan, the decision to move to Florida and leave Dennis behind, starting a new business and the passing of Mom. Now, here I was, a certified fly-casting instructor, learning from one of the best fly fisherman in the world, working on the Orvis guide program and entering a new phase of my fishing business that had unlimited potential. Once again, I am amazed: Dorothy and I couldn't have planned this successful string of events. All we had to do—then and now—was be faithful, follow God's lead and watch our aspirations turn into reality.

We discussed how the many changes reminded us of the first time we stepped out on faith to travel to Venezuela with Ford in 1968, of the horrendous deaths of Dorothy's folks, John and Lucille Hacker, who were killed in a tragic plane crash, of my flights as a missionary pilot for New Tribes Mission. All along, God had led us through good times and bad. In the end, we were grateful for how God had directed our lives and we waited to learn how He would continue to do so.

In January 1994, I launched my Florida charter business. Strategically, I felt I had prepared well, fishing every day during the past eight weeks, improving my fly casting and networking with other guides. I still had a lot to learn but was confident and

Dennis with Action Craft,
Gulf Wind Marine, 1994

excited to start this new venture in my fishing career. I was booked several times a week that first season in Florida. Some customers were from Michigan, but the majority were new customers from the Port Charlotte area. My early contacts with Terry Lynch, Dean Beckstead, Captain Pete Greenan and Captain Sandy Melvin provided an immediate source of credibility that led to customers. I don't actually recall the name of the people on my first charter out of Port Charlotte. This trip was so different from my first paid charter EVER with Hunter Pickens in 1988 when I was trying so hard to do everything right—and not sure I would! I was now an experienced captain—I knew that I both worked well with customers and had a lot to offer them as a result of the experience I had gaining accreditation as a fly casting instructor. I could tell, from my first back-country charter, I was going to like being a fly-fishing guide.

My contacts and networking with other guides also paid off. By the first week of May, I had run sixty-eight charters in Florida. Two things became readily apparent: first, I had hit the sweet spot in the rapidly expanding fly fishing market, where fly-fishing guides and casting instructors were in great demand and, second, that God had picked the perfect location to start my business. The natural beauty and excellent fishing around Charlotte Harbor was a fisherman's paradise. It would be a number of years, and I hoped never, before increased economic development would negatively impact the area.

As with my early days salmon fishing, I made some mistakes learning salt-water fishing in Florida, but with five years of chartering under my belt, the learning curve was much faster. While I ran aground occasionally in the backcountry surrounding Charlotte Harbor and had to push my boat to deeper water to float the boat, I also learned how to pole the boat in windy conditions, when tides were best for fishing and I had discovered where the different species of fish could be caught in largest quantities.

Over the next months, I appreciated the contrast of the equipment and technique used for salmon charters on Lake Michigan and fishing the back country of Charlotte Harbor. The differences were diverse and many. The most obvious was the size of my 31-foot, *True Blue*, weighing twelve-thousand pounds with twin inboard engines, trolling twelve to fourteen fishing lines, with a first-mate and four to six customers in choppy Lake Michigan waters. Compare that with my 20-foot, *True Blue*, in Florida, weighing only one-thousand pounds with a single outboard engine, sight fishing the calm protected waters of the back country with one or two anglers using fly rods with light, twelve- to twenty pound-test leaders tied between the fly line and the fly, and the differences were—not to repeat myself—diverse and many.

Perhaps not as obvious but important, my Florida business was more profitable than my Michigan business. I charged one-third less for my Florida charters than for my Michigan charters but my profit margin was one-third higher in Florida due to the seventy-five percent lower operating cost (fuel, dockage/storage, insurance, maintenance and no first-mate) of my boat in Florida.

These differences in boats, equipment and style of fishing between Michigan and Florida, brought about a significant and unexpected change in my customer base. That winter of 1994, I realized I was no longer a family-oriented business. The casting skill required to fish the back country made it difficult for the novice fisherman. The majority of my customers were experienced fly fishermen/women or people who seriously wanted to learn to be one. I was increasing the size of my overall customer base, as I still had my family-oriented customers in Michigan. The family and recreational orientation that I enjoyed on charters in Michigan was replaced in Florida with fly-casting lessons, often with women and children. I also learned the relationship between the guide and angler was fundamental to a successful trip. While the guide's experience and knowledge were paramount, the angler's ability to see the fish and accurately cast a fly to it was essential if the fish was to be caught. Success was a team effort.

On more than one occasion while poling the boat, I have had to duck as a fly fisherman zinged a fly close to me or stuck me with the hook. Not the way to endear yourself to your guide! I soon learned to explain to the angler not to cast until I positioned the boat for a cast. I would slightly turn the bow of the boat to the right or left of the fish so the angler would not make a back cast directly over me. Of course, an experienced fly fisherman will instinctively know when to cast to avoid hitting the guide, but this was not the case with most of my customers.

What I enjoyed most about my new venue, however, was the tranquility of back-country fishing. The beauty of the area, the birds—herons, ibises and egrets stalking their prey—and the silence except for birds calling and schools of small bait fish and mullet splashing on the water. The goal was catching a fish on a fly, not how many pounds of fish we caught as was often the case with salmon fishing. The experience of seeing the fish, making a good cast and hooking the fish was what it was all about. My new-found skills as a fly-casting instructor coupled with patience and a willingness to teach others—characteristics that had also served me well as a corporate executive —was a perfect match for my new business.

The back country also offered an appropriate time to talk about the beauty of God's creation and about how blessed we were to be experiencing it. Don't get me wrong: I also enjoyed salmon fishing and the people I met in Michigan. The complementarity of fishing both Michigan and Florida was the best of both of those worlds. I know it made me a better fisherman. As when I worked for Ford as a negotiator, there was little inclination to fall into a routine or become bored.

Another difference between Michigan and Florida fishing was weather. In a nutshell, weather was rarely an issue in Florida. As I mentioned in the previous chapter, Lake Michigan can become rough and dangerous, occasionally requiring me to cancel or reschedule a salmon charter. Safety was the deciding factor. In Florida, fishing the protected waters of Charlotte Harbor, I could almost always get out of the wind to fish the backcountry. However, from December through February an occasional cold front with strong northerly winds, would drop the morning low temperatures into the forties. Not cold by Michigan standards but for Floridians, that's long underwear and down jacket time! The fishing was generally slower when the air temperature dropped into the forties and fifties as it also cooled the water. Temperatures would generally climb back into the sixties by mid-day. I learned to plan a later start for the charter to better accommodate most customers. That is not to say I never fished in cold weather, I had customers from Michigan that thought air temperature in the forties was t-shirt weather compared to the near zero weather they had just left. A light jacket and they were ready to go. From April on, thunderstorms would increase in the afternoon, but were generally isolated and moved quickly through the area. Only several times a season would I have to reschedule or cancel due to weather.

The highlight of that first spring (1994) in Florida

was my first tarpon on a fly. I had the day off and decided to take my twelve-weight fly rod and check out Johnson Shoals, a shallow area along the Gulf, one mile south of Boca Grande pass. It was early May and the tarpon were starting to show up in large numbers along the shore of the Gulf beaches. I was idling along the Shoals enjoying the beautiful morning when my mind drifted back to Billy Pate's fly fishing school and where I first learned salt water fly fishing. At the time, fishing in Florida was only a dream that I was hoping might come true one day.

My reverie was suddenly broken when I saw a school of tarpon, maybe a dozen, moving toward me in four to six feet of water. I put the boat in neutral, shut off the motor and waited. The tarpon were swimming slowly toward me, stopping occasionally to circle and stir up sand near the bottom. I used the trolling motor to position myself with the sun at my back for better visibility and prepared for a cast as they approached to within sixty feet of the boat. Standing on the bow, I cast toward the tarpon, but the fly landed too far to the right of the school. I retrieved the fly line and cast again. The second cast landed just in front of the tarpon. I hesitated to allow time for the fly to slowly sink to the bottom. I slowly stripped (retrieved) the fly several inches at a time with my left hand and saw a tarpon move toward the fly—the line came tight. I pointed the rod at the fish while striking hard with my left hand to drive the hook into the boney mouth of the tarpon.

The tarpon exploded from the water thirty feet from the boat twisting and turning, the silver-dollar-size scales reflecting the early morning sun. My immediate reaction, learned while sail fishing with Billy Pate, was to point the rod at the fish allowing slack in the line so the sudden surge of power from the fish jumping would not break the fishing line nor tear the hook from the mouth of the tarpon. Another jump and then another, each one more acrobatic than the others. The tarpon, which I estimated at eighty pounds, then took off peeling sixty yards of line from the reel. In shallow water, less than ten feet, tarpon expend additional energy jumping and tire sooner, making it easier and quicker to land one. In deep water, tarpon often stay deep instead of jumping, conserving energy and making them more difficult to land on a fly rod.

Everything was happening so fast there was no room for error when you have an eighty-pound tarpon on a fly line. A key element when retrieving your fly line after a cast is to ensure the line falls neatly into coils on the deck. When a tarpon bites and frantically swims away from the boat, it is important not to allow the fly line to tangle as it rapidly uncoils from the deck. I instruct my customers to hold the fly line in their left hand away from their body and allow the line on the deck to play out with just enough tension to keep the coils from tangling until the line is back on the fly reel. Most fish are lost when the angler either steps on the fly line or the coils tangle or get caught on the reel. Once the line on the deck is played out and tight on the reel, you can fight the fish using the rod and the reel.

I finally stopped the fish and began to gain line. Being alone, I had to maneuver the boat with the electric trolling motor and fight the fish at the same time. After fighting the fish for about twenty minutes, I started the outboard motor to move closer to the tarpon and regain line. Not so easy when you are steering, shifting gears and fighting the fish. Fishing tarpon on a fly is definitely a two-person operation. Another fifteen minutes and I had the tarpon alongside the boat. I placed my fly rod in a rod holder I had custom-made to hold a fly rod, and with a tight grip on the leader, reached for the tarpon. The tarpon lurched and tried to pull away when the leader broke. The tarpon's raspy mouth had cut the leader just a few inches above the hook. I set back exhausted but happy and content. I was going to release the fish anyway but I wanted to remove the hook before releasing it to assure the fish's survival.

As Dorothy and I were packing to go back to Onekama that spring of 1994, the realization that the condo at Pirates Cove was now our Michigan home finally hit us. We had had the more capacious house in Northville to fall back on and could quickly retrieve items stored there that we had forgotten to take with us to Onekama. The condo didn't have a lot of storage, so we had to be more judicious in what we brought with us from Florida, which was now our home base. Fortunately, in 1985, the fire hall in Onekama had become available for sale and Doug West and I had purchased it. Now, we could store personal seasonal items there for which we had no place in the condo.

Dorothy and I arrived in Onekama just after Memorial Day. It was good to see my friends at the marina again and to catch up on the news in Onekama over the winter. But, socializing was not the top of my docket. There was plenty to do to get *True Blue* ready for another season that was already well booked and for which customers would soon be arriving. I spent the next four days polishing and cleaning the boat, painting the bottom with anti-fouling paint (a special coating that is applied to the hull to prevent algae and barnacles from growing on the bottom of the boat), cleaning and filling fresh water tanks, checking that the toilet and the holding tank worked and other miscellaneous chores to make ready to launch the boat for the season.

Before moving to Florida, I performed these chores of making the boat ready to launch during the winter months. I no longer had that luxury of time. As my cash flow increased subsequently, to avoid the expenditure of time to prepare my boat in Michigan, I paid Onekama Marine to do most of the work of winterizing *True Blue* in Onekama and then getting it ready for summer. These preparations reminded me of one more thing I appreciated about fishing in Florida: the work there of preparing the boat for storage was so easy. It had taken me all of about four hours, before I left Florida, to take my flats boat out of the water and onto my boat trailer, wash and polish the boat and motor, prepare the motor for storage by flushing the engine with an anti-corrosion solution and spraying oil into the spark plug holes and perform other minor maintenance such as greasing the fittings and placing the boat in the garage of my house at Riverwood. That had been it and I was ready to go next fall.

My first trip of the season was a typical offshore

charter of fishing for steelhead on what we call the "scum line" fifteen miles offshore from Onekama. During the early summer months of May and June, as the Lake Michigan water warms from the sun, thermal bars form on the surface in the deeper cold water of Lake Michigan. The deepest part of Lake Michigan, almost one-thousand feet deep, is approximately thirty miles offshore due west of Onekama. In early June, the thermal bars are encountered closer to shore as the water warms from the shoreline westward toward the middle of the lake. When you cross a thermal bar the surface temperature drops from five to fifteen degrees Fahrenheit within a few hundred feet; a surface temperature in the forties would not be uncommon. You can clearly see where the warmer water encounters the colder heavier water and forms the "scum line" where the colder water holds debris and insects that the fish feed on.

Because of this frenzy of feeding in cold water, trolling for the acrobatic steelhead at such a time is exciting and productive, but there is a downside to the colder water. It often produces fog, even on a bright sunny day. *True Blue* was equipped with state-of-the-art radar, so we were prepared for fishing on such a day.

On that day with visibility ranging between one hundred and three hundred feet, my customers were catching steelhead and having a good time when I noticed a target on the radar screen about two miles off my port bow. It was not uncommon to see other boats on the radar. Some were large commercial freighters and others, smaller boats fishing for steelhead. With practice, you can tell the size of vessels

on the radar screen by the size and shape of the target image. This particular vessel looked to be a
smaller fishing boat and was closing at a high rate
of speed, too fast for the restricted visibility, I
thought. Even with radar, a good rule of thumb is to
be able to stop within half the distance of the visibility.

The boat on my radar was obviously travelling at
a cruising speed in the twenty-mile-per-hour range.
As the vessel closed to within one mile of *True Blue*,
I maintained our course to establish the relative
bearing, the clockwise angle in degrees from the
heading of your vessel on a straight line to the other
vessel. If the relative bearing stays the same and the
distance is decreasing, you are on a collision course
with the other vessel. It appeared the other vessel,
now at one-half mile off my port bow would pass behind us. I asked my first mate and the customers to
keep a close lookout. I thought to myself, "My first
trip out! What a way to start the season."

Visibility was about three hundred feet when suddenly out of the fog came a boat headed right at our
port bow. I instinctively turned to starboard trying to
avoid the collision. Just as I thought the boat was
going to hit us, it veered hard to our port. We could
see the bottom of the boat in a tight starboard turn
away from us and heard the deafening roar of the engines as it passed by within one hundred feet of *True
Blue*, taking my three in-line planer boards and lines
with them. Then the day was quiet, except for the
sound of my idling engine.

We were in semi-panic mode. Instinctively, I
asked if everyone was all right and asked my first

mate to hurry and take in the other fishing lines. I didn't want to stop my boat and risk tangling the other six fishing lines in my propellers. There appeared to be no damage other than the loss of the planer boards and one broken fishing rod. As soon as our fishing lines were in, I turned and idled back in search of the other boat. I could see a target on the radar screen about one-quarter mile away and presumed it to be the other boat.

My first mate shouted, "Is anyone out there"?

To which we heard a faint reply, "We are dead in the water."

The mate shouted, "Are you ok?"

"Go to channel 68," was the reply.

I switched to channel 68 on my VHF marine radio just as they were calling me to ask if we were all right. I replied we were and was about to let them know what I thought of their dangerous actions, when the caller said it was Tony Birchmeier on the boat *Bar Tender*. I couldn't believe it! Tony was a respected charter captain and friend from Portage Lake Marine across from Onekama Marine.

I said, "It's me, Denny, on *True Blue*."

"Oh, my gosh, Denny! I'm sorry," Tony said.

Tony went on to say he was with another boat from the Portage Lake Marina, showing the owner how to fish for steelhead. When they started home, visibility was over a half-mile, and he was in the back of the boat putting tackle away. Tony noticed the fog settling in again and asked the owner to slow down which he did, but they were still going too fast for conditions. Tony had just taken the wheel when he saw us dead ahead and veered to starboard while cutting power to the engines. Had he not been at the controls, Lord knows if the inexperienced owner would have been able to avoid hitting us.

My fishing line and planer boards had caught on one of their propellers causing a vibration. Tony was preparing to dive under the boat to see if he could cut the line off rather than go the fifteen miles home on one engine. I told Tony we would stand by until we knew the outcome and offered to help if need be. As upset as I was, I couldn't leave a stranded boat out there, friend or not. I didn't envy Tony diving under the boat in forty-degree water and trying to cut the fishing line from the propeller. About fifteen minutes later, Tony called on the radio to say the line was cleared from the propeller and they were back on two engines ready to head home.

I asked my customers if they had enough energy to fish some more, and without hesitation, they said, "Absolutely!" We fished another hour, catching several more steelhead before calling it a day and heading back to the marina. Fortunately, after a few miles, the fog lifted and we had a relaxing trip back to Onekama at normal cruising speed. Not letting an opportunity to witness pass by, I commented to my customers how fortunate we were to not have been hurt or killed, how Tony had taken the wheel at just the right time. I related some of my experiences and how the Lord had looked after me and my family over the years. They were not all good times, but we knew He was always there with us. I knew these customers understood exactly what I was saying when I got a collective "Amen!"

Tony called the next morning to apologize. He had

a check for me from the owner of the boat for the cost of the fishing gear I lost, plus a little extra, for the difficulty he had caused. Tony said he never saw us on the radar before almost hitting us. We surmised that when the owner of the boat slowed down after Tony spoke to him, the slower speed of the boat caused the stern of the boat to settle lower in the water and the bow of the boat to lift higher, causing the radar beam to point higher above the horizon and miss objects on the water. Tony accepted full responsibility for the near accident, knowing the owner was a novice boater and he was the captain on board. We both agreed you can take nothing for granted when on the water, fog or no fog. I heard from Tony again a few days later. The owner of the boat was so distraught over the incident that he put his boat up for sale and left the marina.

I ran about fifty charters that summer, mostly repeat business. By far, the topic of conversation on the boat was my fishing business in Florida. "Tell us about catching a tarpon. Show us your photos. When is a good time to come fish with you?" The questions went on and on. Some of the customers had actually fished with me in Florida the past winter, and others just wanted to dream about it. In any event, it was a great topic of conversation and enhanced my reputation as a captain.

Luanne and our granddaughter, Emilee, who was now age three, came to Onekama in August for the annual Onekama Marine Shoot Out. Pat was busy at work and stayed in California. The two-day tournament sponsored by Onekama Marine for customers of the marina was a family affair with a pig roast following the tournament. Dorothy and I began fishing the tournament with Luanne and Dennis when we

l-r, son Dennis, Luanne,
Dorothy and Emilee, 1994

first came to the marina in 1983. There was a good weather forecast so we all agreed to take Emilee to her first tournament. Luanne had been on boats with Dorothy and me since she could walk and wanted Emilee to have the same opportunity. Our team of Luanne, Emilee, Dennis, Dorothy and I finished first out of twenty boats. We had a great time just being together and decided Emilee was now a permanent member of our crew.

The good news was Luanne let us know she and Pat were expecting our second grandchild in October. We returned to Florida in late September, and Dorothy flew to California in October to be with Luanne when our grandson, John, was born on October 28, 1994. We were so happy for them and thanked the Lord for another healthy grandchild.

The bad news that fall was we had to put our yellow lab Buffy down. I knew this was coming but it doesn't make it any easier. For the first time in fifteen years, we didn't have a Labrador in our family.

After Dorothy and I returned to Riverwood for our

second winter and told our next-door neighbor, Dot Bittner, that we had to put Buffy down, she felt as bad as we did. Dot and her husband Jack, who were just like family, had moved to Riverwood just after we did. Jack, a World War II Navy fighter pilot and Dot, a nurse, both in their late sixties, moved to Riverwood from Wisconsin after Jack's retirement. They had loved Buffy and had taken care of her when Dorothy and I were away. I was careful to clean up after Buffy but occasionally would miss one. Dot bought some little red utility flags used to mark underground lines and would place them where I needed to clean up.

I have always been fond of animals, particularly of dogs. I still recall when I was sixteen years old we had to put our Great Dane, Colonel, to sleep on the farm, I cried then and I still do now remembering. Not wanting to go through the pain of loss again, I promised myself Buffy would be our last Labrador. However, soon after we returned to Florida and the grief had subsided, I found a kennel that had yellow lab pups available. With encouragement from Dot and Jack, Dorothy and I went to "just look" at the puppies. We left with a yellow female which we named Daisy. Dot and Jack were elated. I made them promise to baby sit Daisy whenever necessary which they were glad to do. The moral of the story is you never "just look" at Labrador puppies if you don't intend to buy one!

In October, I wrote my first article for the bi-monthly Gulf Wind newsletter, *Dock Lines*, and was a regular contributor over the next years. I helped Gulf Wind Marine at the Miami Boat Show and took potential buyers fishing whenever necessary to help sell a boat. Terry Lynch, others in the Gulf Wind Marine staff and I became good friends and enjoyed our time together at the show. Although the Sea Ray boats at thirty to sixty-feet were considerably larger than my flats boat, I occasionally taught a Sea Ray customer to dock and operate their new boat. Over time, I learned to operate larger boats and helped Gulf Wind Marine and Onekama Marine demonstrate boats to potential customers and new owners and move boats for boat shows and winter storage.

My flats boat, *True Blue*, was docked one-mile from Fisherman's Edge Tackle Shop. I first met the owner, Jim Mackey, the previous year but had no idea how important a role he would play in my guide business. Jim was a master at rod and reel repair and sold live bait, shrimp and blue crabs. Many of the guides caught their own live bait, but during the winter when the water cooled, it was difficult for the guides to find live bait and they had to depend on bait shops that bought bait caught elsewhere by commercial operators. I called Jim a week in advance with my fishing schedule, and he would set bait aside for me every morning.

On several occasions, Jim repaired a rod or reel for me while I waited, or when he couldn't repair it in time, loaned me a rod and reel, so I would be ready for the next morning's charter. For a guide to fish every day, it was essential to have a support network for bait, rod and reel repairs and boat maintenance. Thanks to Fisherman's Edge, I only missed one charter for a lack of bait.

I vividly recall that cold, windy morning when I

went to Fisherman's Edge to pick up my pre-ordered four-dozen shrimp. It was around nine a.m. as I had advised my customers we would leave later to allow time for the temperature to warm-up. I became uneasy when I noticed only two cars in the parking lot. Normally, when the weather was cold and bait hard to find the parking lot should be full. I walked through the front door but found no one in the shop. I heard voices in the back, outside the building, where Jim kept his bait tanks. As I stepped outside I was shocked. The ground had been dug up and the bait tanks were tipped over, dead shrimp scattered everywhere. Jim and a couple of guides were frantically trying to salvage a few shrimp.

"What happened? Who would do something like that?" I asked in disbelief. I was thinking the destruction must have been the work of vandals.

Without looking up, Jim replied, "Pigs, those damn pigs."

Wild pigs were a nuisance in Florida at the time, rooting up yards, tipping over garbage containers and anything else that could provide food. The pigs particularly liked to root up sod to get at the grubs. The pungent smell of the shrimp tanks apparently attracted the pigs. Jim had a chain link fence around his back property, but obviously not enough to keep the pigs out. You could clearly see where they had rooted under the fence. Four pigs had gotten in just before Jim arrived at six a.m. and were still there when he heard the commotion in back. Jim chased the pigs away, but it was too late. Bait tanks were lying on their sides, water and shrimp spilling out, sod and mud everywhere. The two guides helping

Jim were able to salvage maybe two-dozen shrimp each that they had picked up. Everyone one else—including me—was out of luck. Fortunately, my two anglers for the day were decent casters with a spinning rod, and we caught trout and redfish on rubber jigs that looked like shrimp. It reminded me to count my blessings. Even bait shop owners have their trials and tribulations.

Chapter 5
Growing My Business and God's Too

The next years of my business growth proved to be enjoyable ones. Gone was the tension of establishing myself in Florida. Any uncertainty about what I might do next was replaced with what I knew very well how to succeed at—by personality and training. That "secret sauce" was developing relationships with others in the fishing community. With more relationships, my business flourished.

In the late-1980s, the recreational fishing industry began a rapid growth in Florida, and with it, came more fishing regulations and advocacy groups. Protecting the grass flats, establishing no-wake zones, controlling the manatee population, banning the use of gill nets and managing gamefish were major topics of discussion by state legislators and user groups. When I arrived in Florida in 1993, there was a growing awareness among fishing guides that they needed a voice in formulating policies and regulations that impacted the fishing industry. In the fall of 1994, approximately twenty fishing guides attended a meeting in Tampa and founded the Florida Guides Association, the first of its kind in Florida. A board of six fishing guides, of which I was one, was elected to direct the organization. Scott Moore, a prominent guide from the Sarasota area, was elected president. By the end of the second-year, membership increased to over seventy guides and the Florida Guides Association became a prominent voice in formulating fishing regulations in Florida. In spite of its humble beginning, the organization still exists today.

In November 1994, I joined the Boca Grande Guides Association. Cappy Joiner, president of the association, had fished the area for over forty years and was a product of the rich history of tarpon fishing in Boca Grande Pass. The sport dated back to the early 1900s when guests at the Collier Inn on Useppa Island went fishing for tarpon in suits and ties and the ladies in long dresses and bonnets. By the mid-1930s, Boca Grande Pass emerged as the premier place in the world to catch a "silver king." Useppa Island, located in Pine Island Sound three miles south of Boca Grande Pass, was purchased by entrepreneur Barron Collier in 1911. He built the Collier Inn and established the Isaac Walton Club, one of the most prestigious fishing clubs in America. Guides hired by the Inn would row sixteen- to eighteen-foot wooden boats to transport the wealthy friends and guests of Mr. Collier to the tarpon fertile waters of Boca Grande Pass.

The Boca Grande Fishing Guides Association, founded in 1988, to protect the natural resources and world-class tarpon fishery surrounding Boca Grande Pass, had thirty plus members, some second- and third-generation guides from the Boca Grande area. Others like myself were transplants from outside of Florida. The association arranged the use of docks on Boca Grande for member guides to pick up and drop off customers, which allowed me to reach a previously untapped customer base on Boca Grande.

I enjoyed the monthly meetings at the Boca Grande Community Center and the banter between the guides which was sometimes heated and at other times, polite and poking fun at each other. The focus of the association was fishing for tarpon in Boca Grande Pass. Fly fishing didn't get much attention. In one of the meetings, a discussion on how to protect the grass flats came up. I suggested they consider no motor zones restricted to poling or an electric motor. The other two fly fishing guides at the meeting, thought it was a great idea but we were shouted down as the majority had larger boats for fishing tarpon in Boca Grande Pass. They didn't want to do anything that would restrict their use of a motor.

I made friends with numerous members who were gracious enough to share information on where and how to fish Charlotte Harbor. Since its inception, the BGFGA has initiated numerous projects and advocated for regulations to protect and promote tarpon fishing in Boca Grande Pass.

In January, I joined the Florida Conservation Association (FCA), a statewide, non-profit organization dedicated to protecting the marine resources and the anglers who pursue them. FCA was one of seventeen organizations from coastal states that made up the Coastal Conservation Association, with over one-hundred thousand members in the US. FCA played a prominent role in the Florida legislature to ban the use of gill nets in state waters in 1994.

At the first meeting to create a local FCA chapter in Englewood, ten miles north of Boca Grande, I met

Ben Kittrell. Tall and lean, Ben was soft spoken, intelligent and loved to fish. Dorothy and I became good friends with Ben, Cheryl and their two sons, and Ben and I fished together as often as we could in our free time. Cheryl was the best cook ever; her cream pies and

Ben Kettrell and new flats boat, 2014

other southern delicacies were delicious. I could never figure how Ben stayed so slim with all that home cooking. Ben was an excellent fisherman and knew his home waters around Lemon Bay and Stump Pass, just minutes away from where I kept my boat at Gulf Wind Marine. Ben came to my rescue on several occasions with advice on where to find local bait and where to go to fish when I was guiding customers in Lemon Bay.

My membership and networking in these fishing organizations significantly accelerated my knowledge of marine resources in Florida and allowed me to become an active participant in issues affecting the fishing industry.

During the mid-1990s, I finally accepted the benefit of having a web site and a cell phone as marketing tools. Some of the older generation, like myself, were slow to make the switch but it didn't take long to become a believer. Like so many other innovations, it's hard now to imagine life before the Internet and cell phones.

I had developed skin problems over the past several years from the sun, and by the mid-1990s, the condition had gotten worse. I was using sunscreen and covering up more with a hat and long-sleeved shirts and pants, but the damage had already been done. Fishing in Venezuela, Australia and Brazil where the sun was intense had taken its toll. I understood this was something to keep an eye on but I resolved not to let it interfere with my fishing.

In the winter of 1995, I was busy every day with charters and fly-casting seminars. Evenings were often taken up with meetings at local fishing clubs and guide association meetings. One night a week, I taught a fishing course to eighth graders at Lemon Bay High School in Englewood. The kids were enthusiastic, but I think I enjoyed the class more than the kids, whom I found to be fun to be around. I poured much time and energy in these "extra-curricular" activities as I have always applied myself one hundred and ten percent to anything I was doing. My dad used to say, "If it was worth doing, it was worth doing well." In addition, I believe it is my responsibility to use the abilities God gave me to the utmost if I am to be an ambassador for Christ.

Phil Benton, past president of Ford and my former boss in Dearborn, had just retired to Boca Grande and called me for a charter in February. The day we went out was a cool windy one, but we had a great time chatting about old times at Ford and our mutual friends. We both laughed when I reminded him how the general managers at Ford asked me not to bring up boating in their meetings with Phil as he preferred talking about boating rather than their business priorities. (Phil still had a boat of his own.) One thing we both still had in common—every time we heard Ford mentioned our ears picked up and we wanted to know what was going on. We agreed, however, we wouldn't want that responsibility again! That was then, this was now. I told Phil I felt my leaving Ford at age fifty-five and starting a new career charter fishing was the right thing for me. I related how I believed Ford had provided me the opportunity to travel the world as a mission field and now my charter boat was my mission field. Phil nodded and said, "I know what you mean. We both have been blessed." Phil chartered with me several more times over the ensuing years.

I had just returned from a charter and was putting my boat on the hoist at Gulf Wind Marine when a gentleman walked up and introduced himself as Larry Hardy, bullpen coach for the Texas Rangers baseball team. Larry was staying in a condo next to Gulf Wind Marine and he wanted to book a charter. That day was the beginning of a new friendship and of an unanticipated flow of new customers. Larry was in his fifties and looked like he could still pitch in the major leagues. He had been a star pitcher for the University of Texas and had played on several major league teams before his coaching career. The Charlotte County Baseball Stadium in Port Charlotte had been the spring training site for the Texas Rangers since 1988.

Larry and I made our first fishing trip on February 22. He was an excellent fisherman and loved being on the water. Over the next five years, I could count on twenty to thirty charters each spring from Larry and other ballplayers. As an all-star first baseman with the San Francisco Giants and Texas Rangers, Will Clark would be the best known. Roger Pavlik and Bobby Witts, both starting pitchers, were also regulars, fishing several times each spring.

In 2003, the Rangers moved to a new spring training center in Arizona, and I lost touch with most of the players. I missed fishing with them and going to the practice games as they were great people to be around, laughing and joking. Remembering my own ambitions during the days when I was a ball player at Michigan State University and on an Army team, I relished the thought of getting paid to play a game. Several were Christians and readily shared their faith as to how God had blessed them with the skill to play baseball. Larry Hardy called the summer of 2005 when the Rangers were in Detroit playing the Tigers and invited me to a game and dinner afterwards. Unfortunately, I couldn't make it due to charters. I heard later Larry had retired from baseball and was enjoying life fishing in Texas.

My fishing world expanded in March 1995 when Don Beck, a retired businessman from Wisconsin, called me about a charter. "Jim, at Fisherman's Edge, recommended I call you for a charter. How about next week", he said? To which I replied, "Great! At what time and where should I pick you up?" That was the beginning of a long and lasting friendship. Jim had told Don I had lived and fished in Venezuela, Australia, New Zealand and Brazil, and that's all it took to trigger a phone call from him. Don and his wife Ann had hunted and fished extensively throughout the world, and after his retirement in the late 1980s, they bought a condo in Placida, a small, unincorporated community on the water near Gulf Wind Marine where I kept my boat.

Our first charter together was on March 14. Don caught a few redfish on spinning tackle, but what we both enjoyed the most was the conversation. Don and I had much in common—we were the same age (sixty-one at the time), shared a love for fishing and had travelled extensively around the world. Balding, but trim and athletic, Don was an excellent fisherman. By the time I left Florida to move back to Michigan in 2005, ten years later, Don had chartered with me over one-hundred times. He was also the source of many additional charter referrals. In addition, Don and I made six overseas fishing trips together which I will talk about in subsequent pages.

One evening, Don and Ann invited Dorothy and me for dinner at their condo to see their safari trophies. The condo was beautifully decorated in an African décor with numerous mounts of wild animals in natural settings, the focal point was a life-size male lion resting near a small, six by four foot, blue acrylic pool of water, lily pads and all. The lion looked so real we were afraid to reach out and touch it!

In late April 1995, I had my first serious encounter with a hammerhead shark. During the spring tarpon season, sharks are abundant around Boca Grande Pass looking for a tarpon to eat. When a hooked tarpon tires, it becomes easy prey for a shark and it is not uncommon for an angler to lose a tarpon to one. My customer had hooked a large, one-hundred-plus-pound tarpon, and after a thirty-minute fight, had the tarpon alongside the boat. With the eighty-pound test, six-foot leader, in my left hand, I was leaning over the side of the boat to remove the hook with the pliers in my right hand, when the tarpon exploded from the water, drenching me with salt water. The leader was ripped from my hand and when the fishing line came taut it almost pulled the unsuspecting angler, still holding the rod, off the boat and into the water.

Simultaneously, a ten-foot hammerhead shark swooshed within two feet of the boat in pursuit of the tarpon. Wanting to give the tarpon a chance to elude the shark, I reached up grabbing the fishing line as it screamed from the angler' reel and cut it with my pliers. Fortunately, as I always wore leather gloves when releasing a tarpon due to their sharp gill plates and raspy month, the line coming off the reel cut into my glove instead of my hand. I have seen serious cuts to guides and anglers inflicted by fishing line rapidly peeling off a reel. As I sat for a minute to catch my breath and wipe the salt water from my eyes, I looked at the angler and said, "Nice catch." He

139

replied, "Which one, the tarpon or the shark?" We both laughed. It didn't appear that the shark caught up with the tarpon as there were no telltale signs of a struggle or scales and blood in the water. A side note, the world record one thousand two hundred and eighty-pound hammerhead shark was caught from a flats boat in Boca Grande Pass May 23, 2007.

After the excitement settled down, my customer and I resumed fishing. I smiled to myself thinking back to the mid-1970s when Dorothy, the kids and I were fishing for yellow fin tuna in Bermagui, Australia. Sharks were also plentiful in the waters around Bermagui, and we would occasionally lose a hooked tuna to a shark bite. On one occasion, as I was gaffing a sixty-pound tuna next to our boat, Dorothy had to hit a shark on the nose several times with my boat hook to keep it from taking a bite out of our fish!

In May of 1995, Steve Gibson, sports editor for the Sarasota *Herald*, called to ask if we could get together for an interview. Steve, an avid fly fisherman, said he had heard about my fly-fishing background and would like to do an article for the paper. I readily agreed as Steve was regarded as one of the premier sport-fishing writers in Florida.

The following week Steve and I fished Charlotte Harbor together and had a great time telling each other stories of our fishing exploits. The following Sunday, May 8, the headline of the Outdoor Section of the Sarasota *Herald* read, "Worldwide Experience Prepares Denny Blue". The entire page was an article about my fishing background, picture and all. That article did wonders for my future as a fly-fishing guide. Steve was good enough to follow up with five additional feature articles on me over the next several years.

A service I had instituted for my customers during the 1995 season was to pick them up by boat whenever possible. It was normal practice for customers to meet their guide where he launched or docked his boat. Initially, I did the same, asking my customers to meet me at Gulf Wind Marine. It occurred to me that many of my customers either had homes on the water or were staying at a hotel on or near the water. Case in point, I had many customers from Palm Island Resort and Boca Grande where I could easily pick them up with my boat in less than half the time it would take them to drive to Gulf Wind Marine. I addition, I did not have to provide driving directions. While picking up and dropping off customers added time to my day, this convenience proved to be a big plus for my customers and resulted in more repeat business. The 1995 season, I ran one hundred and twenty charters in Florida and did not schedule charters in Onekama until mid-June due to the number of trips I had in Florida.

On the drive back to Michigan, Dorothy and I discussed the uncertainty of starting a new business and identifying a new ministry. We agreed it was not always smooth sailing, but it was apparent, after two full seasons of living and fishing in Florida, this is where God wanted us to be. As had happened so many times in our marriage, stepping out on faith and trusting that God is in control has turned our hope into reality. We learned early in our marriage that, when God closes doors, we stay put, and when he opens doors, we move through them. Everyone needs to find a niche in life, and spiritually we find it when we receive a ministry from God.

Pat, Luanne and the grandkids moved back to Michigan in June 1995. The real estate market in California was depressed forcing Pat to look for other work. Dorothy and I suggested they move into the condo in Onekama until they decided what they were going to do. They gladly accepted. It was great having them around during the summer, especially the grandkids, Emilee and John. Pat helped me on *True Blue* that summer. We both enjoyed our time together. By September, Pat still hadn't found a job so he and Luanne enrolled Emilee in kindergarten at the Onekama Public School. John was only two years old—not old enough for school. Dorothy and I encouraged Pat and Luanne to stay at the condo until Pat found a job as we would soon be headed back to Florida, and it would be nice to have them watch over the condo.

That fall in Florida, I began to write a weekly fishing article for the Boca *Beacon*, the weekly newspaper for Boca Grande. The *Beacon* had a large circulation in Lee and Charlotte counties and reached an exclusive segment of readership who were potential customers. The weekly articles on fishing became popular with readers prompting positive letters to the editor and so I remained a contributor until 2004.

Fly fishing can be a snobbish sport if you let it. Having the most expensive fly rods, reels and gear is part of the ambiance. That is not to diminish the almost-spiritual experience that many anglers—including me—have for fly fishing. It has been said that, "fly fishing is to fishing as ballet is to dancing." The movie, *A River Runs Through It,* can't say it any better. Poling the backcountry, the morning sun rising over the mangroves, herons and egrets quietly stalking their prey in the mirror-like water—not a sound except for the occasional call of a bird or animal. Red-

Dennis with redfish, 2003

fish tails protrude from the shallow water as they forage for crustaceans. The blazoned black spot on the redfish tail and the bronze, tinged with indigo blue, of the scales reflecting the sunlight would get your heart pounding. My customer, fly rod in hand, making a perfect cast to a redfish and then the excitement of the hook-up and playing the fish as it streaks across the shallow water, spooking other unsuspecting fish, in its vain attempt to free itself. All this culminating in the thrill of releasing the fish to fight another day and the satisfaction of the accomplishment.

Now that's what fly fishing is all about!

I started fly-tying in my spare time in 1995. It goes with the territory. In fact, fly-tying can become the goal. It is another dimension of fly fishing to create an imitation of the bait and insects the fish feed on using natural and artificial materials such as deer hair, feathers and chenille. Some fly-tiers are artists, but I never got that good. Eventually, I did learn to tie all my own flies, and even did a few fly-tying demonstrations at fishing shows. Nothing is safe from a fly-tyer's quest to find a new material for his flies. I would often stop and examine road kill to harvest fur and feathers from an unfortunate squirrel, deer or bird. Even the hair of my trusty yellow lab Daisy was used in my quest to find the perfect material for a fly. I never had enough time to keep myself stocked with my favorite flies. As I got more into fly fishing, I also had many flies given to me by manufactures and customers that helped keep me in stock.

It was October 1995 when Don Beck, who was aware of my time in Brazil and Venezuela when I worked for Ford, asked me if I still had contacts in South American to fish peacock bass. I had once told him Brazil and Venezuela were the two best places in the world to fish for peacock bass. Don then explained he was interested in setting up a fishing trip with a couple of friends and would like me to come along as their travel guide and translator. After further discussion, I agreed to check into the availability of an outfitter and get back to him. Just the thought of returning to Brazil to fish again after fourteen-years got me excited. How would Brazil have changed since I left it to return to the US in 1982?

I informed Dorothy of my discussion with Don, and she thought going was a great idea. She was happy playing golf every day and it provided her time to help out with programs at our church. I checked with several fishing services in Manaus, Brazil, where I had worked in the early 1980s establishing a new television manufacturing plant for Ford-Philco Brazil and found an outfitter that would be perfect. The *Amazon Queen* was an eighty-five-foot, three deck river boat set up to accommodate twelve anglers, two to a cabin. We would sleep and eat on the boat and fish from eighteen-foot aluminum skiffs with outboards. Each skiff would have its own guide with two anglers. These skiffs were towed behind the mother ship when we moved from one location to another. Trips had to be booked in advance so I talked to Don as soon as I had gathered the information and we agreed to schedule the trip to Manaus the following January.

That January 1996, Pat was hired by Ford Motor Company, for which we were all thankful. During the work-week, while he completed a six-month sales training program, Pat stayed with our son, Dennis, at his home in Walled Lake about thirty miles from Detroit. Luanne and the kids stayed in Onekama to keep Emilee in school and Pat commuted from Walled Lake to Onekama on weekends until he finished his training program the following June.

Based on the recommendation of the *Amazon Queen*, I suggested tackle and lures for Don and the rest of the group to take on the trip. Spinning and bait casting rods and reels capable of handling fifty-pound test braided line was essential due to the heavy cover we would be fishing. The lure of choice was a six-inch long, floating plastic lure, known as a buzz bait. It had small propellers on the front and the back to create commotion in the water as it was

145

retrieved. The technique was to cast the lure among the fallen stumps and bushes that lined the shore

Amazon Queen, Brazil, 1996

and retrieve as fast as possible with big sweeps of the rod creating a turbulence on the water similar to a fish feeding on bait. Bright orange, yellow and green were the preferred colors of the lures. I took my eight- and nine-weight fly rods in hopes of getting a record peacock bass on six-pound test tippet (leader). Preparing for the trip brought back memories of my time fishing for peacock bass in Venezuela and Brazil during the 1970s and the early 1980s when Dorothy and I lived and worked in those countries for Ford.

When I worked in Manaus in the late 1970s, the population was approximately six hundred thousand. At the time of our trip in 1996, it was one million and today, over two million. Located in the middle of the Amazon rain forest near the confluence of the Rio Negro and Rio Solimoes that form the Amazon proper, Manaus is nine hundred miles inland from the Atlantic Ocean and geographically isolated with transportation mainly by air and boat.

Manaus has an interesting history, having been the richest city in South America during the 1800s due to the rubber plantations. Following the demise of the rubber boom in the early 1900s, the city fell into poverty, the world-famous opera house closed and electrification of the city by generators was ended. Manaus was only a shell of its former self until the 1960s when a free trade zone initiated an economic recovery that now provides the sixth largest economy in Brazil. The opera house was re-opened in 1997.

Don Beck, Tom Balisteri, Don Volk and I left Miami at midnight on January 5, 1996, and arrived at the Edwardo Gomes International Airport in Manaus at five a.m. Eastern Standard Time the following morning, having covered a distance of two thousand four hundred miles. It was a short night with not much sleep, but everyone was wide-awake and ready to go when we were greeted at the airport by a representative of the *Amazon Queen*. At 6 a.m. on a Saturday morning, there was not much traffic as we drove through Manaus. I recognized several places, but there had been substantial growth since I was last there in 1982. After a thirty-minute ride to the *Amazon Queen*, docked on the Rio Negro, we had breakfast and were introduced to eight other anglers who would be sharing the boat. Scanning the river-front brought back great memories. Boats, large and small, plying their trade, the fragrant smell of fruit, vegetables and flowers mixed with the pungent scent of the riverfront and fishermen unloading their catch. At this time, on a Saturday morning, sixteen-years ago, I would have been embarking upriver in a small wooden boat with a local fisherman for a day of fishing peacock bass.

The *Amazon Queen*, remodeled in 1989 as a floating hotel, had all the comforts of home. We departed Manaus at noon for our seven-day trip on the Rio Negro. The next morning after a breakfast of local fruit, home-made biscuits and bacon and eggs, we boarded our skiffs and headed out to fish.

Don Volk and I fished together the first day. I had previously fished with Don in Florida and so I was mindful of his careless casting. I reminded Don to look over his shoulder before casting to be sure no one was behind him. Don said, "I promise to be careful! Don't worry." I had an uneasy feeling this wouldn't be the last time Don and I would have this discussion

We hadn't fished fifteen minutes before Don had a heart-stopping strike when a peacock bass (*tucunare* in Portuguese) cleared the water a few feet from the boat. Similar in appearance but unrelated to the large-mouth bass caught in the US, it is black, yellow and orange in color. Peacock bass are hard fighters, and the strike is a ferocious bite. I had

Don Volk with peacock bass, Brazil, 1996

several strikes on my eight-weight fly rod with an orange fly but couldn't stop the peacock bass on my lighter fly tackle before they reached the cover of fallen trees and broke my light six-pound test leader.

Most Brazilian outfitters practice catch and release to protect the peacock bass from over harvest. However, the guides kept enough for a fresh fish dinner our first night on the *Amazon Queen*. It was delicious baked in a lemon sauce. That evening, sitting around two large tables for six, everyone was relating stories of the fish that were caught. I could only tell of the fish that got away. I applied too much pressure to try and stop the fish and others broke the leader when it became entangled in the bushes. I had brought four dozen large flies but I had already lost a dozen that first day. The fish preferred orange and yellow colors, of which I had only two left, so the cook let me use some food coloring to dye my remaining flies orange and yellow.

Dennis with peacock bass on fly, Brazil, 1996

The second day fishing everyone but me caught fish. I lost five or six nice fish in the bushes again. The third day Don Beck and I fished together. Recalling my days fishing in Mexico, when I used a bait with no hook to tease sailfish to the boat before casting a fly to the sailfish, I suggested to Don that we remove the hooks from his buzz bait, and when a fish struck the lure, he keep retrieving and tease the fish closer to the boat. If Don could coax a peacock bass further from the bushes with repeated strikes at his buzz bait, it would give me a better chance at landing a fish after hooking it. Several casts later, the water boiled behind Don's hook-less buzz bait, the fish struck a second and a third time as Don continued to retrieve. When the fish was perhaps fifty feet from shore, I cast my fly to the swirl on the water where the fish last struck at the lure and on my second strip the fly line stopped with a thud. A large peacock bass jumped out of the water with my fly in its mouth and the fight was on. The fish headed for the cover of the fallen trees but as we were further from shore I was able to stop the fish before it made it to the bushes. I played the fish in open water and after a ten-minute battle brought the fish to the boat. The peacock bass weighed fourteen pounds on my certified hand scale, just ounces short of the world record on six-pound tippet. Don and I were elated, exchanging high-fives before taking pictures and releasing the fish. I caught and released several smaller peacock bass that day using the same technique, each one a memory.

Back at the mother ship that evening, I received the accolades of my fellow fishermen, and of course, took several bows. I decided to put the fly rod away satisfied with what Don and I had accomplished, even without catching a record. The remainder of the trip I caught several more peacock bass near twenty pounds on spinning tackle, but none as rewarding as my fourteen-pound fish on the fly. I was not a fly fisherman when I fished for peacock bass in Venezuela and Brazil, in the 1970s and 1980s, not taking up the sport until 1990 when I fished with Billy Pate in Mexico. I think of the hundred-plus pea-cock bass I had caught and released in those early years, many in the twenty-plus-pound range on light tackle and wondered how many would have been records today.

During our seven days on the *Amazon Queen*, five of which were devoted to fishing, we proceeded up the Rio Negro about sixty miles. It was beautiful, iso-lated country, reminiscent of the venues over which I had flown in Venezuela. We passed only four or five huts along the river during the entire trip. These were inhabited by local families living off the jungle. After the fifth day of fishing, it was time to head back to Manaus as it would take us all night and the bet-ter part of the next day to arrive on time to catch our flight back to Miami.

It was a great trip with good food, excellent fishing and pleasant, comfortable accommodations. When Don Beck, Tom and Don Volk wanted to do it again next year, I agreed. For me, it was like old home week coming back to Manaus to fish for peacock bass. It brought back memories of when we built the Ford-Philco plant there in 1981. I would have liked to spend more time there but our schedule didn't per-mit and so returning the next year appealed to me. I was pleased with how quickly my Portuguese had come back. By the time we left, I was conversing with the locals like I had never left.

My trip to Brazil with Don Beck and friends de-veloped into something I had not foreseen. This fishing expedition which had seemed at the time to be a one-up occurrence capitalized on my background in international travel and language ability. Then sometime during that trip, I began to entertain the thought that expanding my fishing business from guiding customers locally to bringing them to exotic destinations around the world could be a logical next step. The more I thought about it, the more I concluded, "Why not expand my fishing charters—and my ministry—to a broader arena?"

The downside to these exotic trips was the time and effort it took me to arrange the logistics: suggesting the proper fishing tackle and personal items to take with us, the travel itineraries, interim accommodations, the outfitter to service us and destination particulars from lodging to taxis. From a business point of view, it was reasonable to charge any time and expense to the fees I was collecting. When I did so on the Brazil trip, I realized I had just broken even on my expenses. I attributed the significant time and effort devoted to arranging the trip to its being a first-time experience. With each additional trip, my learning curve would surely be less steep. Back in Florida, word had gotten out that I was now running an international guide service, jet setting to wherever my clients wanted to go. When asked about international fishing, I would just smile as perception is half the battle won and then add, "Any place you want to go to?"

Dennis came to Florida over Easter 1996 and caught a nice tarpon with spinning tackle. He was not yet into fly fishing—that would come later. As always, we had a great time together, his work was going well and he was enjoying his own house in Walled Lake. We both agreed moving out of our house and into his own was the best thing that could have happened for him. Being on his own was a maturing experience. At this time, he was still a single man.

Life at Riverwood was good as Dorothy played golf every day and we both had great friends and neighbors. Several Riverwood residents fished with me when their families came to visit. I didn't play golf but was grateful Dorothy did as her eager involvement in the sport led to absences from the house and these blocks of time provided me the opportunity also to absent myself in order to pursue my own passion of fishing and not feel I was infringing on our time together. I know she felt the same, as when I had a few days off, Dorothy would ask, "Isn't it time for you to go fishing again?"

When we again didn't return to Onekama until mid-June in 1996, I realized the emphasis of my business had definitely shifted to Florida. Most of my Onekama business was now repeat customers that booked the same time each year with only a few new ones that were referrals by friends. Many of these repeat customers were my former friends from Ford who fished with me over the years: Jack Hall, Pete Pestillo, Phil Benton, Don Kummer and John Slosar to name but a few. Joe Bugeia was my most frequent customer, salmon fishing with me in Onekama twice a year for twenty-five straight years. I knew Joe for most of my thirty years at Ford. A true friend, Joe passed away in 2015. His legacy is his family, his wife Mary, sons, grandsons and brother-in-law that

came with him for most of the years we fished together. Fishing on *True Blue* was a family affair.

Of increasing concern for salmon fishermen on
the Great Lakes was Bacterial Kidney Disease, BKD.
First reported by the Michigan Department of Natural Resources in 1994, the disease was having a negative impact on the survival of salmon in Lake
Michigan. I promised my customers I would keep
them informed of future developments regarding
BKD in my newsletter at the end of the year.

Having Luanne, Emilee and John staying with us
for a second summer was fun for Dorothy and me.
Pat was still living with Dennis in Walled Lake during
the week and would come to Onekama on weekends.
Dennis came with Pat as often as he could to spend
time with us and do some fishing. Dennis still had
several close friends in Onekama with whom he liked
to keep in touch.

Pat finished his training at Ford in June 1996,
and two months later, was assigned to the Ford sales
office near Cincinnati, Ohio. He and Luanne found a
nice house in Lebanon, Ohio, a small town of about
twenty thousand, a half hour from Pat's office and
they made plans to move there before school started
in the fall. Dorothy and I would miss having them
with us at the condo but we were glad that they were
getting back on their own. Pat and Luanne moved
into their new home in Lebanon in September 1996.
Pat and Luanne shared our Christian belief that "All
things work together for good to those that love God,"
Ro 8:28. The previous several years had been a test
of their faith as they relocated from California, and
Pat started a new career with Ford but they main-

tained a positive attitude and never lost faith that God was in control of their lives.

Dorothy and I returned to Florida in September 1996. No sooner had we gotten unpacked than Dean Beckstead from Palm Island Resort asked me if I would take the owner/editor of *The Angling Report*, Don Causey, for a few hours fishing as part of research to flesh out an article he was writing on the Resort. I readily agreed to support Dean as my customer base at Palm Island had continued to grow, thanks to Dean's support. The next morning, I met Don Causey at the Palm Island docks. Don was an avid fly fisherman who had fished the world. *The Angling Report* had a large subscriber base of fly fishermen and focused on educating the travelling angler on when and where to fish based on the reports of the subscribers. Don, an excellent fly fisherman, caught several snook and red fish as we talked about our overseas fishing experiences before we headed in for dinner at the Resort. Don suggested we keep in touch and perhaps we could work together on some overseas fishing trips in the future. Little did I know at the time the significance of that request. I thanked him for the offer and told him I hoped we could fish together again. Based on the stellar recommendation Palm Island Resort and I got from Don in his January 1996 issue of *The Angling Report*, he must have enjoyed our trip also. Meeting Don Causey and sharing his enthusiasm for overseas fishing re-enforced my perception of the growing market for guided fishing trips abroad. Was international fishing something I should pursue more actively?

Walter Hamm, a well-known fly fisherman from

Sarasota, whom I had met previously at a fly fishing seminar in Sarasota, called to ask if I would be his guide in the Gasparilla Island Fly Fishing Tournament on November 26. The tournament, whose proceeds went to local charities on Boca Grande, had become a prestigious event for fly fisherman in the area. As I knew he was an excellent fisherman, I felt we would make a competitive team. Normal practice for a charity tournament was for the guide to donate his time for fishing the tournament. The fisherman/sponsor paid the tournament entry fee which was donated to the charity organization. The fisherman often tipped the guide for his services, especially if he and the guide had good fishing and placed well in the tournament.

The one-day tournament was conducted on a catch and release basis and adhered strictly on the honor system. Points were awarded for each species of fish, five-points for trout, ten-points for redfish and fifteen-points for snook. The morning of the tournament was windy and overcast, not good for fly fishing. By noon, Walter had released a few trout and a redfish, nothing to brag about yet. With the tournament ending at two p.m., we decided to try one more spot before heading back to the tournament headquarters. No sooner than I began poling when Walter hooked something large. At first, we thought it was a big snook. The water was murky from being churned by the wind, and it was hard to see what we had, but after a few minutes, we knew we had hooked something bigger than a snook. After a twenty-minute fight, Walter had the fish to the boat. To our surprise, it was a cobia—a fish you usually don't catch in the backcountry. This cobia measured thirty-eight inches, a great catch on a fly rod. We took pictures and released the fish before heading back for the weigh-in.

After an excellent lunch, attended by sponsors and participants, at the Pink Elephant Restaurant on Boca Grande, awards and prize money were given to the top three boats. Walter and I came in third out of a dozen boats, missing out on first place by only five points. We pleaded our case for the cobia we released, which was the biggest fish of the tournament, but unfortunately only trout, redfish and snook got points. Nonetheless, we were both pleased with our participation.

On January 7, 1997, true to our plans of the previous year, Don Beck and I made our second trip to Brazil to fish on the *Amazon Queen.* The fishing was even better than in 1996. Our group of four—beside Don Beck and I, there were Don Volk and Tom Balisteri—caught over one-hundred peacock bass several of which were over twenty pounds. I caught numerous peacock bass on the fly rod using the "bait and switch" technique Don and I had mastered, but we did not make a record catch. On this trip, I noticed that Don Volk was not careful when he cast. He was

Dennis, Florida, 2000

sloppy in his execution, and I was giving him a wide berth whenever I was near him. I kept reminding him to look around to see who was nearby before he cast, and I would give him pointers on how to control his line better. One evening, the captain arranged for us to have dinner on a sand bar in the middle of the Rio Negro, white table clothes, grilled fish, wine and all the trimmings. Nice!

I had planned one minor change to this trip: instead of coming back to Manaus by boat, we flew back in order to have time to sightsee in the region. Because of that, the *Amazon Queen* dropped us off at Barcelo, a town of about eighteen thousand residents on the Rio Negro. Barcelo was noted for its exotic tropical fish which it exported around the world. A charter flight flew us back to Manaus in an hour and a half instead of the seventeen hours by boat. This allowed us time in Manaus to sightsee (which I had sorely missed on the prior trip) and have dinner before our flight left at midnight for Miami. We took a taxi to the Ford-Philco plant. but didn't go in for lack of time. From the outside the plant looked the same as I remembered it. I could image walking inside the plant and greeting old friends—would any still be working there? But, I preferred to remember it as it was when I left Brazil in 1982. I was thinking on the way home how blessed I was that I could return to fish the Rio Negro and see Manaus again. After returning to Florida, Don Beck wanted to try fishing peacock bass in Venezuela instead of Brazil the following year. We both agreed it would be a new adventure, and Don would let me know soon what his schedule was so we could set a date and make specific plans. Don Volk wanted to join us also.

The second trip to Brazil was a success from Don's point of view—and a whole lot of fun for both of us, but I had growing doubts about the viability of guiding overseas trips as a business. This trip to Brazil was again not profitable in spite of efficiencies learned from the first trip. I had invested too many hours in the planning and preparation for getting us to Manaus to fish. Most importantly, I didn't enjoy performing the tasks of a travel

Don Beck with Peacock Bass, Brazil, 1996

agent—what I enjoyed was to be on the water guiding my clients. The upcoming trip to Venezuela with Don would be my third guided trip to an overseas location. Venezuela would be a new venue, and with my experience on previous trips, this fishing expedition would be a good opportunity to confirm the viability or the lack thereof of my revised business plan to take on international fishing expeditions. I would wait until after the trip in 1998 before reaching a decision.

I was at the Miami Boat Show in February 1997 when I met Scott Deal, owner of the Maverick Boat Company, which manufactured Maverick and Hewes flats boats. Scott told me his company was introducing a brand-new seventeen-foot flats boat, named the Pathfinder, the following year. Scott claimed the boat would float in only four inches of water and said his company would be looking for reputable guides to buy the boat at factory price. In return, I would promote and market the boat to my customers and at boat shows. My current Action Craft flats boat that I used in Florida handled two anglers comfortably, provided a stable fishing platform and had plenty of live-well capacity to recirculate water and keep bait alive. The Action Craft's twelve-inch draft was its only negative feature. The one-thousand-pound boat made it difficult to fish the backcountry on low tides. I had been casually looking at other flats boats that were lighter and had less draft to get my fly fishing customers farther into the back country where only very shallow draft boats could go and the new Pathfinder might be the answer I was needing. I decided to wait for a test ride before making up my mind to buy. The ride, however, would not be available until the following year.

I didn't run my first trip in Onekama until June 26, 1997—partially because Luanne, Emilee and John were not staying at the condo that summer and I was still busy with charters in Florida. Another reason, however, was the salmon fishery had been going through a couple of difficult years due to BKD that had reduced the salmon population about 30 percent. Programs had been put in place by the Michigan Department of Natural Resources (MDNR) to stop the spread of the disease, and its efforts were beginning to have a positive effect. Charter reservations were down, however, on Lake Michigan by between twenty percent and fifty percent depending on the port. In my December 1996 newsletter, I had advised my charter customers of the decrease in the salmon fishery and suggested they book from late-June to September, when the salmon fishing would be at its best. This timing would increase their opportunity to catch fish. Because of this recommendation I did not have reservations until late in June and I had no reason to leave Florida early.

I was fortunate my customer base was not focused on how many fish they caught but on their overall family experience. I lost a few customers because of BKD, but for the most part, the regulars kept coming. Other charter boats in the area whose clientele was more focused on size and number of fish were not as fortunate and several closed operations due to lack of business. The Michigan Charter Boat Association also suffered. It had reported two-hundred and fifty members in 1979, and that number had grown to nine hundred members by 1989. Then it experienced a gradual decline to approximately five hundred members by 2000. Not all of the reduction was attributable to the BKD. There was also a decline in the forage base for salmon which reduced the number of fish. Also contributing was an overall reduction in the numbers of people participating in fishing charters in the US.

The good news as I write this is that the salmon fishery and the number of charter boats have made a comeback over recent years. Once again, salmon provides a profitable business opportunity to charter boat operators.

Dorothy and I were back in Florida by the end of September 1997. The pattern of four months in Michigan and eight months in Florida (roughly forty to fifty fishing trips in Michigan and one hundred to one hundred and twenty fishing trips in Florida) was a perfect balance for me. In 1997–1998, I had one hundred and twenty-five trips on the books through mid-June. I really enjoyed the people I met and came to know many of them as friends more than as only customers. During the 1997 Florida season, I fished with Blaine McCallister, a professional golfer on the PGA tour and Mike Mularkey, former professional football player and NFL coach.

We continued to be involved in activities at the Assembly of God church where several fishing guides I knew were also members. The church was involved in a large building program, which it completed in the fall of 1997, our fourth year there. The first Sunday in our new building, some four hundred members marched in, single file, singing *Amazing Grace*. What was also "really amazing" was the church did not owe a penny on the new building due to the savvy of our pastor in fundraising and the dedication of the membership to give financially to the Lord's work. Dorothy and I had come to know and socialize with many of the five hundred members in the church. The music program was the most accomplished of any church we attended. The week-long Christmas pageant, with live donkeys, camels and sheep attracted several thousand spectators from the Port Charlotte area. No matter the country, the state or the church we attended, Dorothy and I have been blessed by the Christian love and fellowship of brothers and sisters in Christ.

Fishing has always been a passion, but over time, I had come to realize my business was not just about catching fish. My boat, I realized, was my mission field. I was careful not to sound "preachy" and instead let my actions and words reflect my walk with Jesus. I was following Matthew: 5:16: "Let your light shine before others, that they may see your good deeds and glorify your Father in heaven." I think Christians too often view a mission field as being far away, but our ministry of witnessing can be directed to the neighbor next door and to the people you encounter each day.

As 1998 approached, it was time to finalize plans for Don Beck, Don Volk and Bob Voell and me to take our Venezuela trip. I was a bit unsure about Don Volk as I had first-hand experience of his being careless when casting. The previous year in Brazil, I had given him plenty of room and kept reminding him to look around before he cast. Nonetheless, Don Beck and I decided to let him join us as he was a friend of Don and Bob and they enjoyed his company. I would grow to regret this decision to accommodate Don Volk.

I planned to lead them to the Guri Reservoir which is a large body of water, one thousand six hundred and twenty-one square miles, covering what used to be forests and now is excellent habitat for peacock bass. When I worked for Ford Venezuela from 1969 to 1972, my fishing buddy Joe Semester and I had flown on fishing trips many times in my plane. I recalled fondly the excellent peacock bass we had caught on those fishing trips to the Guri Reservoir, the Cunaviche and Cinaruco Rivers. Naturally enough, my thoughts also drifted back to my days volunteer flying for New Tribes Mission in the Amazon Territory of Venezuela. On one of those flights to support the many missionaries who dedicated their lives to reaching the unsaved for Christ, we had discovered a previous unknown tribe of primitive Indians.

Fishing tackle we required for the Guri Reservoir was much the same as we used in Brazil. The fish are more numerous but smaller—ten to fifteen pounds—instead of the fifteen to twenty pounds we had found in Brazil. I would compare the Guri Reservoir to a large self-contained inland lake where the fish get smaller as the population grows and the forage base diminishes. In the vast expanse of rivers in the Amazon basin, Mother Nature is not so impeded by boundaries.

We left for Venezuela on January 8, 1998, for a nine-day trip with five days devoted to fishing. Flying from Miami to Caracas, we boarded a connecting flight to Ciudad Bolivar, four hundred and ten miles southeast, and stayed overnight. Passing through the Caracas airport, I noticed its deterioration and the armed guards everywhere. For the past several years the Venezuelan economic and political situation had been deteriorating, and the negative effect on the country was evident.

The next morning, we made the seven-hour trip by road from Ciudad Bolivar to the fishing camp. The road was two lanes and bumpy, a long hot ride in a dilapidated van with no air conditioner. The accommodations at the fishing lodge were basic as there was no air conditioning and large spiders roamed about. I joked that the spiders were big enough for us to hear them walking, but no one laughed. We had screens on the windows—fortunately—as the mosquitos were bad at night. The food was basic but good. We all had stayed in worse accommodations at one time or other and, if the fishing was good, we would be happy despite the lodging.

The boats were old aluminum eighteen-foot skiffs with sixty horsepower outboards. The guides couldn't speak English, but they knew how to fish which seemed most important. My own Spanish was rusty, but I was confident it would come back soon. In the following days, we were pleased to discover the fishing to be excellent with lots of ten-pound fish. We were releasing up to twenty fish per person each day. I caught several on the fly, but as in Brazil, the fish preferred the noisy, topwater baits. It didn't take long for my Spanish to come back, and I was in constant demand from my three

Dennis with Peacock Bass,
Venezuela, 2001

"*gringo*" companions as a translator. Meals turned out to be excellent as were the lunches packed for us each day. After dinner, it was get-ready-for-the-next-day and early-to-bed. Just as we were about to turn out the lights, I would remind everyone to keep an eye out for the spiders. One night, I was awakened when Bob Voell was roaming around with a flashlight. "I think I heard one!" he said.

Things took a turn for the worse on the third day. The boats had basic VHF radios necessary for safety. Don Beck and I were fishing together. It was about three p.m. when I heard a call come over the radio to our guide in garbled Spanish. I couldn't make out exactly what was said due to the poor radio reception, but it had to do with an accident. Our guide turned to us and said that one of the other anglers had been hooked by a lure and the boat crew needed help. I translated the message to Don Beck who groaned and said, "I bet it's Bob Voell who's hurt! I had a feeling we shouldn't have let Bob fish with Don."

Don Beck had been fishing with Don Volk since we arrived two days previously and had commented to me how pleased he was with Don's casting. "I think your coaching has helped," Don said. The evening before our fateful third day, Bob, and Don Volk, who were close friends, decided they wanted to fish together despite my lingering concern and promised they would be careful. Don Beck looked at me and said, "Why not, I had no problems fishing with Volk the past two days."

As I feared at the time, Don Volk apparently had not followed through on his promise to be careful. We motored fifteen minutes to the other boat, and there was Bob with a lure attached to the top of his head, pinning his hat in place. It looked funny, a large bright orange and yellow lure with spinner blades on each end, setting on top of Bob's head, but I knew the situation was deadly serious. Apparently, Bob stood up just as Don was casting and "wham", both sets of treble hooks sunk into the top of his head.

Don Beck and Don Volk had been friends for years and hunted and fished together all over the world, but that didn't stop Don Beck from chastising Don Volk for his carelessness. Don Volk was apologetic and obviously humiliated by the situation, but what could he say other than, "I'm sorry." To his credit Bob defended his friend and said, "It was my fault, I was sitting in the back of the boat changing lures and stood up just as Don was casting."

From my own experience, whenever I have two anglers casting on my boat, I watched them closely and repeatedly reminded the anglers to look over their shoulder before casting. Over the years and despite my careful observation, I have had several experiences removing hooks from customers and myself from careless casting and have had other minor injuries.

I had a well-stocked first-aid kit that I carried on my boat in Florida and with me on overseas trips. After surveying the damage to Bob Voell, with both sets of treble hooks embedded into the top of his head, I knew he should see a doctor. We had to cut Bob's hat off around the lure so the wind wouldn't pull on the hat while motoring back to the fishing camp. He was obviously in pain and I was concerned he might go into shock.

The owner of the fishing camp had been contacted by radio and was waiting to drive Bob to the closest medical facility, a two-hour drive. Initially I planned to go with Bob as the interpreter, but as the owner spoke fluent English and Don Volk, who was feeling responsible, insisting he go with his friend Bob, I stayed at the camp. Having spent much time in the interior of Venezuela as a mission pilot in the 1970's, I was concerned as to the quality of medical care Bob would receive, but it was the best available. Travelling to remote places overseas to fish is an unforgettable experience for most anglers. However, a minor injury which could be readily treated in the US can be serious if not fatal in many of these remote locations due to lack of transportation to medical facilities and of proper medical care once there.

Don Volk and Bob left the fishing camp for the medical facility at five p.m. At ten p.m., dinner was over and there was yet no word from them. There was not much we could do but wait and pray for Bob. About twenty minutes later, the van returned to camp. Bob's head was in a bandage, they had to surgically remove the hooks and stitch up the wounds. The doctor gave Bob antibiotics and said he should have the stitches removed when he got back to Florida the following week. Thankfully, there were no bad feelings or animosity among our group now that Bob was safely back. Everyone was just relieved and glad to see them. The owner graciously provided Bob and Don Volk with a hot meal of roast pork, beans and rice, after they returned. Bob slept in the next morning while the rest of us went fishing.

The final day Bob went fishing with Don Beck and caught the biggest fish of our trip. Don Volk and I fished together and had a great time catching peacock bass. Don's casting was impeccable as he continually looked around before casting and at times waiting for me to move so as not to cast near me. I complimented Don on his casting etiquette. He was quite for a moment, then looked me in the eye and said, "Honest, Denny, I looked behind me before casting and Bob was sitting on his seat changing a fishing lure; he must have stood up just as I turned to make my cast. I have been extremely careful with my casting; Don Beck can confirm that from the days we fished together." I replied, "I believe you Don and so do the others. I think we owe you an apology for jumping to a conclusion before knowing the facts." With that, Don breathed a sigh of relief and smiled.

Dennis with Piryara,
Venezuela, 2001

I think we all had a better understanding of feeling empathy for one another after the trip. I know I did.

Overall, we had a great time despite the accident, and we left on a positive note. To take us back to Ciudad Bolivar, a forty-five-minute flight, I had asked the owner of the camp to arrange for a charter flight, to save Bob Voell the unpleasant seven-hour trip by car. The plane, an Antonov An-2 made in Poland, is popular for its cargo carrying capacity and short field landing and takeoff performance in the underdeveloped countries of the world. With a dual-wing span of sixty-feet, a body length forty-two feet and a one thousand and ten horsepower radial engine, the plane could take off in less than one thousand feet. Inside, the cabin was large enough to stand up in with jump seats that folded against the fuselage. It reminded me of being on a bus. The noise from the engine was deafening, and it was hard to converse with one another, but we all agreed it was worth the entire trip just to ride in a plane like that.

Unfortunately, after we returned home from our trip, Bob had an infection in the wound on his head and came down with a severe case of the shingles that the doctor attributed to unsanitary treatment.

l-r, Don Volk, Don Beck, Bob Voell and Dennis, Venezuela, 2001

No doubt, the unsanitary conditions and lack of proper medical care after the accident contributed to the infection but that is a risk of fishing remote areas around the world. I will write more about my own experience with a severe infection while in the Bahamas in a future chapter.

The week following my return from Venezuela, I spent time analyzing this third trip and came to the same conclusion that I reached after my two-trips to Brazil—my new business model was not working. Preparing for the trip to Venezuela was time consuming, and the trip itself had been stressful due to the deteriorating economy and the political unrest in that country and to the serious hook injury to Bob Voell. I broke even on my cost for the trip, but more importantly, I was convinced I no longer wanted the role of travel agent and being responsible for the entire trip.

At the moment, I resolved to either find a more profitable business model or give up guiding overseas fishing, but I was to figure out a third approach to international fishing in just a few months.

Through the Eyes of a Fisherman

Chapter 6
Fun Fishing Years

I have observed five stages of a fisherman's life: 1) catching the first fish—any size of fish will do; 2) catching lots of fish—the more the merrier; 3) catching bigger fish—bragging rights; 4) catching fish with lighter tackle and by fly fishing—it's the challenge that counts; 5) catching fish is not as important as the experience. Applying these five stages to my own life, I notice: 1) catching blue gill in a river near the farm where I grew up in the 1940s; 2) catching perch, bass and walleye in Lake Erie in the 1950s and 1960s; 3) catching black marlin and tuna in Australia in the 1970s; 4) catching salmon in the 1980s and sailfish and tarpon on a fly in the 1990s; 5) not so much catching now as an experienced charter captain and fly casting instructor but teaching others how to fish.

As the charter captain, I had come to understand my job to be teaching people to fish, to pay attention

173

to the conservation of the species and to enjoy the company of the people on the charter. After I understood the five stages, it became easier for me to deal with my customers at their current level and to lead them to the next. That's where I had arrived at in the late '90s—and I was enjoying it immensely. I had arrived at the stage where I gave back and shared knowledge and experiences with others. These years were what I now call my "fun fishing years."

The idea of expanding my business to international fishing, which I had pursued since 1996, had proven a failure by the winter of 1998, but even after the difficult Venezuela trip, I had to acknowledge that international fishing—minus the business component—remained satisfying to me. I enjoyed the experience of travel to new and challenging places and fishing for different species of fish, but I had now seen enough of this new business line to know it was both unprofitable and stressful. My passion for leading fishing charters was rooted in teaching others how to fish and in being a Christian witness. This passion did not include becoming a travel bureau: being the booking agent, the outfitter and the interpreter responsible for the good time of a group of fishermen. Following my trip to Venezuela in January 1998 I realized I could not—and did not want to—continue to conduct these trips. The irony was Don Beck and his friends Bob Voell and Don Volk were having a great time, and I was also—when we were fishing together. It was the work leading up to the fishing and the "buck stops with me" responsibility that I didn't enjoy. I no longer wanted to put up with the big difference between leading a charter and going on a fishing trip with friends.

How could I solve this dilemma?

In little time I came up with a good solution. My companions on these trips would be family and friends rather than customers. While I still brought my experience to bear on planning the trips and did most of it, I made sure my companions knew I was asking them to be fellow fishermen. People paid their own expenses, and it was understood that I was not their hired guide—although I obviously continued to guide them. With this change, the pressure was off me both to make the work into a business and thus profitable and to be responsible for the safety and pleasure of my companions who were not customers.

In all, I made seventeen international fishing trips during the period of 1996 to 2002. Except for the added stress of the first three, I enjoyed each and every one of them. As a ministry, the seventeen fishing trips I made during this period were a success. As a businessman, I continued to calculate possible expenses and income and had to conclude I could only have covered my expenses on three or four of those seventeen trips. Even with discounted accommodations I received from the lodges and which I could resell at the going rate, I would not have turned a profit. The reason was always the same: for every hour I spent fishing on a guided international trip with customers, I spent three or more hours with administrative and logistical duties. Without this office work—which I contributed to family and friends, it would have been difficult, if not impossible for customers to get to the exotic venues to fish and be accommodated there. There was no way, I became sure, that I could turn this fun experience into a business that supported itself.

My Florida business, however, was doing well. With more and more positive reviews from satisfied customers, the success of my fly casting seminars, the fishing shows I attended, the media attention I garnered and experience with overseas travel, my reputation within the fly fishing industry was solid. That reputation provided me access to discounted overseas fishing trips offered by lodges and outfitters to promote their business. The more people who booked trips at the lodges, based on my referral, the more discounts I would receive from the lodges. In return, I shared the discount with friends travelling with me—some of whom were also my Florida customers.

After the Venezuela trip of January 1998 that had led me to refocus, I didn't have to wait long to try out my new international fishing model. Don Causey, editor of *The Angling Report*, with whom I fished at Palm Island Resort in 1996, called me just after my return from Venezuela and advised me of a special two-for-one rate at the Casa Blanca Fly Fishing Lodge on Ascension Bay on Mexico's Yucatan Peninsula. I was not familiar with the Casa Blanca Lodge, but I felt the discount offered a low-risk opportunity to check out new fishing waters and it permitted me, at a very affordable price, to discover a new fishing experience. The offer was good for only the coming two-weeks, however, so, if I wanted to take advantage of the discount, I needed to act promptly.

I contacted my good friend Chuck May and asked him to go with me to the Yucatan. Dorothy and I had first met Chuck, his wife, Nancy, and their three children around 1984 at the Pirates Cove Condominium Association in Onekama, where we both owned a condo. Over the ensuing years, we became close friends and spent much time together socializing, fishing and sharing our faith.

In the winter of 1997, the house directly across the street from Dorothy and me in Riverwood came up for sale, and Chuck and Nancy bought it. We often joked among ourselves that we couldn't have had better neighbors.

Chuck was recovering from rotator-cuff surgery on his right shoulder but the opportunity to go fishing in the Yucatan at half the cost so caught his fancy that he didn't hesitate to agree to come along. On March 7, 1998, we flew from Miami to Cancun, Mexico. It was a two-hour flight to the popular tourist destination on the northeast coast of the Yucatan Peninsula, followed by a forty-five-minute charter flight from Cancun to the Casa Blanca Lodge on Ascension Bay. The lodge, located at the entrance of Ascension Bay overlooking the Caribbean, had first class accommodations and guides that would please the most discriminating fly fishermen. Chuck did his best casting with a sore shoulder and between us we caught numerous bonefish each day.

Ascension Bay is located in the Sian Ka'an Biosphere Reserve with abundant lush foliage and white sand beaches. The United Nations in conjunction the Mexican government designated the region as a biosphere reserve in 1986 to protect the unique flora and fauna and the Mayan ruins. Based on my visit, I realized the Casa Blanca Lodge would be a perfect future trip to recommend to my fly-fishing customers at their own expense and I resolved to get the word out to people about fishing with me under the new arrangement when I returned home. I was careful to remind people to mention my name when booking with a lodge so that I would get a credit for the referral. They paid full price at the lodge, but then I always shared my referral discount with them and this, in effect, lowered the cost for their trip. This process worked well as it assured I would continue to receive discounts to share with others. The discounts varied by location and season, from free all-inclusive trips, to discounts of up to fifty percent from one to four guests. (Airfare was not included.)

The new approach worked so well that I was gaining a local, word of mouth reputation as a clearing house for international fly fishing trips. Several people booked fishing trips with me in Florida so as to get my recommendations on where to travel internationally to fly fish. Ironically, abandoning charter leadership for international trips led to acquiring more customers in Florida!

I was relieved and elated! The contrast between the fun fishing trip to Casa Blanca, and the guided trip to Venezuela where Bob Voell had been "hooked" was like night and day. Even with the difference in the number of anglers, the location and the travel arrangements between how I had done it and how I was doing it now, it was clear to me that not being in charge and responsible for the successful outcome of the trip was a big relief. Profit was no longer my motive, but having new, fun fishing locations with friends became my focus.

In mid-April 1998, Jody Moore and I motored along the beach on a warm and sunny morning in Florida looking for tarpon. Jody, a contributing editor for the *Florida Sportsman Magazine*, had been referred to me by a friend. He wanted to do an article on catching a tarpon on a fly, and it was my job to provide him with that first-hand experience. Jody, his photographer and I were slowly motoring along the beach near Boca Grande talking about what to expect when he hooked a tarpon. In the process of helping him, I spotted a ripple in the calm water and the dark shape of a school of fish.

"Those fish are too small for tarpon," I said.

Jody agreed and thought it might be a school of permit. As we moved closer with the trolling motor, Jody said, "Holy cow! It's a school of Jack Crevalle. They look like they are maybe fifteen to twenty pounds each."

Jody Moore and Dennis,
Jack Cravelle, 1998

Jody quickly laid his twelve-weight fly rod down and picked up his nine-weight fly rod, prefect for catching that size fish—or so he thought! The fish were moving slowly near the surface, Jody made a perfect cast to the side of the school and stripped slowly. Nothing! He retrieved his green and white, Clouser minnow fly (so named after Bob

Clouser, the developer of the fly) and cast again. On the third strip, the line became tight. There were no jumps, typical for a Jack Crevalle, just a long, fast run that took over fifty yards of line off Jody's reel. Jack Crevalle, pound for pound, fight harder than any comparable fish I know and are prevalent along the Gulf beaches. I have often targeted them with fly fisherman as Jack Crevalle readily take a fly but I have never caught one over ten to twelve pounds. After about twenty minutes of give and take, Jody, wet with sweat, had the fish close to the boat. Each time I reached for the tireless fish, it moved several yards away, the possibility of a break in the twelve-pound test leader increased by the minute. Jody finally eased the fish close enough for me to get a firm grip on the tail with my gloved hand and ease the Jack over the side of the boat. At that, the magazine's photographer who had accompanied Jody took a few pictures for the eventual article.

I weighed and measured the twenty-four pounds, thirty-seven-inch Jack Crevalle and released it back to the water. Jody quipped, "Maybe I should have used my twelve-weight rod. This fish fought harder than a tarpon." We wondered out loud if this could be a record on twelve-pound tippet (leader) and Jody said he would check with the International Game Fish Association (IGFA) to be sure. (Jody found out later the fish was not a world or state record, but still a great catch by any standard.)

Jody rewarded me for my guiding with a center-fold photo and feature article in the April 1998 *Florida Sportsman Magazine*. You can't buy that kind of advertising!

I have been a member of the IGFA since the 1970s. Dedicated to the conservation of game fish, ethical angling, research, education and record keeping, the IGFA is one of the largest and most influential fishing associations in the world. For an angler looking to catch a world record, finding a guide familiar with IGFA fishing regulations and application requirements is essential. Detailed information such as length of leader, fish measurement, weight, photos, certified weigh, names of angler, witnesses and captain are required on the notarized world record application. A mistake on the application can disqualify a world record catch. Several of my customers requested that we fish using IGFA rules in anticipation of catching a world record species.

My 1998 summer in Onekama was busy with salmon charters and seeing old friends and customers. With my growing interest in fun-fishing trips overseas, I contacted international booking agents and outfitters looking for new places to fish for different species in addition to my salmon charters. Jim Mrozinski, owner of Onekama Marine, told me he was considering a new franchise with Rampage Yachts, a well-known manufacturer of offshore fishing boats, and thought I might be interested in trading my Tiara for a new Rampage. I told Jim I had little interest in changing boats as I had in mind to update my Florida Action Craft, whose twelve-inch draft made low-tide fishing hard. In July, Dorothy made news in the golf world by placing second in the Golf Association of Michigan Seniors Championship. I was proud of what she had achieved and suggested to Dorothy that perhaps I should get some of the credit for fishing everyday so she could practice while I was fishing.

When Dorothy and I returned to Riverwood in October 1998, my first order of business was update my Florida boat. In February 1997, while at the Miami boat show, I had met Scott Deal whose company was introducing a brand-new seventeen-foot flats boat that he had claimed would float in only four inches of water. Very soon after returning south, I called Scott who confirmed his company's new seventeen-foot Pathfinder with a sixty horsepower Mercury outboard was ready for a test ride. The next day, I drove the one hundred and sixty miles to the factory in Ft. Pierce and liked what I saw. The boat was three feet shorter and seven hundred pounds lighter than my Action Craft. With one small bait well for shrimp and two water-tight compartments for fishing tackle and life jackets, it would be ideal for myself and two anglers. When I took the boat for a test ride, I found it was easy to pole and it ran in four inches of water as announced. The major drawback was that the flat bottom of the boat would make for a bumpy and wet ride in rough water. I might have to forgo tarpon trips on the beach when the water was too rough.

After considering the pluses and minuses and the attractive price, I decided to give the Pathfinder a try and made arrangements to buy the boat which I would pick up the following week. Because I had already announced I was selling my Action Craft, I had a buyer waiting. My first customer on the new Pathfinder was Don Beck, and after adjusting to the cramped space, Don told me how much he liked the boat. He liked it so much, in fact, that he bought one which I ordered for him direct from the factory.

I spent several hours with Don Beck to improve his fly fishing casting stroke, and he was now doing fly fishing on his own using his new Pathfinder when not chartering with me. Don and I teamed up and took second place in the 1998 annual Gasparilla Island Fishing Tournament that November. We caught the most

Pathfinder, 1998

fish in the tournament but, because standing was awarded based on the total inches of the fish caught, we came in second. You would have thought there was a million dollars at stake, but apart from a small trophy and a picture of the top three finishers in the *Boca Beacon* newspaper, all the proceeds from the tournament went to charity. Hey—egos are important to fishermen!

Winter tides are the lowest of the year in Charlotte Harbor. Some mornings when a strong northeast wind prevailed, the back country was hard to reach at low tide. With the four-inch draft of my Pathfinder, I could run almost anywhere I wanted to go, even on the low tides. The shallow water forces the fish into the deeper pot holes, and if you can reach the pot holes on low tide, it is, as they say, "Like shooting fish in a barrel." As the tide rises, the fish begin to move back out over the flats, and tailing redfish feeding on crustaceans are easy targets. For about two hours after low tide, it is a fly fisherman's dream. Sometimes I would get out of the boat and wade in six to twelve inches of water pushing the boat and angler into casting range of a pothole. I knew of only a half-dozen other guides that could get to the areas where I now fished with my new Pathfinder.

It was not unusual during low tides to see boats aground with their inexperienced owners waiting for a higher tide to refloat their boat. I knew of several people that had spent the night in the backcountry after running aground, or not being able to find their way out in the dark. One morning while fishing with a customer in the backcountry, I came across a boat that appeared to be abandoned. On closer inspection, I saw a man was lying in the bottom of the boat, shivering and covered with mosquito bites. He related how he became disoriented, the tide had receded, and he couldn't float his boat. By the time the tide came back in, it was dark and he couldn't find his way out. The mosquitos were so bad that he had gotten out of the boat and into the water. With just his face above the water, he had been able to protect himself somewhat from the mosquitos. Clad only in a tee-shirt and shorts, he became hypothermic and was in a state of shock when we found him lying in his boat the following morning. I provided a jacket, a candy bar and a drink of water to revive the man and then, as I towed his boat to deeper water, I contacted a local towing service by radio. The service took him to safety on Boca Grande.

On February 25, 1999, we were blessed again

when Luanne gave birth to her third child, Grace. Luanne and Pat were still living in Lebanon, Ohio, and Dorothy went there for two weeks to help Luanne with the baby. We now had three grandkids—who would have thought it! Dorothy and I agreed grandchildren are special and give us a new definition of love.

That winter, using the Pathfinder was great fun in Florida and my fly fishermen loved it. One morning, Don Beck and I were skimming across the flats when suddenly we ran out of water and came to a sudden stop. Fortunately, I had the steering wheel to hold onto, but Don, who was sitting beside me, went flying to the front of the boat. I instinctively reached out and grabbed him by the leg as he was catapulted from the seat or he would have gone headfirst into the water.

That spring, I began to see the down side of my Pathfinder. It was really a two-man boat, myself and only one customer. Some of my regular customers who wanted to take a family member or friend found the boat too crowed for two anglers. There were also days when I couldn't fish the beach for tarpon as the flat bottom was neither comfortable nor safe in one to three-foot waves. I borrowed a friend's flats boat a few times to allow me to take an extra angler or get onto the beach for tarpon.

I began to doubt the wisdom of my choice of the Pathfinder and started to look for other options. Hell's Bay Boat Works was started in 1997 by Hal Chittum, a well-known Florida guide and founder of H.T. Chittum and Company, a retailer of fishing tackle and casual clothes in Florida. Hell's Bay used a new technology building the hull with Kevlar and carbon fiber instead of fiberglass. The benefit was a lighter hull, rigid and almost indestructible. The boat was expensive compared to my Pathfinder built of fiberglass, due mainly to the material cost and the labor-intensive production process. I called Hal in April 1999 and discussed my requirements for a new boat, and he concluded the Hell's Bay boat would be just what I was looking for. He would get me on their guide program so as to extend an attractive price to promote the boat. I told Hal I would be heading back to Michigan in June and we agreed I would come to visit the factory in Titusville, on the east coast of Florida, two hundred miles from Port Charlotte, when I returned to Florida in October.

We always looked forward to getting back to

l-r, Dennis, Dennis (son), Pat and Luanne, with salmon

Onekama; deep down inside it was still where our roots were. One of the highlights of the summer was the annual Onekama Marine Shoot Out, a family-oriented two-day fishing tournament followed by a pig roast. Only boats docked or stored at Onekama Marine could participate. At the tourna-

186

ment's peak, over twenty boats competed. Luanne, Pat and Dennis fished with me every year, with Emilee, John and Grace joining in from the time they could walk. It was a family event we all looked forward to each summer. On a few occasions, family ties were strained when Luanne and Dennis complained to Dorothy that they were not going to fish with Dad again because he shouted at them!

"Don't feel bad," she replied, "your dad shouts at me too when we are fishing together."

Luanne and Dennis never understood the difference between my being excited and my shouting at them. I think it reminded them of being scolded when they were growing up. The grandkids, however, never seemed to mind my "shouting." They were as excited as I was when we had a fish on. In the end, the entire family kept coming back. We did well in the tournaments, winning a few times, but the memories we generated are what really counted. Unfortunately, the tournament ended in 2007 due to dwindling participation. The younger generation doesn't have the passion for fishing that my generation did. There are too many other attractions to complete for their free time and money.

Another annual event was started when our granddaughter Emilee went to the Covenant Bible Camp for the first time in 1999. The camp, located next to Onekama Marine and operated by the Covenant Church, is a faith-based, one-week program for children ages seven through high school. As John and Grace became of age, they too attended the camp each summer. The grandchildren never missed a year of camp through high school.

In 1999, Onekama Marine became a dealer for Rampage Yachts. Rampage had a reputation as an offshore saltwater fishing boat and was looking to expand to the freshwater market on the Great Lakes, Onekama Marine would be their first Lake Michigan dealer. That summer, Jim Mrozinski and I discussed the possibility of my buying a Rampage—as we had discussed for a while now, but I still had no interest in selling my thirty-one Tiara for a new boat, particularly as my increased business in Florida pointed to a future for me there rather than in Michigan. And my travels overseas did not require a new boat.Neither Jim nor I realized however how involved we would become with Rampage in the not-too-distant future.

The previous year, 1998, my son Dennis had taken a position with Michigan Blue Cross/Blue Shield. In the spring of 1999, he graduated from Eastern Michigan University with a bachelor of science in facilities management. For his graduation present, I wanted to take a trip to Alaska with him before Dorothy and I returned to Florida in September. In August, I took him to Alaska. We flew from Detroit via Seattle to Anchorage, where we spent the night. The next morning, Dennis and I flew in a twin-engine commuter plane to Port Alsworth, an hour southwest of Anchorage on Lake Iliamna.

The lodge, Fishing Unlimited, was located on Lake Iliamna, which is home to some of the best trout and salmon fishing in Alaska. Everything about the trip was first class—rooms, food, guides and fishing. Each morning, two to four anglers, depending on the size of the float plane, flew to a different lake or river to fish. The pilot, who was also our guide, would land on a river or lake, taxi us to shore and we began fishing. Regulations at the Lodge were "catch and release" to help preserve the fish. Dennis and I caught Dolly Varden, grayling, rainbow trout and silver salmon depending on the location. As usual, we were in competition for who caught the most and the biggest fish. One day, Dennis and I flew to Kodiak Island, two hundred miles south of Port Alsworth, and fished a remote inland lake for Dolly Varden and grayling. The weather was typical Alaska, sun, clouds, rain and cold all in one day. The scenery was beautiful. Flying over the rugged terrain of the Katmai National Park and along the Gulf of Alaska, we saw numerous moose, bear and caribou and schools of silver salmon swimming into the rivers along the coast.

The highlight of our trip was not the fishing, however. At times, we fished rivers frequented by brown—a.k.a. grizzly—bears who were also looking for fish. Anglers had to move out of the water on occasion to let the bears go by—no one argued over territory with them. Brown bears frequent coastal regions of southern Alaska feeding on spawning salmon and have an average weight of around nine hundred pounds, with a few exceeding twelve hundred pounds. The guide gave Dennis and me instructions on what to do if we encountered a bear: we were to wave our arms and shout and, under no circumstance, to turn and run.

On our third day of fishing, Dennis and I saw several brown bears at a distance, but they were as yet nothing to be concerned about. Dennis and the guide were fishing one side of the river, and I had crossed to the other side to a different spot. The river, about one-hundred feet wide, was quite deep and difficult to cross. However, I had found a shallow area a few hundred feet upstream where it was safe to cross to the other side. I moved back down river directly across from where Dennis and the guide were fishing and waded into the river about forty feet from shore. I was focused on catching rainbow trout when I looked up and saw a brown bear walking along the riverbank toward me. The bear, about one-hundred feet upriver from me, moved into the tall brush boarding the river and disappeared so I went back to fishing.

Suddenly, I heard Dennis and the guide shouting. I looked up. There on the river bank directly in front

Grizzly bear taken by Dennis, Alaska, 1999

of me was a very large brown bear. My first reaction was not panic but awe. I had a camera hanging from a strap around my neck, and without thinking, put my fly rod under my arm and started taking pictures as the bear slowly walked down into the water directly toward me. The bear had its nose pointed to the water looking back and forth for fish. It didn't acknowledge I was there. As the bear moved closer, I heard Dennis shout, "Wave your arms and shout at the bear". The guide was running to the shallows where I had crossed the river earlier, shouting as he ran. He was armed with a forty-four-magnum revolver strapped to his side.

I was mesmerized by the sight of the bear and continued to take pictures as the bear advanced to within fifteen feet of me, I could have reached out and touched the bear on the nose with my fly rod. I couldn't back up as the river was too deep and swift. It was then I realized the potential danger with the bear on one side and deep swift water behind me. I slowly put my camera down and shouted as loud as I could. The bear stopped and looked up at me intently for what seemed an eternity. Then it turned and slowly retreated to shore and disappeared in the tall grass. I stood motionless for a few moments to regain my composure; my heart was pounding as I realized the seriousness of the situation that had just ended. Cautiously, I walked to shore watching for the bear as the guide made his way toward me along the river bank. The guide who still had his revolver drawn as he approached me, had a stern look on his face. He was half mad, half glad to see me in one piece. The guide admonished me for not shouting at the bear sooner, but then he acknowledged that taking a stand, facing the bear and not panicking was the only response I could have done.

Back at the Lodge, I was the center of discussion, not for catching fish but being so careless as to almost get eaten by a bear. (The pictures turned out great by the way!) Dennis and I caught lots of fish that week, and Dennis swears he caught more than

I did—but that shows how wrong Dennis can be! Overall it was the most enjoyable and memorable trip I have ever been on—thanks to the bear and my son. I will never forget it.

Upon our return to Riverwood in October 1999, I called Hal Chittum at Hell's Bay Boat Works and arranged to visit the factory in Titusville which is on the Atlantic coast, a four-hour drive from Port Charlotte. After a brief meeting with Hal and his staff, I tested an eighteen-foot flats boat with a sixty-horsepower outboard motor and was impressed how soft and dry it handled rough water. I polled the boat in windy conditions and liked how easy it was to maneuver. The hull weighed only four-hundred pounds due to the Kevlar construction and could easily take two anglers plus myself. I was sold! The only problem was the factory had fallen behind in production due to technical problems with the new hull molding process. Hal said it would be better to delay the delivery of the boat until they had all the bugs worked out. We agreed I would contact him after the first of the year and decide then on a build date.

In November 1999, Chuck May and I made our first trip to Deadman's Cay on Long Island in the Bahamas. Once again, Don Causey, who because of his position as editor of The Angling Report had heard of the place, had recommended it to me. He said the area was not well known but was getting excellent reports from anglers who had fished there. Getting to Deadman's Cay was not easy. It involved a flight from Miami to Nassau and then a connecting flight to Deadman's Cay. The connecting flight ran only twice a week but that was not dependable.

Accommodations were basic but clean: three separate apartments in a one-story cement block building with a metal roof. Meals were delivered to the door by a local restaurant. The food was good but not always delivered on time. The owner, Sam Knowles, his uncle and his cousin were our guides. What we experienced in the next five days was why Deadman's Cay was receiving excellent reports. Bonefish everywhere! Chuck and I each caught ten to fifteen fish

Dennis with bone fish,
Deadmans Cay, 1999

per day—either sight casting from a boat or getting out of the boat and wading to the fish.

Bonefish are one of the most sought-after game fish in the world. Small in size, three to eight pounds, but tenacious fighters with lightning speed that can readily take fifty to one-hundred yards of line off your reel as they "rooster tail" across the shallow flats. Aptly named, "grey ghost of the flats", bonefish can appear and disappear as a mirage due to the changing reflection of the sun off their silvery scales. A fisherman requires stealth, good eyesight and casting skill to catch one. Sam was an excellent guide in all respects and had the sight of an eagle. The fish averaged around four pounds, while a few were in the six-pound range. The price for a week all-inclusive was one thousand dollars plus airfare. Some of the better-known fishing resorts charge that much per day. We both agreed it was worth a trip back with our wives the following year.

As it turned out, Deadman's Cay would become an annual event, not as a destination to take customers as I was no longer doing that, but to relax and have a good time with our friends Chuck and Nancy May and George and Ruth Bell who went every year with me. Dorothy went with me only one year but it was clear she would have rather been golfing. She did catch a few bonefish, but I knew from prior experience, fishing was not her passion. She enjoyed the friendship, sight-seeing and the card games after dinner but the fishing she could do without. So that was her last trip with us. We often joked about Dorothy suggesting I go fishing when my being around too much interfered with her golf and vice-versa with my fishing. It worked fine for us without either Dorothy or me feeling neglected by the other. Dorothy used my time away fishing to accept invitations to golf tournaments in different states. Texas, New Mexico, California and Georgia come to mind, which enhanced her reputation as a championship golfer. She viewed the opportunity to meet different people through her travel and golf as her ministry to witness to others about Christ in the same manner I used my work at Ford and my career as a charter captain as a ministry. We both sought day to day opportunities to be ambassadors for Christ.

Ben Kittrell, my friend from Florida, went with us for two years and became an excellent fly fisherman. The only downside to Deadman's Cay was getting there. I don't recall a year that we didn't miss a flight or were delayed going or coming. Deadman's Cay was my busman's holiday with friends. There was no pressure and my only agenda was to enjoy the fishing and my friends.

Of the several hundred bonefish I have caught, my most memorable catch was a twelve-pound bonefish in Islamorada, Florida with my good friend, Captain Jim Bennett. Dorothy and I were on a weekend rendezvous in Islamorada with a group of friends from Onekama, and Jim offered to take Dr. Ed Barlan, a mutual friend from Onekama, and me bonefishing.

We hadn't been fishing for ten-minutes when Jim spotted several bonefish from his perch on the poling platform. I made a per-

fect cast just in front of the unwary fish and no sooner had the shrimp hit the water than the fish was hooked. Jim and I knew the fish was big after it sped across the flats taking seventy yards of line off my reel. After fifteen minutes of give and take, I had the bonefish in the boat. It was the biggest I had ever seen, weighing twelve pounds on Jim's

l-r, Jim Bennett and Dennis, 12-lb. bonefish, Islamorada, 2000

certified scale. There were shouts of excitement and high-fives all around for my "once in a lifetime" catch.

The accolades had hardly died down, perhaps ten minutes had gone by, when Ed hooked a large bone-fish, which—it's hard to believe—also weighed exactly twelve-pounds on Jim's certified scale! Jim said they were two of the largest bonefish he had ever caught as a guide and both had been hooked on the same day!

I know we had an outstanding guide and Ed and I were experienced fishermen, but what are the odds of catching two "once in a lifetime", twelve-pound bonefish on the same day? I know what I believe as I said, "Thank you, Lord."

In February 2000, I arranged for Don Beck, Tom Balisteri, his son Jim and me to make a trip to Golfito Bay in the southernmost part of Costa Rica, bordering on Panama. The area, adjacent to the Cordova National Park and the Golfito Wildlife Refuge, had just opened to tourism and fishing. We stayed at Crocodile Bay Resort, a newly constructed facility capable of handling twelve guests in luxurious accommodations. A friend of mine recommended I get in touch with Todd Staley who used to guide in Florida and was now the director of fishing at Crocodile Bay. Todd was excited for us to come and he arranged a discount for all four of us. Perhaps in view of what he had offered me, he asked if I could teach the local captains the bait and switch technique for catching sailfish on a fly. I was pleased to do so. Don and I had previously discussed my new "fellow fisherman" business model, and he thought it was a great idea especially with the discount we received on the trip.

On February 9, we flew from Miami to San Jose,

the capital of Costa Rica. I knew San Jose well from my previous trips to Quepos, Costa Rica in the 1980s when I was fly fishing for sail fish. I took our group on a sightseeing tour of San Jose. Afterwards, we had dinner that evening. The next morning, we flew to Puerto Jimenez, two hundred miles south of San Jose, where Crocodile Bay Lodge was located. The one-hour trip on a twin-engine commuter plane confirmed the natural beauty of the rain forests and mountainous terrain of Costa Rica. Golfito Bay, edged with tropical rainforests and partially separated from the Pacific Ocean by the Osa Peninsula, is a nature lover's paradise. The Bay is surrounded by seventeen national reserves constituting about three percent of Costa Rica's land area.

Crocodile Bay Resort had one twenty-eight-foot boat with a single diesel inboard capable of getting to the sailfish grounds in the Pacific Ocean. Several other smaller boats were used to fish in Golfito Bay for snook, rooster fish, snapper and grouper. Don, Tom and Jim decided to fish Golfito Bay while I went offshore with a one of the lodge's captains and two mates to show them the bait and switch technique used by Billy Pate.

My "students" and I set up our teaser rods and started a westerly troll looking for signs of bait fish that sailfish feed on and for birds to alert us of fish feeding in the area. I demonstrated to the mates how to rig a hook-less bait to tease a sailfish to the boat and once the sailfish is close to cast a fly to it. During the morning, we saw a few sailfish, but none came to inspect our baits trolled behind the boat. About noon, a sailfish appeared behind one of the hook-less

baits. The mate quickly took the rod and began to retrieve (tease) the sailfish. He did so slowly at first
until the fish saw and got a scent of the bait and then
the mate was coaxing the sailfish to the boat. The
captain put the boat in neutral just as the mate lifted
the teaser bait out of the water, and I made a perfect
cast just to the right of the sailfish. Before I could
start retrieving line, the sailfish turned, took my fly
and accelerated completely out of the water—thus
living up to its name! When I hooked the fish it was
airborne twenty feet behind the boat. A couple more
hook sets, forcefully jerking the fly line with my left
hand, and the fish was solidly hooked. After an aerial
display consisting of numerous jumps out of the
water, the fish ran from the boat and then dove deep
into the water.

The inexperienced captain was having trouble
maneuvering the boat so I could apply maximum
pressure on the fish. It is important when fighting a
large fish to keep a tight line directly from the fishing
rod to the fish. When a fish swims alongside and toward the front of the boat, increased drag is placed
on the fishing line being pulled sideways through the
water creating a bow in the fishing line. I hurriedly
tried to move around the boat to keep a direct line to
the fish as I was giving instructions to the captain in
Spanish. In a short time, the captain was doing a
good job keeping the fish directly behind the boat
where I could apply maximum pressure and keep a
tight line directly from the rod to the fish. Unfortunately, the sailfish had taken over one hundred
yards of line off the reel during the first few minutes
of our trial-and-error maneuvering of the boat. We

would soon learn that proved to be a costly mistake.

After about thirty minutes, I had the fish close to the boat, swimming slowly alongside just below the surface. I asked one of the mates to take the fish by the bill, lift it aboard for pictures and release it. There was a brief discussion with the captain to take the fish back to the Lodge for mounting as it would be the first sailfish on a fly at Crocodile Bay Lodge. I preferred not to but would let the captain decide after we had the fish in the boat.

One of the mates took the six-foot leader in hand and was gently leading the sailfish to the boat while the other mate leaned over the side to take hold of the bill when the leader broke. For a moment, the fish didn't realize it was free and continued swimming slowly alongside the boat just a foot under the water. We all stared hopelessly at the one hundred plus pound Pacific sailfish as it slowly swam off and down out of sight. The water was so clear we could see the blue iridescent colors of the sailfish thirty-feet below the surface.

A collective groan went up. Technically, we had released the first sailfish caught on a fly at Crocodile Bay. We agreed it was officially a release as we had the leader in hand, but we wanted the photos or the fish to prove it. The hook was just inside the mouth and the raspy jaws of the sailfish had weakened the eighty-pound leader during the prolonged fight. I had let the fish take too much line during the initial stage of the fight while I was instructing the captain how to keep the fish behind the boat. The added time it took to bring the fish to the boat was the deciding difference. Had we been able to keep the fish closer to the boat initially and land it sooner, the leader would likely not have broken.

Word had spread by marine radio that we had caught and released a sailfish, and by the time we got back to the dock, a crowd was gathered to welcome us. There was talk with Todd Staley about officially acknowledging the catch, but we unanimously decided against it. We felt it was better to wait for a subsequent catch when we might have photos for documentation. Until then, we would rely on the memory of the first sailfish on a fly at Crocodile Bay Lodge. The rest of the trip was anticlimactic for me. Our group caught numerous other fish during the week. Tom landed a respectable rooster fish, and his son Jim took a sixty-pound yellowfin tuna. All the guests at the lodge pigged out on fresh sushi and grilled tuna over the next couple of days.

By coincidence, Larry Dahlberg, TV personality and host of "Hunt for Big Fish" was in Costa Rica at the time filming a show about Crocodile Bay. We got to know him quite well over the week and learned a lot from his experiences around the world. We liked everything about the place and would highly recommend it to others. At the end of the week, I thanked Todd for hosting us, and he in turn appreciated the instruction I gave his captains in the bait and switch technique.

In May 2000, just before returning to Onekama, Chuck May and I made a three-day trip to Guatemala to fish sailfish on the fly at the Fins n Feathers Inn. We flew from Miami to Guatemala City where we spent the night at the Hilton Hotel, compliments of the Fins n Feathers Inn. The next morning, we were met by a representative of Fins n Feathers and transported sixty miles by van to Iztapa, a small fishing village of about two thousand residents, on the Pacific coast. The trip of one and a half hours on a modern four-lane highway through tropical forests and active volcanos was scenic and to some degree incongruous to the extreme poverty in the country. On

Dennis with sailfish,
Guatemala, 2000

the van with us were four anglers from Brazil with whom I had a great time trying to polish up on my Portuguese. I actually wasn't too bad considering I had not spoken Portuguese for several years.

The Inn was surrounded by a high wall with armed guards at the gate. Crime and poverty were a problem, and the political situation unstable in the country. Once inside Fins n Feathers, we found it to be very nicely decorated with an open veranda and dining room overlooking the marina. The accommodations and food were excellent. The next morning, we left the marina at seven and proceeded about a mile along an inland waterway along the coast to an inlet leading to the Pacific Ocean.

The entrance to the open water of the Pacific was

dangerous with large swells breaking as they came ashore. The channel was lined on both sides with large boulders that helped break the high waves crashing in from the Pacific. When the captain saw a lull in the breaking waves, he applied power to the large diesel engines in the boat, and we exited the channel against the incoming ten-to-twelve-foot swells. After a half dozen, large swells, we cleared the channel and moved into the open ocean. I have been through entrances like that before in Australia. They are exciting to negotiate, but you must know what you are doing.

Our captain used the same bait-and-switch technique we used in Costa Rica, where the charter fleet in Quepos was setting phenomenal records for sailfish releases. Ten releases a day per angler was not uncommon. Chuck and I didn't reach our high expectations but nonetheless had excellent fishing over the three days we were there releasing a dozen sailfish each.

As I always liked to do when visiting a new location, I wanted to visit the neighboring community. Chuck and I walked into the small village of Iztapa to visit with the locals. The village of about two hundred people had an open-air bar and restaurant, a produce market and a general store. A few chickens, dogs and a pig roamed the dusty unpaved streets. The people were friendly and easy to converse with in Spanish. They were preparing to expand the only school in town to accommodate more students as the increase in tourism from fishing was bringing people to the area to work at the new jobs.

At the end of May, soon after my return to Florida,

Dorothy and I traveled up to Onekama. Just two weeks later, Dennis and I left for another one-week trip to Fishing Unlimited Lodge in Alaska with our good friends, Chuck and Nancy May and George and Ruth Bell. Once again Dorothy chose golf over fishing. As Dennis and I left the house to drive to the airport, I can still hear her saying, with a smile on her face, "Have a good time! See you when you get back." The Mays and the Bells were as im-

Dennis with silver salmon, Alaska, 1999

pressed with the lodge and the fishing as Dennis and I had been on our trip the previous year. We had a great time with them and saw a few bears again but had no encounter as close as mine the previous year. Dennis got Chuck to agree with him that he caught more fish than I did on the trip—how wrong can he be two years in a row! Upon returning to Onekama, I was booked for two-weeks straight with salmon charters as I caught up on the charters I had postponed to make the Alaska trip.

July 2000 turned out to be a big month for Dorothy. She won the Michigan Senior's Golf Championship, which proved the pinnacle of her golf career. Dorothy's golf had improved significantly since our return to the US in 1982. Playing regularly at the

Washtenaw Golf Club in Michigan and at Riverwood in Florida, where she was club champion multiple times, Dorothy had improved to a three handicap. She was playing in numerous tournaments, travelling around the country and tough to beat in competition. I'm glad I didn't take up golf. I don't think I could handle being second all the time.

No sooner had I returned to Florida in November 2000 when I picked up my Hell's Bay flats boat and had Gulf Wind Marine mount a sixty-horsepower Mercury outboard and electric trolling motor. (The same week I bought my new Hell's Bay I sold my Pathfinder to a friend.) I finally had the boat of my dreams; the Hell's Bay would do all that I needed. It floated in four inches of water, poled like a leaf on the water, was quiet, had an adequate live well, would handle two anglers plus myself and was comfortable and dry in open water. I could fish the back country and still do tarpon trips along the shore of the Gulf beaches. I had several customers who would fish tarpon in the

Dennis poling flats of Charlotte Harbor with Don Beck fly fishing for snook, 1999

morning and then fish for redfish in the back country in the afternoon.

Also, in November, the Mays, Bells and Ben Kittrell and I made our annual trip to Deadman's Cay for one week. The results were the same: lots of bonefish, a great time with friends and a delay in our airline schedule to get home.

In December 2000, Don Beck and I made another trip to the Guri Reservoir with Larry Schantz and Kevin Rowe, two mutual friends. The trip was more laid back and a lot of fun, primarily because Larry and Kevin are not hard-core fisherman. I also reminded Don that I enjoyed the trip more not being in charge and responsible for the outcome, to which Don jokingly replied, "I never knew you were!" We did catch a lot of fish but that was not as important to Larry and Kevin as the camaraderie. There were lots of kidding each other, with Kevin taking most of the ribbing. He was a Canadian and claimed he had caught more fish than any of us. An international banker, Kevin had spent most of his working life in the Far East and was now retired. Larry was a retired physician who later fished salmon with Don Beck and me in Onekama. Our friendship was entwined with a mutual fishing acquaintance neither of us were aware of at the time. Neither Larry nor I could know how in a few short years he would no longer be with us.

It was on fishing trips like those to Brazil and Venezuela that I was reminded how my passion for fishing had provided me a ministry to witness for Christ all over the world. Often during long days on the boat with other fishermen, meeting local guides and over dinner in the evening, our discussion turned to faith. I was mindful that not everyone believed as I did and I let the Holy Spirit provide opportunities to do or say the right thing.

Instead of going to Deadman's Cay in 2001, Ben Kittrell and I went to the Mangrove Cay Club on Andros Island in the Bahamas. A good customer of mine was a founding member of the club and gave me a free one-week trip. I called Ben to see if he wanted to go and split the cost of a second trip. He jumped at the chance, and Ben and I left for Andros Island the week of February 7, 2001. The weather was not good, very windy and rainy, but we caught fish and the accommodations were first class. Ben and I agreed, for the money, we still preferred Deadman's Cay. The Mays and Bells had maintained our annual tradition by going to Deadman's Cay, but that year they went without us. Their report of the excellent bonefishing confirmed that Ben and I should have gone with them instead of to the Mangrove Cay Club.

The following May, 2001, Chuck and I went back to Fins n Feathers in Guatemala and released thirty-one sailfish on the fly over three days, not counting the ones that got away. Had we been physically up to the task we could have exceeded that number significantly. Each day after hooking a dozen or more sailfish each, Chuck and I tired and fished for mahi-mahi, a smaller but hard fighting fish, beautifully colored, fun to catch and great eating. Overall, the accommodations, the quality of the boat, the captain and his crew, the weather and my friend, Chuck, offered the best saltwater fishing trip I have ever been on. A few years later, an angler at Fins n Feathers released a phenomenal fifty-seven sailfish on the fly in one-day.

The summer of 2001 turned out to be a busy one and not just with charters. Jim Mrozinski of Onekama Marine, ever mindful of setting me up with a Rampage Yacht, had called me in Florida. Rampage Yachts would give me a discount on a thirty-foot Rampage in return

2nd & 3rd from left, Chuck May and Dennis, Guatemala, 2001

for representing them in salmon tournaments. It would be a big investment of my time and money and would take time away from my overseas trips. I would have to equip the new boat with downriggers, rod holders and other fishing gear necessary to fish salmon. Dorothy and I talked it over, and as has always been the case when I had to make a major decision, we asked the Lord to pave the way.

Dorothy and I arrived in Onekama the first week of June 2001 without having made any decision, but things soon began to fall into place. Jim confirmed the discount on a new Rampage, and a friend at the marina wanted to buy my Tiara. Several sponsors agreed to provide me with downriggers, rod holders and electronics in exchange for representing them on the Tournament Trail. How could everything I needed have fallen into place so easily—well, of course, I knew the answer and so did Dorothy. I bought the Rampage one week and sold my Tiara the following. It took another week to mount downriggers, electronics and rod holders, and entirely set up. I ran my first charter on my new Rampage on June 20, 2001.

I was sad to see the Tiara go. Dorothy and I had bought the boat new in 1982, when we had come home from Brazil. We had many fond memories of *True Blue*, as we called the Tiara, cruising and fishing with the kids over the past twenty-years, and she had become part of the family. The name on the new Rampage was, guest what? *True Blue II*. I had to redo my business cards, brochures and web site with new pictures. This update was needed anyway. Rampage helped me in a new marketing program to promote Rampage Yachts via *True Blue II*.

Our numerous bonefish trips to the Bahamas had started me thinking about establishing a fishing business in the Bahamas. Dorothy and I had discussed it occasionally—she was all for it if there was a golf course nearby. The trips would be short, maybe three days to a week, so we wouldn't be away from Riverwood for long periods of time. Our neighbors, Dot and Jack, would be glad to watch Daisy when necessary. This business would be different than the guided fishing trips to international locations I had initially planned where I was the travel agent, outfitter and interpreter. I would have a fixed base of operation in the Bahamas where customers would come to fish. The customers would arrange for their own airfare, I would handle local accommodations, provide fly fishing tackle and a guided charter at an all-inclusive fee. Much easier, simpler and hopefully, more profitable.

I had fished enough in the Bahamas over the past several years to know I could do a good job on my own. In fact, Sam Knowles, our guide at Deadman's Cay, wanted me to come and help him out. I ruled out Deadman's Cay, however, as it was difficult to reach due to the infrequent and unreliable air transportation. I was thinking of a location in the northern Bahamas, Bimini, Grand Bahama, Andros or Great Abaco. Those islands offered quality accommodations and

Rampage 30 with Dennis, 2001

were easily accessed from Florida. I already had enough customers in Florida to guarantee a good business so finding the right location was the first step.

After some research, I settled on Great Abaco, the largest of a group of islands forming the Abaco Islands, one-hundred and eighty miles east of Ft.

Lauderdale, in the northern Bahamas. It could be reached by a thirty-minute commercial flight. Marsh Harbor, a town of about five-thousand which serves as the area's commercial center, is known throughout the Caribbean as a prime tourist destination. It offered excellent accommodations and was serviced by major airlines. Marsh Harbor was home to several international big game fishing tournaments. The Marls, located on the east side of Great Abaco Island, is a vast area of shallows and mangrove stands similar to the area I fished in Florida. It is one of the most productive waters to catch bonefish in the Bahamas and a thirty-minute taxi ride to the east of Marsh Harbor. Abaco Beach Resort and Boat Harbor Marina, one of the most prestigious resorts in the Bahamas, had excellent marina facilities and was a twenty-minute walk into Marsh Harbor. The offshore Atlantic fishing was a thirty-minute boat ride west of Boat Harbor Marina. I wondered if there would be a market to combine backcountry fishing and offshore fly fishing in the same package.

One of the industries targeted for foreign investment by the Bahamian Tourism Agency was fishing. I already had a twelve-month Bahamian transient permit for boating and fishing, which I obtained when I cleared customs in Bimini. I decided to wait to make a formal application for a business permit until I was sure I would be committed to a business venture in the Bahamas.

After considering alternatives, it occurred to me that taking my new Rampage to the Bahamas would make more sense than buying another flats boat. I already had a boat that was sitting in storage during the winter in Michigan. I could take customers fly fishing for game fish on *True Blue II* and contract with a local guide in Marsh Harbor to use his boat for bonefishing on the Marls until I knew more about the area.

The first week of December 2001, Don Beck and I made our third and last trip to the Guri Reservoir in Venezuela. We were accompanied by Tom Balisteri, and his son, Jim, who had both been with us on our trip to Crocodile Bay Lodge in Costa Rica the previous year. It is worth noting that, for the most part, Don's friends were also my friends. Thanks to Don, almost everyone he knew had fished with me as a customer over the years. Don was not only a good friend and customer, but he was also a great booking agent! None of the four of us were disappointed with the Guri Reservoir as the fishing was as good as ever with each of us catching ten to fifteen peacock bass a day. As we were departing to fly back to Ciudad Bolivar on the same Antonov An-2 airplane that we had used the year before, the owner of the lodge confided that things were not well in Venezuela and he wondered how long he would be able to stay in business. Tourism had dropped dramatically, and the economy was on the verge of collapse. We shared his concern and hoped we would have an opportunity to come again, knowing it would not be likely under the current economic and political conditions.

Arriving at the airport in Caracas from Ciudad Bolivar, we were told our flight back to Miami had been rescheduled to the following morning due to mechanical problems with the airplane. The ticket agent advised us we could wait at the airport for the delayed flight or pay for our own accommodations elsewhere. With all of the armed guards standing around the airport, it was apparent to me this was not the time to make a scene with the airlines over who should pay for overnight accommodations, especially as we were foreigners. I strongly suggested to my friends that we look elsewhere.

We found a hotel near the airport, at our expense, and having the afternoon free hired a taxi and drove to Macuto, a city of eighty thousand, thirty-five miles north of Caracas on the Caribbean Coast, noted for its beautiful beaches, resorts and big game fishing. When Dorothy and I lived in Venezuela in the late 1960s, we stayed at the Macuto Sheraton Resort where Dorothy and the kids spent time on the beach while I went fishing for striped marlin on a local charter boat. The area had been a mecca for expensive sport fishing yachts visiting from the US and the Caribbean during the peak of the marlin season.

What I saw was only a remnant of what I remembered had been Macuto. Several of the resorts and marinas were closed, and the area was in deterioration. You could vividly see the negative economic impact the political situation was having on the country. We were told by the taxi driver that travel was becoming difficult and unsafe in the country, tourism had diminished, unemployment was increasing and the availability of basic staples like food and clothing were scarce and expensive.

Dorothy and I had the good times and great friends while living in Venezuela. It was sad to see the negative changes that were taking place in this once prosperous and beautiful country. Thirty-one years previously, in July 1968, Dorothy, Luanne and I first arrived in Venezuela at the same airport. I recalled my time flying for New Tribes Mission, the tragic loss of Dorothy's folks, John and Lucille Hacker, in a plane crash and subsequent internment in Maracaibo on March 16, 1969, and the happiness Dorothy and I felt with the birth of our son, Dennis, in Valencia on July 5, 1969. Emotionally, I was leaving a part of myself and my family behind. When we departed from Caracas on December 12, 2000, I knew it would be my last time in Venezuela.

Dennis came to Florida for Christmas 2001 to introduce us to his fiancée, Donna Bajtka. They had been going together for over a year and were planning a summer wedding in Onekama. She was a lovely young lady, and we looked forward to welcoming her into our family. It was Donna's first time fishing in Florida, and she enjoyed seeing the dolphins and doing some back-country fishing. Dorothy and I were happy for Dennis to have found such a nice young lady to be his future wife. Dorothy confessed to me she was relieved. Dennis was thirty-two, and she was beginning to wonder if we would ever have grandkids from his side of the family!

The winter of 2002 went by quickly. I was busy with charters, fly casting lessons and planning to take *True Blue II* from Michigan to Florida in the fall. I didn't realize how much was involved in taking a boat thousands of miles across inland waterways. The route would take me from Onekama across Lake Michigan to Chicago then along the inland waterway system to Florida. Having the right maps, learning how to transit locks, overnight stops at marinas and fuel management were just a few of the details I would have to become familiar with. Everyone that had made the trip advised that preplanning was ninety-percent of the success of the trip. Good planning, good trip – bad planning, watch out!

That winter, as I was planning my trip to Florida the following year, I encouraged Dorothy to come along, even if only for a few days. I could drop her off at a predetermined location along the way. From there, she could fly back to Michigan. As I thought she would, Dorothy smiled and said she preferred staying home to look after Daisy—she left off the part about playing golf every day. We both knew the answer before I asked, but I wanted to be polite. Dorothy commented how blessed we were to still do the things we enjoyed at our ages of sixty-nine and sixty-six. We both had been active all of our lives and blessed with good health. Why let a physical number such as age slow us down? (A word of advice to the younger generation: get a good night's sleep, eat well and stay physically active.)

Dick and Shirley Osborne, friends from Michigan and Riverwood, owned a forty-two-foot Sea Ray in Michigan. When I told Dick that I was taking my boat to Florida, he asked to accompany me in his Sea Ray. We agreed it would be safer and more fun to do the trip together and began co-operating on plans. I told Dick it would be September before I could leave due to my charter season and we would keep in touch over the summer to finetune our plans.

The summer salmon season was busy, as I ran my usual forty charters and continued planning my trip cruising *True Blue II* to Florida and then on to the Bahamas. In addition, I fished several tournaments as a representative of Rampage. My agreement with Rampage required I fish three salmon tournaments with my Rampage, pass out marketing material and provide test rides to potential buyers referred by Rampage. We did well in the tournaments which we fished with charter customers, missing first place in one tournament by just a point.

The highlight of our summer was Dennis' marriage to Donna Bajtka on September 21, 2002. Donna grew up in Manistee, and her dad and her mom (Gordon and Barb) were still living there. Tragically, Barb passed away in 2014 from cancer. Dennis and Donna were married at the Catholic Church in Manistee. With Tom, Joann and many nieces and nephews belonging to the Catholic faith and Dorothy and I attending numerous churches during our travels overseas, we understood there are doctrinal differences in denominations. Our advice to Dennis and Donna was to focus on a personal relationship with Christ and the inspired word of God and to join a denomination that shared these beliefs.

Their wedding reception was held at the historic Ramsdale Theater in Manistee. Built in 1902 during the lumber boom in Manistee, the theater now provides arts and cultural entertainment and is available for social events. Donna and our son-in-law, Pat, have been like a daughter and a son to us, loved like our own children.

So, ended my "fun fishing years." I would make one more trip to Deadman's Cay and to Alaska the following year but starting in 2003 the emphasis changed from fun fishing to taking *True Blue II* to

Florida and setting up a fishing business in the Bahamas. I didn't realize it at the time, but my forthcoming trip to the Bahamas with *True Blue II* would become a humbling experience and initiate a change in the future of my fishing business.

Chapter 7
Bahama Bound

It was a cool, windy day, September 27, 2002, when I departed Onekama with *True Blue II* on my trip to Florida and the Bahamas. I was about to begin an odyssey filled with adventure, danger and excitement, an odyssey that would change the direction of my fishing career and initiate a new phase of my life. I had been planning this trip to establish a fishing business in the Bahamas for the past year and felt I was well prepared for all contingencies. I could not have imagined, however, the challenges that I would encounter over the next several months. Was it faulty planning or had I overlooked important details—like including God in my plans?

When I had talked to Doug West several months prior to my trip, he jumped at the chance to accompany me to take *True Blue II* to Florida and share the costs. Doug would be a great companion—not only is he fun to be with but he is a knowledgeable boater.

Doug and I, accompanied by Dick Osbourne and two of his friends in his boat, were filled with anticipation as we left Onekama for Chicago. It was rough cross-

l-r, Doug West, Dennis and
Dick Osboune

ing Lake Michigan with winds out of the southwest at fifteen to twenty miles per hour and seas three to five feet. It took us ten hours to cover the one-hundred and sixty miles from Onekama to Waukegan, Illinois, where we spent the night. The next morning with the lake now calm, we travelled the remaining fifty-miles south to the Chicago Harbor Lock and entered the Calumet River, the start of the Mississippi River System that would take us south to Florida.

The route took us over the Illinois, Ohio, Mississippi, Cumberland and Tennessee Rivers and the Tennessee-Tombigbee Waterway to Mobile, Alabama, a total of one thousand and eighty miles. I had no idea how interesting and vital the Ohio and Mississippi river systems are to our country. Millions of tons of cargo and numerous industries and cities are totally dependent on these river systems. In addition, we found the history and culture of the "river people" to be intriguing. We met people living on boats of all shapes and sizes who follow the sun from Minnesota to Florida and back each year, some working along the way as needed to sustain themselves. We also met captains moving expensive yachts for their owners to southern destinations.

Barge traffic and locks were our biggest challenges. Barges on the Mississippi River, moving forty-six million tons of cargo per year, are interconnected by steel cable and can stretch to twelve hundred feet long and two hundred feet wide. Propelled by a pusher tug, the barges were difficult to pass without creating even a minimum wake. The tug had little tolerance for even little wakes. A wake of one or two feet could overflow the low side of a tug and drench the powerful diesel engine, up to eleven thousand horsepower, installed below the deck. Not a good way to make friends with the captain of a tug!

We passed through seventeen locks in total. Commercial boats and barges have preference in entering the locks that open on a schedule. Sometimes we would be directed by the lock master to immediately enter the lock and other times we waited up to four hours to transit through a lock. Being squeezed between the lock wall and a barge that could crush your boat like an egg shell was unnerving at times. By the time Dick Osbourne and his friends, and Doug and I got to Mobile, we were old hands at transiting locks.

There were so many interesting places to see and visit along the way. From little marinas like Hoppies, consisting of six barges tied together on the river bank, to luxurious marina resorts, marinas meet every need of the transient boater. On one stretch of the lower Mississippi, it is over four hundred miles between fuel stops. This is too far for most pleasure boats to go without refueling. A cell phone call to a local vendor, Kidds River City Fuel Service, at Cape Girardeau, Missouri, is required to schedule a fuel stop. There, a small barge, anchored to the shore with steel cables, substituted as a dock while the fuel was delivered to the boat by a sixty foot hose from a fuel truck parked on the road. That is one appointment you don't want to miss as docking there for the night is not permitted. There were some marinas that didn't even show on the map and others that are heavily promoted as stop overs. We were forced to anchor out one night in a small cove as we misjudged our time to the next destination and didn't want to run the river after dark as barge traffic continued to be heavy.

Early morning fog occurred frequently during the trip, making it difficult to start on our way before nine a.m. One morning, Doug and I were anxious to get going and so we departed at seven a.m. I had put in many hours fishing in the fog on Lake Michigan using radar and GPS chart plotters and so I felt I was prepared to negotiate our way through the fog on the Mississippi. I was not prepared however for the myriad of unfamiliar objects on the radar screen. Tugs and barges often appeared as one large blob on the screen blocking out channel markers and other boats. By the time the fog lifted at nine a.m., Doug and I were exhausted, and we had only covered ten miles in two hours. We wished we had stayed in port and decided we had done our last "early start." Fortunately, Dick Osbourne and his friends had stayed in port as Dick was not comfortable cruising in the fog.

A week after our departure, on October 3, 2002, Hurricane Lili made shore near New Orleans and worked its way north up the Mississippi River for several hundred miles, dumping four to six inches of rain along its path. Dick and his two friends along with Doug and I stayed an extra day at Green Turtle Marina on Kentucky Lakes waiting for the rain to subside, but after we set off, we still encountered numerous logs and trees washed into the river by the storm's heavy rains. This debris slowed our progress for a few days.

Just after entering the Tennessee Tombigbee waterway, two days after the hurricane, I hit an underwater object and bent a propeller that I had to change at the Demopolis Yacht Basin in Demopolis, Alabama. Fortunately, I had a spare prop with me. As it was late in the afternoon, the five of us decided to spend the night at the Demopolis Yacht Basin, and by morning, with the new prop in place, we headed south, two hundred and forty miles, to Mobile, Alabama where the members of our two-boat flotilla spent the night. Dick and I had found it was difficult to travel together due to the barge traffic and the locks, but we kept in touch by cell phone and radio. We'd determine an overnight destination to have dinner and to discuss plans for the next day. That night, Mobile was our regrouping point.

Unfortunately, an unexpected problem at his own business forced Doug to fly home the following morning. We decided that one of Dick Osbourne's friends would ride with me to replace Doug. The next morning, after Doug arranged for a taxi to take him from the marina to the airport, Dick and I steered our boats east along the Gulf of Mexico on the Intracoastal waterway to Apalachicola, two hundred and fifty miles east of Mobile, where we spent the night. That evening Dick, his friends and I ate at a restaurant that only served oysters, twenty different ways! I don't remember how many dozens we ate, but it was a lot.

The following morning, our two boats left at daylight for the two hundred and twenty mile run across the Gulf of Mexico to Clearwater, Florida. We were out of sight of land most of the time but enjoyed the trip as we saw loggerhead turtles, dolphins, rays and various other marine creatures during the nine-hour crossing. I had navigation equipment on the boat, but I still relied on my compass, time and speed—just in case. This was a carryover from my days flying in Venezuela.

Dick and I stayed the night and refueled in Clearwater. The next day, October 13, we ran the last one hundred miles from Clearwater to Gulf Wind Marine in Cape Haze where I would keep *True Blue* II until making the trip to the Bahamas. Dick arranged to keep his boat at another marina near Boca Grande. Terry Lynch and the folks at the Gulf Wind Marine were glad to see me again. Terry thought I looked out of place on *True Blue II*, which was more than twice the size of the smaller flats boat I used in Florida.

It had taken Dick and me seventeen days and one thousand eight hundred and twelve miles from Onekama to Gulf Wind Marine. We agreed it was a trip of a lifetime and a test of our boating skills, but worth every minute we invested. I regret we hadn't had more time to stop along the way. It could easily take twice as long to see everything.

That fall was busy with charters, but I scheduled my Florida charters to allow three open weeks in December to take *True Blue II* to Marsh Harbor in the Bahamas. As I was preparing this trip which I considered to be a bit exploratory, I contemplated the feasibility of starting another venture, this one to be focused on chartering in the Bahamas. I wasn't sure why, but I wasn't embarking on this new venture with the enthusiasm that I experienced with my other business start-ups. Maybe, even after a couple of months to recuperate, I was still tired from my long trip with *True Blue II* from Michigan.

I was soon to find out the wisdom of my negativity.

Doug West, who had a twenty-six-foot boat and condo at Port St. Lucie on the east coast of Florida, flew back from Michigan to accompany me to the Bahamas in his boat. I was delighted to have him follow along for the safety and the company. Doug's brother-in-law, Don, crewed for Doug on his boat and my good friend and fishing buddy, Chuck May, crewed on *True Blue*. (Chuck also shared the costs.) Chuck and I left Gulf Wind Marine on December 4 for Ft. Meyers and the Okeechobee Waterway east across Florida to Port St. Lucie, a distance of one hundred and sixty-six miles. We spent the night in Clewiston on Lake Okeechobee at Roland Martin's Fishing Resort and then on to Port St. Lucie the following day where Chuck and I met up with Doug and Don at Doug's condo to spend the night. The four of us excitedly discussed our plans for an early departure the next morning for Bimini, the westernmost island in the Bahamas. Unfortunately, the morning

223

forecast was for high winds and rough seas, which could delay our departure.

The morning of December 6, the wind was blowing twenty-five knots out of the northeast with wave height six to eight feet. The Gulf Stream, like a large river, about fifty-miles wide, runs to the north along the Atlantic coast of Florida at five miles per hour. With six- to eight-foot waves running to the south into the five-mile-per-hour current, the Gulf stream is extremely dangerous. While we were eager to leave (it is only sixty-five miles from Port St. Lucie to Bimini), the negative weather forecast convinced us to delay our crossing.

We waited two days for the wind to subside. Time was beginning to weigh heavy on all of us, the weather delay was eroding our tight schedule for a return to Florida before Christmas and increasing our eagerness to get started for Marsh Harbor.

The forecast on December 9 was for a north-east wind at ten to fifteen knots and for two-to four-foot waves. Again, this was not the ideal weather we had hoped for, but it was safe crossing weather and Doug and I were anxious to get our boats running and begin our trip. We departed at nine a.m. to ensure we made the crossing in the daylight. During the first half-hour, both Doug and I made good time before entering the Gulf Stream about five-miles offshore. There, the waves increased to three to six feet with occasional eight-foot waves. My thirty-foot Rampage was designed with a planing hull to rise up and glide on the water when enough power—that is, speed—is applied, but at a slower speed, with the boat not on plane, the waves would crash right over the bow. I decided to run at a higher speed to keep my boat on plane and stay on top of the waves.

Doug was having trouble keeping up with me in his smaller boat which simply did not have the power of my Rampage. We lost sight of Doug for about an hour during the roughest part of the crossing. Doug called several times on the radio to say it was slow going but he and Don were still making headway. Cell phones were of no use unless you had an international phone plan to use the Bahamian telephone system, which was expensive and not that reliable.

As Chuck and I moved out of the Gulf Stream into two- to three-foot waves on the Bahamian Bank, I slowed down to wait for Doug. I tried calling on the radio but got no answer. After a half hour, Chuck and I became concerned. I was about to turn back to look for Doug and Don when we saw Doug's boat on the horizon. Visibility was limited to two or three miles due to the haze, but with my Fuji 750 x 50 binoculars, I was sure it was Doug. I finally made radio contact, and Doug said he was so busy steering to keep on course he didn't hear our calls. The four of us pulled into Alice Town on Bimini wet and tired but happy to be there. The trip which should have taken two and a half hours had taken four. With six to eight-foot seas crossing the Gulf Stream, you could say it was a rough way to start our trip.

Our group cleared Bahamian customs and obtained our transit and fishing permits at the Compleat Angler Resort and Marina where I had made reservations for the next two nights to give us a day to rest and look around the island before continuing our journey to Marsh Harbor. Bimini, with a population of about two thousand, became famous when Ernest Hemingway spent many days on the island

during the 1930s. We were told his book, *The Old Man and the Sea*, was based on his experiences fishing in Bimini and Cuba. Attached to the hotel was a museum containing memorabilia of Hemingway's time there. Tragically the hotel and museum were completely destroyed by fire on January 13, 2006—a little more than three years after our visit.

l to r, Don, Doug West and Chuck May, Bimini, 2002

It was a beautiful calm morning as we departed Bimini and cruised north toward Freeport on Grand Bahama Island, a distance of seventy miles. Doug decided he and his brother-in-law Don would do some fishing along the way and meet us at Flamingo Bay Marina on Grand Bahama where we were to spend the night. About an hour into our crossing to Grand Bahama, I felt a bump and slight vibration from the starboard engine. I slowed to idle speed to confirm the vibration was from the starboard side of the boat. Whatever I hit didn't feel big enough to do much damage. I figured it was perhaps a piece of rope or sea weed wound around the shaft. To unwind the entanglement, I put the engine in reverse and revved it, but after several attempts, I could still feel the vibration.

Shutting the engines off, I donned a swim suit and a snorkel mask, and I got into the water to inspect the running gear. As I had suspected, there was a piece of rope wound around the starboard shaft and propeller, probably from a lobster trap. Although the water was crystal-clear and warm, it was difficult to cut the rope with a knife as the boat moved up and down and from side to side in the ocean swells. To complicate the task, I could only stay down a minute or two before needing to come up for air. Chuck stayed in the boat cheering me on, but good friend and Riverwood neighbor that he was, he did not offer to trade places.

The second time down, with the boat tossing, I cut myself on the left forearm with my knife, the cut was bleeding but it didn't appear to be serious. I still had a task to finish so I went back down several more times before disentangling the rope. Back in the boat, I wrapped my arm in a towel to stop the bleeding, and Chuck took over the helm. After several minutes, the bleeding stopped. The wound didn't look too bad and seemed to be more of a puncture than a cut. I placed antibiotic cream on it and applied butterfly stitches, which I carried in my well-stocked first-aid kit, to hold the wound closed and promote healing. Back underway, I turned to Chuck and said, "After the rough crossing a couple of days ago and the rope on the prop today, do you think God is trying to tell us something"? We both laughed as we went on our way.

After we had pulled into the Flamingo Bay Marina at Freeport, Grand Bahama, the dockhand helped us tie up. Chuck mentioned the rope incident and my cut. The dockhand's eyes widened, and he admonished us, "Mon, you don't want to be in those waters bleedin'. There's sharks all over! Lucky you didn't get eaten."

Somebody was protecting me!

Our two boats crossed into Grand Bahama Island through a narrow canal that bisects the island near Lucaya and headed fifty-miles northeast across the Little Bahamian Bank to Walker's Cay, the northernmost cay of the Bahamas. The Bank is shallow, averaging about ten feet in depth, and is pocked with coral reefs. There were no marked channels, just open water. The wind was out of the northeast at twenty miles per hour creating three- to four-foot waves and milky water that made it impossible to see more than a few feet into the water. With the waves directly off our bow and the spray from the wind making it hard to see, I decided to slow *True Blue II* down to ten miles per hour in hopes of dodging any reefs we might encounter. The trip, which normally takes two hours, stretched to five. That was my first but not my last encounter with the strong prevailing northeast winds and the negative impact it would have on my business plan. The Walker's Cay Resort, where we stayed, has a rich history of game fishing dating back to the early 1930s. Unfortunately, in

2004, two years after this trip, Walker's Cay was devastated by a hurricane destroying most of the buildings on the island, including the resort.

The next day, Chuck and I, followed by Doug and Don, headed sixty miles south to Green Turtle Cay, a small island three miles long, noted for its beautiful beaches and the Green Turtle Resort and Marina where we had dinner and spent the night. It was a good place to relax after an exciting and sometimes stressful four-day trip from Florida's Port St. Lucie. The following morning, we cruised the thirty-five miles south and passed Spanish Cay, Guana Cay, Man-O-War Cay and entered into Marsh Harbor. The northern Bahamian bank is a beautiful area, dozens of sparsely inhabited Cays with white sand beaches surrounded by emerald colored water and boarded to the east by the deep blue of the Atlantic Ocean. You could clearly see the bottom in thirty feet of water.

We arrived at Marsh Harbor on December 13, 2002. The three-hundred-mile trip from Port St. Lucie had taken five-days. I had reserved a slip for Doug and me at the Boat Harbor Marina through April and was given a discount by the marina and the Abaco Beach Resort for bringing customers to the area. The marina had excellent facilities for transit boaters who were sure to enjoy the swimming pool, the showers and the lounge. While Doug, Don, Chuck and I stayed on our boats, we enjoyed the amenities the marina had to offer. We alternated eating at local restaurants and cooking dinner on the grill at the marina.

The next day, we made the twenty-minute walk

into Marsh Harbor itself. The place was perfect. It had several good restaurants, many opportunities for shopping, and plenty to do for visiting anglers. I contacted a local bonefish guide, by the name of Sam, who was recommended by a friend in Florida, and arranged for him to take Chuck and me bonefishing. Doug and Don, not wanting to go bonefishing, took Doug's boat and did some fishing of their own and exploring around Marsh Harbor.

Chuck and I not only caught several nice bonefish but had a great time just being with Sam who had an easy-going personality. Initially, I had thought of leasing Sam's flats boat to take my clients bonefishing myself, but after fishing the area with Sam, I realized there was still a lot for me to learn about fishing the Marls. I was already busy trying to learn offshore fly fishing with *True Blue II*. For now, I decided to contract with Sam to take my clients bonefishing while I concentrated on offshore fly fishing.

My business plan was to provide three-days fishing and four nights' accommodations at a package price. Airfare would be arranged and paid for separately by the customer.

Doug found a local Bahamian captain to be my first mate on *True Blue II* and show us around the area. Doug and I, along with Chuck and Don, fished offshore a couple of times with our local captain and enjoyed it. The water was a deep cobalt blue, yet you could easily see thirty feet down into the water. Just a half-mile west of Man-O-War Cay in the Atlantic Ocean was a reef teaming with numerous fish, many I couldn't identify. A fly fishing paradise, I thought, as my customers could sight cast to numerous species around the reef.

As I soon learned, however, the prevailing northeast winds during the winter would make it difficult to fish offshore. One of the local charter captains told me he lost about thirty percent of his charters to weather from January to April. In contrast, the Marls on the leeward (west) side of Abaco was protected from the northeast winds, making for excellent bonefishing almost every day.

A twinge of doubt entered my mind! Had I failed to do my homework or was I charging ahead with MY plans instead of God's. I was aware of the prevailing northeast winds in Florida making offshore fishing difficult during the winter months but I hadn't made the connection to the Bahamas. Was I ignoring these blips on the radar screen as insignificant bumps in the road instead of the gentle nudging of the Holy Spirit to rethink my plans? Overall things seemed to be coming together and *True Blue II* was already in Marsh Harbor. I resolved I would wait to see how things developed. I began to ask myself, "Why am I really here?" The answer to that question would become clear over the next three months.

Chuck and I flew back to Florida on December 18, in time for Christmas. Doug and Don stayed in Marsh Harbor a couple of extra days to fish before flying back to Port St. Lucie in time for Christmas with their wives.

On January 20, 2003, I had the biggest surprise of my life. Dorothy suggested we go to the golf club for dinner to celebrate my seventieth birthday with our neighbors, Jack and Dot Bitner. Jack and Dot went into the restaurant first, and as Dorothy and I entered the restaurant, the first person I saw was Lu-anne! What was she doing in Florida? I glanced around the room—there was my brother Tom and his wife, Joann, Chuck and Nancy May, Doug and Bonnie West, Tom and Phyliss Hunt, George and Ruth Bell, Gary and Laura Miserlian, Bill and Marge Johnson, Ben and Cheryl Kittrell, Dick and Shirley Osborne and a host of other Riverwood neighbors. Once again, my dear wife had put one over on me! She and Nancy May had organized the surprise birthday party without a shred of evidence to tip me off on what was about to take place. Thank you everybody. It was a birthday I will never forget.

George Poveromo, host of the popular TV show *World of Saltwater Fishing* and host of the National Saltwater Seminar Series, had invited me to make a presentation on back country fly fishing for his Florida seminar to be held in Sarasota on January 27, 2003. The seminars, held in several states noted for saltwater fishing such as Texas, Louisiana and Virginia are hosted by George with presentations by fishing experts from the host state.

Due to advanced media coverage, there were over five hundred people in attendance for the Sarasota seminar. It was a great experience meeting George and the other presenters and gratifying to be included in the seminar with the six other fishing experts from around Florida. A reception followed the seminar where presenters mingled with attendees, answered questions and thanked them for their support. A number of attendees, including several of my customers and friends, gathered around after the seminar to ask questions about fly fishing. I ended up scheduling a fly fishing seminar in Sarasota and booked several fly-fishing charters.

My Hell's Bay flats boat was working out great, I had one hundred and thirty charters scheduled from October 2002 through May 2003. It would be another busy season, particularly as I worked around my trips to Marsh Harbor in the Bahamas.

I had been promoting my Bahamas fishing trips with customers the past couple of months and already had three charters scheduled for February and March 2003. It was important that I book the Bahamas trips as far in advance as possible to allow me to schedule time away from my Florida business. I was fortunate to find a commuter flight from Port Charlotte to Fort Lauderdale and on to Marsh Harbor, about a three-hour trip including a change of flights at Fort Lauderdale, that made it possible for me to leave home the day before and return the day after my charters in the Bahamas. In addition, Bahamasair had a promotion to buy a book of six or more round trip tickets to the Bahamas for half-price. I could fly from Port Charlotte to Marsh Harbor and back cheaper and in less time than I could drive to Fort Lauderdale and back!

My first charter at Marsh Harbor was for early February with Don Beck and a friend of his for two days in coastal waters and one-day bonefishing. From the day Don arrived, the wind blew hard from the northeast. Getting to the offshore fishing grounds in the Atlantic through Man-O-War Channel, near Marsh Harbor, was impossible when the wind blew hard from the northeast. The ocean bottom rises from three thousand feet to less than one hundred feet onto the Bahamian Bank a mile from shore. As the ocean swells encounter the shallow water of the Bank, large waves are created that make passage through the channels unsafe. It ended up that Sam ran three bonefishing trips on the Marls that were protected from the northeast wind.

Don and his friend had a great time. Accommodations and food at the Abaco Beach Resort were excellent, and they caught lots of bonefish with Sam. It didn't seem to bother Don that I lost two charters and money on their trip!

The next two trips to Marsh Harbor with different customers followed the same pattern, too windy to get off shore but the bonefishing on the Marls was great. On one of the trips, I did manage to fish two days around the channel at Man-O-War Cay with *True Blue II*, and my customers caught Spanish mackerel, barracuda and numerous exotic-colored reef fish on the fly. They had a good time in spite of the wind, but that's not what they came for, they were hoping for game fish such as tuna or sailfish on the fly.

I ended up cancelling the fourth trip I had scheduled to Marsh Harbor in March based on a high wind forecast. The logistics and weather were proving too difficult to overcome. Each trip I booked was for three-days fishing; it was difficult for me to extend the trip due to my tight schedule in Florida and the added cost of changing airline tickets. I decided not to schedule any customers to Marsh Harbor after mid-March as I was booked every day in Florida.

Another oversight on my part was the best time for pelagic gamefish in the Bahamas was from April through October when the winds were calmer and the ocean temperatures climbed into the seventy to eighty-degree range. I entertained the idea briefly of leaving *True Blue II* in the Bahamas so as to fish the summer months in the Bahamas instead of salmon fishing in Michigan. But then a totally predictable emotional reaction set in: just the thought of not going back to Onekama to fish salmon made me uneasy. What was I thinking? — And then it hit me — the uneasiness I felt and the seemingly unrelated obstacles I had been encountering since I left Florida were God telling me not to establish a new venture in the Bahamas. It was time to have a talk with Dorothy to reconsider my apparent ill-conceived business plan.

Financially, my venture to Marsh Harbor didn't cover my professional costs. Over the three months *True Blue II* was based there, I got paid for two-days of fishing, the booking fees from Sam and the Abaco Beach Resort and several generous tips from my customers for arranging the trips. Sam, on the other hand, thought it was great bonefishing with my customers and wanted them to come back next year!

On the plus side, Dennis and Dorothy came to Marsh Harbor on visits, and we snorkeled, went bonefishing, cruised the islands in *True Blue II* and had a great time together. Doug, who had also left his boat at Boat Harbor Marina, came to visit several times and we fished and hung out together. We had several productive days catching snapper, grouper, wahoo and mackerel. All of this family and friends time for little money out of my own pocket.

My brother, Tom, came from Frederick, Maryland,

in late March 2003 to help me take *True Blue II* back to Port Charlotte. We spent two-days sight-seeing. Doug, too, had decided to take his boat back home and so he and a mutual friend, Tom Hunt, followed my brother and me when we departed Marsh Harbor on April 1. On our way back, still in the Bahamas, the four of us stopped one night at Green Turtle Cay and a second-night at The Old Bahamian Resort on the west end of Grand Bahama Island. I wanted my brother to experience other ports and the great Bahamian food.

The third day, we crossed the Gulf Stream. The weather was perfect. Sun and calm winds followed us on our way to Port St. Lucie from the Old Bahamian Resort. What a contrast to four months previously when we crossed the Gulf Stream in eight-foot waves going to Bimini.

Doug, his friend, Tom Hunt, my brother and I cleared US customs by VHF radio at Port St. Lucie and spent the night with Doug and his wife Bonnie at their condo before Tom and I headed on to Gulf Wind Marine the next day. It was the longest my brother, Tom, and I had spent together since leaving high school. We had had eight-days of enjoying the scenery, the journey and each other's company.

The trip itself and the time with my family and friends made it worthwhile. I would do it again, but not for business. The trip to the Bahamas reinforced how fortunate I was to have of sources of income in addition to my charter business. My Ford retirement and investments provided me a financial cushion to attempt these business ventures without risking my financial future. In March 1998, just five-years earlier, I had made the decision to take the business aspect out of my guided overseas trips and changed the focus from profit to fun fishing. Would this too be a better approach for the Bahamas? Perhaps, but for what reason? I was already travelling overseas and fishing exotic locations, including bonefishing in Deadman's Cay every year with my friends. I was beginning to realize this was just another version of what I was already doing and that it was the Holy Spirit nudging me to stay in Florida.

When I got back to Riverwood, I shared my reservations with Dorothy about expanding my charter business to the Bahamas. I related to Dorothy that, just prior to leaving Florida for the Bahamas the previous December, I hadn't had the enthusiasm I had had starting previous business ventures and was not sure why. Neither of us remembered, when we had discussed expanding the business to the Bahamas a few months earlier, talking about how fishing with *True Blue II* in the Bahamas would be a new ministry of serving God's purpose. This is a fundamental question we have always asked in the past before undertaking a new venture, and when we have done so, we have arrived at answers which we never doubted were God's will guiding our decisions.

Looking back, we could see how subtly we had left God out of our decision. When we had moved to Florida in 1993, we were at first hesitant with our decision and prayed for direction. Subsequently, we were imbued with the rightness of this decision to go to Florida. This confidence, which we felt was given us from the Holy Spirit, indicated to us that we had found a new ministry and were about to make the right decision. God opened doors as to where we were to live and do business to serve His purpose. But when I had planned extending my business to the Bahamas my main goal now seemed to have been to enhance my reputation as a fisherman and perhaps it was the ego's last attempt to counter the fact I was getting older and no longer able to keep expanding my business. I had made my decision on what was best for me, ignoring the numerous obstacles God had placed in my path, and not how it would serve God's purpose of expanding my ministry.

Dorothy agreed that ego has a way of asserting itself and that perhaps my goal was self-gratification instead of God's purpose. She has always been quick to perceive God's lead in our lives and suggested maybe we both were getting too complacent with the "good life" and not thankful for the blessings we already had. Even after forty-years as Christians, we needed reminding about how important it is to keep God first in our lives. It is generally when all is well with life, that you are most vulnerable to moving away from God and relying on your own wisdom. Proverbs 3:5, "Trust in the Lord with all your heart and lean not on your own understanding." The good news: I never lost the subtle guidance of the Holy Spirit. It was just that, for a short while, I wasn't paying attention to that guidance. With this understanding, I humbly asked the Lord to forgive me for being so shortsighted. As a bonus, I was also reminded not to be quick to judge others when they stumble. "There but for the Grace of God, go I." I remembered why I titled Chapter Five of this book, "Growing My Business and God's, too."

It was seven a.m. April 10, 2003, just a week after my return from the Bahamas to Gulf Wind Marine with *True Blue II*, as Ed Marinaro, Jay Hodson and I pulled away from the dock for the first day of the prestigious Red Bone Celebrity Tournament. Jay, a customer of mine from Palm Island, was sponsoring my boat in the tournament being held at Palm Island Resort. The Red Bone is one of the most prestigious charity fishing tournaments in the country with all money going to the Cystic Fibrosis Foundation.

I would be guiding Jay and his friend Ed Marinaro, former NFL running back, member of the college football hall of fame and star of the television series "Hill Street Blues." Other celebrities fishing in the tournament were actor Jim Sikking, novelist Randy White, NFL quarterback Steve Berg, NFL quarterback Earl Morrall, astronaut Bruce Melnick and NBA center John Havlicek. During the pre-tournament dinner, Dorothy and I socialized with the celebrities, listening to their stories and getting to know them. I was

l-r, Dennis and Earl Morrall,
Redbone Tournament, 2002

pleasantly surprised Earl Morrall was in attendance as we had played baseball together at Michigan State in 1956 after I returned from the Army. We chatted about our careers and family and took a few pictures together.

Sponsorship for the thirty-two boats in the tournament was two thousand dollars a boat, which went to the cystic fibrosis charity. Each boat had a team consisting of a captain and two anglers. An Instamatic camera and measuring board were given to each team to record their catch with a photo of each fish on the measuring board. Back at the dock, each team turned their camera over to the judges. The pictures were developed by a local photo shop, and the results posted within an hour after docking.

Winners would be determined by the total inches for each species of fish caught by each team over the two-day tournament. On the first day, we caught three small speckled trout and a redfish, with the total inches placing us in the middle of the standings. That evening, Palm Island Resort sponsored a delicious dinner of barbeque ribs and chicken. Highlight of the evening was a presentation by Bruce Melnick about his career as an astronaut. He had spent over three hundred hours in space before retiring in July 1992.

On the second day, everyone was struggling to catch fish due to the high winds. At two p.m. with only an hour left in the tournament, we moved to one last location. On the first cast, Ed Marinaro, who was athletic, six-foot four inches and two hundred and thirty pounds, and who, at age fifty-three, looked like he could still play NFL football, hooked a large fish casting a lure designed to imitate a shrimp. I knew immediately, when the fish jumped and rapidly pulled line off the reel, that it was a snook (which is also known as robalo in Spanish). I poled frantically to keep the boat away from the mangroves and shouted for Ed to gently apply pressure on the spool of the reel with his left hand to slow the fish down. Just as the fish was about to enter the mangroves, where sharp oyster shells would have surely cut the fishing line, the fish turned away, the tide was low and the water too shallow for the snook to go any further toward the mangroves. Ed slowly gained line and moved the fish to the boat where I took hold of it by the lower lip with my left hand and around the tail with my right hand and lifted it into the boat. It was big—over thirty inches, I guessed. Such a great shout went up from Ed, Jay and me you would have thought we had won the Super Bowl. I took pictures of the fish on the measuring board and released the thirty-five-inch snook to fight another day. This fish could put us high on the leader board!

As it happened, Ed Marinaro was the master of ceremonies at the banquet that night. After a delicious dinner, it was time for the presentation of the awards--a.k.a. "the Academy Awards." There was much speculation about who had won, but no one knew the final standings. Founder and tournament director Gary Ellis gave Ed a sealed envelope to open for each award. There were numerous awards for different species and biggest fish. Ed announced the name of each winner and this announcement was accompanied by applause from the audience. After Ed graciously handed out the awards for biggest redfish and speckled trout, it was time to open the sealed envelope for the biggest snook.

After doing so, he smiled to the crowd. "Well, folks, it looks like Yours Truly has this one," thrusting his hand into the air among cheers from fellow competitors. Gary Ellis then stepped forward and presented Ed the award for biggest snook.

Next came the awards for best angler and best guide. Smiling and waving to the crowd, Ed announced that he and I won those two awards! We were obviously excited and acknowledged the applause with waves and bows to the audience.

Ed is a funny, gregarious person and never at a loss for words, but when Gary Ellis handed him the envelope for the last award of the evening, the prestigious celebrity grand champion award, Ed was silent after opening the envelope. After a moment gathering his thoughts, he started out seriously, "Ladies and gentlemen, the winner of this year's Academy Award is Ed Marinaro, (pause) oops, wrong award." When the laughter died down, he then continued with a loud voice and big smile. "This year's winner of the celebrity grand

l to r Ed Marinaro and Dennis,
Grand Champion,
Redbone Tournament, 2002

champion award is (pause) (pause) Ed Marinaro!" He thrust his arms into the air with a loud shout. It brought the house down with laughter. Everyone stood cheering and applauding. He motioned me to the podium and gave me a big hug. I was so happy for all of us. Jay, our sponsor, came up and hugged us both. It was a day I will never forget.

Later that evening, after the awards had been presented, I shared with Ed and Jay the odds of having a customer (Jay) I met four years ago, sponsor me in a tournament at Palm Island fishing with a celebrity (Ed Marinaro) who was the master of ceremonies and won the celebrity grand champion of the tournament with me as his guide. I related how I believed it was not chance, but it was God directing the circumstances to bring us together and share this experience. Ed acknowledged this was a special experience for him. Considering the many other awards he has won over the years, his words made winning special for all of us.

The end of April 2003 provided another special catch, maybe not as prestigious as the Red Bone Tournament two weeks previously, but just as gratifying. My companions on that trip were Nancy May and Suzi Lynch. The May and the Blue families have been friends since we both moved to Onekama, socializing, sharing our Christian faith, and travelling together on numerous overseas fishing trips. Suzi Lynch, the daughter of my friend Terry from Gulf Wind Marine, was one of my first fly-casting students in Florida and loved to fish. Suzi, a school teacher who loved the outdoors, became quite proficient with numerous fish caught on the fly rod.

I had scheduled a fly fishing trip with Suzi for the end of April and asked Nancy May to come along with us. I enjoyed fly fishing with women as they paid attention to what you were saying. (Men, on the other hand, like to do it their way—right or wrong.) The tides were low that morning, and we were blind casting into pot holes hoping for a bite. I was poling along a shoreline when I spotted a large snook tucked next to the mangroves in a foot of water. The fish lie motionless, basking in the sun, waiting for an unsuspecting prey for breakfast. I pointed out the fish to Suzi as I quietly poled into casting range. I stopped the boat by pushing my pole into the soft bottom and whispered to Suzi to make a cast. On her first cast, the fly line tangled around her foot and the fly fell hopelessly short of the snook. I quietly said, "Relax, take your time and try again." The second cast was better but short of the fish. "Once more," I whispered, Suzi cast again but still short of the fish.

We were about sixty feet from the fish, and I was afraid to move closer for fear of spooking the fish. I asked Suzi to let Nancy try a cast. Nancy quietly got to the front of the boat and prepared to cast. I was expecting the fish to spook at any moment, but it lay motionless. Nancy made a cast, and it landed close to the mangroves but behind the fish. I whispered, "Retrieve slowly and cast again further to the right." The next cast was right on target, about five feet in front of the fish. The fish didn't react. I told Nancy not to move the fly as it settled to the bottom. After maybe fifteen seconds, I said to Nancy, "Just a short twitch of the fly."

As the snook moved slowly toward the fly, I said,

"Another short strip." The fish pounced on the green and white fly." I shouted, "He's got it." With the shallow water preventing the snook from seeking shelter in the mangroves, it instinctively accelerated away from the mangroves looking for deeper water and a place to seek cover.

From my vantage point on the poling platform, the snook looked like a torpedo as it accelerated across the flats just under the surface. Nancy played the fish expertly, not allowing the fly line to tangle on the initial run. After several more shorter runs, Nancy gradually worked the fish to the boat. I used my Boca Grip, a device to hold a fish by the lower lip and lift it from the water and handed it to Nancy for a photo. The snook measured thirty-two inches, a real trophy on a fly. I sympathized for Suzi not being able to reach the fish, but she was sincerely happy for Nancy, as I knew she would be.

Nancy May with snook,
November, 2003

Having caught numerous bonefish, Nancy was just better prepared to cast to this fish. I'm still not sure if I was happier for Nancy because of the big fish or that she could brag to Chuck about her trophy catch.

Nevertheless, it was a great day.

I had a commercial boat transporter pull my Rampage back to Michigan at the end of April. I had intended to cruise *True Blue II* back to Michigan on the intra-coastal water way north along the east coast to New York, the Erie Canal to Lake Ontario, the Welland Canal to Lake Erie, north to Lake Huron and finally Lake Michigan to Onekama. It would have been a great trip but I just didn't have the time to make the twenty-plus day trip by water. The decision was clinched when I found, based on fuel prices, it was cheaper to transport the boat by land than to make the trip by water.

Dorothy and I returned to Onekama on June 15 to get *True Blue II* ready for the salmon season. I hadn't realized how much Onekama and salmon fishing had become such an important part of my life until my glimpse, earlier in the year, of what life would have been like had I left *True Blue II* in the Bahamas. The workers at Onekama Marine were preparing to launch *True Blue II* as I stood on my dock watching. I inhaled deeply as I glanced at the clear blue sky over head, the ripple on the water glistening in the sun, the sand dunes capped by green trees surrounding the shoreline and thought to myself, "This is God's country! How could I even think of giving this up?" It has been years since I was so excited about the start of a salmon season in Onekama.

Since the inception of the Tournament Trail in 2000, professional salmon tournament fishing had been growing rapidly. There was a significant increase both in the number of tournaments on Lake Michigan and in tournament prize money. Total payouts at most tournaments ranged from thirty to fifty thousand dollars and was based on the number of participants paying into the tournament entry fees.

Tournament fishing requires a different approach, mentally and strategically, than chartering. Fishing a tournament with customers is the safe approach as you get paid for two days of charter for the tournament, plus a possible share of the winnings no matter where you finish in the standings.

The down side is that customers are not professional fishermen and make it difficult to compete with the professional tournament teams to place well in rankings that win the money. I didn't realize it at the time, but with the Rampage Company helping me with expenses, tournament fishing was to become a lucrative part of my salmon fishing business in the near future.

Tournament Trail and the Tournament Trail Magazine were officially created in 2000 by Fred Mac-Donald and his son, Scott, to promote salmon tournaments at different ports around Lake Michigan. A big man, about two hundred and forty pounds, with a big heart, Fred was a successful charter captain before establishing Tournament Trail. By 2003, Tournament Trail magazine, had increased from a few pages to over eighty full-color pages highlighting each tournament and its circulation reached over fifty thousand. It was the largest tournament fishing magazine on the Great Lakes.

By the 2005 season, the Tournament Trail had grown to fifteen individual port tournaments in three states, Michigan, Indiana and Wisconsin, all bordering on Lake Michigan. In addition to providing administrative and marketing support for each port, Tournament Trail also introduced the 333 Championship Series where participants weigh in their three biggest fish at each port tournament with prize money and points awarded to the top ten finishers. Points are accumulated throughout the tournament season ending in September. The participant with the most points is declared the winner of the 333 Championship Series with a sizeable cash payout that could reach over ten thousand dollars. This was in addition to other prize monies a crew might have won at individual port tournaments during the summer.

With so much repeat business, in both Florida and Michigan, my chartering had become like a family reunion. I was seeing my old friends again, people I know and care about. Customers whose children had been young when I started chartering in 1988 now had married children, and in some cases, grandchildren who fished with me regularly. As I have said before, it wasn't about the fishing—it was about the people. I have mentioned many times that focusing on families was the single biggest reason, apart from God, for the success of my business. The results speak for themselves.

I effected a last trip to Deadman's Cay in the Bahamas in November 2003. This expedition was unforgettable but for the wrong reason. The Mays, the Bells and Ben Kettrell, my fishing buddy from Florida, and I were making our annual visit to fish with Sam Knowles. The second day of fishing I got a cut on my heel from a shell in my wading boot. I have had numerous cuts and nicks wading in bare feet while fishing in Florida and they all eventually healed, but this one didn't. By the time we were ready to come home four days later, my right foot was infected and very painful.

When we arrived in Miami at about mid-night, I could hardly walk. The redness and swelling had spread up into the calf of my right leg. After a four-hour drive to Port Charlotte, I went directly to the emergency room at four a.m. The doctor performed a blood test and minor surgery on my heel to see if there was a foreign object still in the wound and he put me on the strongest oral antibiotic he could give me. The doctor said it was a bacterial infection and could be very serious if it continued to spread. He sent me home with strict orders to soak my foot in a solution he gave me and to report back the next day. If there was no improvement, he would admit me to the hospital and start an intravenous antibiotic treatment. Fortunately, by the next morning, the swelling and the pain were subsiding. The doctor recommended I stay with the current treatment which I took for over a month before the wound was healed. While my foot was mending, I missed maybe six charters. It wasn't that many years ago that I wouldn't have missed any charters—well maybe one or two, but the point is you don't heal as fast when you get older. Something to think about, if you are older, before you do anything foolish.

In February 2004, I caught my biggest snook ever on a fly. Don Beck invited me on a two-day fishing trip to the Ten Thousand Islands, a thirty-mile expanse of mangrove islands, one hundred and fifty-miles south of Boca Grande on the Gulf of Mexico.

On the second and final day of fishing, our guide worked his way back to a small lake in the middle of a mangrove swamp. Don had been doing most of the fishing and was on the bow of the boat when our guide saw a large snook cruising the shoreline.

Don, being the consummate gentleman, handed me the rod and said, "You give it a try."

I felt intimidated by my favorite customer who wanted me to show him how it's done. I also knew the guide, who was now peering down at me from the poling platform, had worked hard to find a big fish for us and did not want Don nor me to miss this opportunity to catch a big snook. The tables were turned: how many times had I scowled at customers when they failed to make a good cast after all my effort to find a fish for them. I swallowed hard. Then, I cast the fly toward the fish. To my relief, the fly landed right in front of the snook, and before the guide could say, "You spooked him," there was a big splash and the fish was hooked.

I struggled to stop the fish before it reached the mangroves, and after a ten-minute fight, had the snook in the boat. The fish measured thirty-four inches, a great catch on a fly. A week later, the guide sent Don a newspaper article from the Naples *Sun Times* featuring a photo of me and my big snook on the sports page. Don graciously passed the article on to me, and we are still great fishing buddies. What would fishing be without a little competition!

The summer of 2004, I fished four Tournament Trail events with my thirty-foot Rampage placing in the in the top five finishers twice and winning three thousand dollars in cash and prizes. When I tried scheduling charter customers to fish with me during the tournaments, it did not take long to realize I needed my own high-powered tournament team if I was going to win big money prizes. After I was able to get George Peplinski and his son, Chris, to fish with me, I started winning.

In August, I fished a tournament with my friend Chuck May and George and Chris Peplinski in Sturgeon Bay, Wisconsin. We placed a respectable fourth, winning twelve hundred dollars in the tournament.

Following the weigh-in on Sunday, we left Sturgeon Bay for the sixty-five-mile trip to Frankfort, Michigan, where George, Chris and I had another tournament the following weekend. I learned to fish salmon with Dorothy, Luanne and Dennis in Frankfort in 1983 with our 31-foot Tiara, our first *True Blue*, and here I was again, twenty-one years later preparing to fish a professional salmon tournament in our new Rampage, *True Blue II*.

I had just returned to Onekama from the Frankfort tournament, where we placed a respectable third, when Jim Mrozinski called to let me know that Rampage Yachts was working on a new thirty-three-foot sports yacht to be introduced to the dealers in the spring of 2005. Jim was planning a trip to the Rampage factory in Wilmington, North Carolina in a couple of weeks and asked me to come along.

I told him I would talk to Dorothy, and when Dorothy and I spoke, we agreed it wouldn't hurt to look. It would be a fun trip for me to see the factory and inspect how the boat is constructed. We would then assess whether a door was opened to purchase a new boat. In September, Jim and I flew to Wilmington, North Carolina to visit the new, state-of-the-art factory and test the Rampage 33. The boat performed impressively whether it was trolling, cruising at high speed or moving though rough water. Rampage was targeting the high-end offshore fishing market for serious big game fisherman.

I liked what I experienced.

That evening at dinner with the general manager and the sales/marketing manager of Rampage, Jim and I discussed pricing of the boat and Rampage's possible sponsorship to have me fish in the Tournament Trail. Rampage Yachts was investing money to expand their presence in both the saltwater and Great Lakes markets. The general manager asked Jim and me to put together a proposal to market Rampage Yachts on Lake Michigan and get back to him in two-weeks.

To add to my general excitement, Donna called in October 2004 to let Dorothy and me know she and Dennis were expecting their first child in February. We were excited for them and the thought of being grandparents again. Luanne and Pat had three children and were not planning for more, so Dorothy and I were counting on Dennis and Donna to keep the grandkids coming.

Dorothy and I had some thinking and praying to do about our future in Florida. I would be seventy-two on January 20, 2005. Poling the boat everyday was beginning to take its toll physically, and I had some serious skin problems from too much sun over the years. To add to these negatives pulling us towards an exit, Florida house prices were sky rocketing, making it tempting to sell at a profit. Would the demands of a new boat and a sponsorship agreement with Rampage Yachts be too taxing when added to the current demands of my existing Florida business?

If we returned to Michigan and gave up the Florida business, the purchase of the new Rampage began to make more sense. It was hard, however, to contemplate giving up the back-country fishing that had become such a rewarding part of my life. Also, Dorothy would no longer have the golf course she had enjoyed at Riverwood. We would have to say goodbye to the many neighbors and friends we had made over the past twelve years. We agreed, under the circumstances, the decision to retire the business and leave our home in Florida would not be an easy one. However, this time Dorothy and I felt we were not charging ahead without involving God. It looked as though God was nudging us back to Michigan to be close to our new grandchild and to transition to a ministry in Onekama.

Step one would be to see if Rampage would accept the offer Jim and I were preparing to present to them. Over the next several weeks and further discussions with Rampage Yachts, Jim and I reached an agreement on the purchase of the Rampage 33 and a sponsorship plan. Rampage Yachts would sell me a boat at a reduced price and sponsor me on Tournament Trail for the next five years. Rampage would pay my expenses for the tournaments, accommodations, meals, fuel and entry fees plus a stipend for my time representing Rampage and the cost of my charter fee for each day of the tournament. In return, I would represent Rampage at the tournaments, give test rides to potential customers, represent Rampage at boat shows and allow the use of my name and a testimonial statement for Rampage marketing and advertising. Onekama Marine would also contribute to the sponsorship money, provide boat maintenance and vehicle transportation for the tournaments and take my thirty-foot Rampage in trade. I would keep any and all prize money I won at the tournaments. The expected delivery of my boat would be May of 2005.

With details of an agreement worked out, Dorothy and I agreed, after closing the door on my effort to start a business in the Bahamas, God had opened a door for us to purchase this boat and return to Michigan. However, I was still not ready to let go of my business in Florida and move back to Michigan. I wanted to see if I could still continue operating my Florida and Michigan businesses as I had done for the past twelve years. I guess I was not ready to admit I was getting too old to have a business both in Florida and in Michigan.

We returned to Florida in late October. About two-weeks after our arrival, I was giving a fly casting demonstration using my left hand when I felt a sharp pain in my left shoulder. As I had gotten older, aches and pains were not unusual, but they normally went away in a day or two. This one didn't. The next week poling my boat was difficult. Whenever I raised my arm the pain came back with increasing intensity. The doctor confirmed it was a tear in the rotator cup and scheduled surgery the following week. Reluctantly, I rescheduled my charters for the next two months, but the increasing pain convinced me it was the right thing to do to give myself time to have surgery and a decent recovery.

The surgery went well, and after six weeks of therapy, I was back at fishing. During my six-week hiatus from fishing, I kept busy tying flies, working on my fly casting with my right hand and hanging around Gulf Wind Marine. With me underfoot, Dorothy couldn't wait for my shoulder to heal!

That was the good news. The bad news is my surgeon questioned how long my shoulder would hold up poling a boat every day and suggested I think about giving up guiding. I thought, "Funny, that was the same thing my dermatologist told me about my increasingly serious skin problems." My surgeon, quipped, "Guiding is a young man's profession, why don't you just let them do it and retire?" That's not what I wanted to hear the doctor say, but the rotator cup therapy was long and painful, and I didn't want to go through that again. Dorothy agreed with the doctors and noted this was perhaps another more painful nudge by God that it was time to give up my fishing business in Florida and go back to Michigan.

Dorothy reminded me of my ill-conceived business plan taking *True Blue II* to the Bahamas just two years earlier as an indication that God didn't want us there. She also believed it was the first step in opening the door to our return to Michigan. Having a new Rampage and fishing salmon tournaments instead of being on the water every day with fly fishing charters was God's way of making it easier for me to get out of the sun and quit poling. One nudge, not so gentle, came with my rotator cup surgery and then another nudge, this one sweet, came with the announcement by Dennis and Donna of a new granddaughter due in February. Luanne's oldest child, Emilee, was fourteen, John twelve and the youngest, Grace, was now six, so for Dorothy and me, it would be like starting grandparenting all over again with Dennis and Donna's first baby.

"Do you really need any more convincing?" Dorothy insisted, looking at me intently. As always Dorothy was right: God was telling me I was getting older and it was time to re-focus our ministry back to Michigan. We decided to put our house on the market when we returned to Florida in the fall.

Dorothy and I targeted to be in Onekama by May 2005 for the arrival of our new boat. Chuck and I had discussed selling our homes in Florida several times over the past months so it was no surprise for him to learn of our decision to put our Florida house up for sale. Without hesitation, Chuck, who had maintained a residence in Onekama, said he and Nancy would do the same. We both decided to wait until our return to Riverwood in the fall to tell our friends that we would be selling our homes and moving back to Michigan.

The hardest part was telling Don Beck. He was disappointed Dorothy and I would be leaving Florida but understood. Don, being my age, knew what I meant when I said, "It is too physically demanding at my age to poll a boat every day in the hot sun." Don and I had many fond memories fishing together and we had become close friends., My last trip with Don in Florida was on April 11, 2005. I don't remember if we caught any fish, but as always, we had a great time. Don had never fished salmon with me in

Michigan, and I suggested, if he was really a friend, he and Ann would come to Onekama and fish during the summer. Don smiled and said, "We'll see."

With Dorothy's approval, I closed on the new Rampage 33 on May 6, 2005 and began outfitting our new boat with downriggers and electronics for the salmon season. We decided to continue the name *True Blue*, but without the numerals. I ran my first charter in the new Rampage on June 30. *True Blue* was the queen of the tournament fleet, a blue blood, no pun intended! It was a busy first summer fishing six tournaments and running thirty-five

Rampage 33, 2006

charters. George Peplinski and his son Chris agreed to fish the tournaments with me, and Dennis filled in when work permitted. Frank Baker, a young man who loved to fish and had just graduated from high school, was my new first mate and fished with us during the tournaments.

That first summer with my new Rampage was a shake-down period. I spent it getting to know the boat and the new electronics. Each time I went to a tournament, we drew a crowd as Rampage was a beautiful boat and not a well-known brand name on the Great Lakes. I passed out brochures to people at the tournaments and invited them to come on board to inspect the boat. I even took a few serious potential buyers for a test ride.

In my previous sponsorship contract with Rampage Yachts from 2002 to 2004, Rampage had paid my tournament expenses and I booked charters to fish tournaments. Under my new contract, Rampage Yachts and Onekama Marine would pay my expenses and pay me a stipend to fish tournaments for them. I would need a top-notch tournament team to place well in the tournaments. Fishing tournaments requires a different strategy than fishing charters. In tournament fishing, catching fish is the number one objective, period. Catching fish on a charter is also the goal, but not the only goal, you don't have to have the biggest box of fish to have a good time and enjoy the experience of a quality charter. In tournament fishing every fish could amount to the difference between winning and losing.

As with any sport, competing at the top level takes dedication and hard work. Preparation begins Monday the week of the tournament, checking the boat and fishing equipment, making motel reservations and coordinating schedules with team members. On Wednesday, we depart for the tournament destination which can be from ten to one hundred and twenty miles from Onekama. Thursday and Friday are pre-fish days, developing a fishing strategy, checking weather and local fishing reports on where the fish are biting and the "hot baits."

Attendance at the captain's meeting Friday night is mandatory. The rules for the 333 Championship

Series are the same for every tournament; rules for the host port tournament may vary somewhat based on local preferences. Greeting friends and fellow competitors is always a highlight, followed by side bets and camaraderie.

Saturday morning comes early—by 3:00 a.m.! — after only a few hours' sleep at best. Contenders make a quick stop for ice, hot coffee and donuts on the way to the boat and then conduct a check of fishing rods and reels one more time to be sure all is ready for the day's fishing. At five-forty-five a.m., tournament boats gather at the pier heads to be ready for the six-a.m. shotgun start. I was always awed by the sight to be had as we waited. The eastern sky, along the shore, blushing pink from a rising sun. The bright stars still twinkling overhead in the night sky, and the red, green and white navigation lights of the boats accentuating by the dim light of the morning.

Tournament rules state all boats must stay within an imaginary arc of one-quarter mile of the pier heads prior to the official start. Anticipation builds as the tournament director starts a ten-second-count-down over the VHF radio and then— "Gentlemen, it is six a.m. The tournament has officially started, be careful and good luck!" Up to one hundred and twenty boats from eighteen to sixty feet in length fan out from the pier heads under full power. The noise is deafening, like thousands of horses charging for the horizon, steep waves created by the wake of the boats, come from every direction making it difficult to steer. If that doesn't get you excited, nothing will! I have had numerous people tell me the shot gun start was the most memorable part of the tournament.

Most tournaments are two-day events based on the state fishing regulations. Fishing is from six a.m. to two p.m. The number of fish that can be weighed varies somewhat from tournament to tournament, but never more than the state regulations permit. Winners are determined by ten points a fish and a point a pound. Following the weigh in on Sunday and presentation of awards, we head back to Onekama to get ready for our Monday morning charter and begin preparation for the next tournament.

Our granddaughter, Carey was born on February 19, 2005, and was already two months old when we first saw her on our return from Florida in April. What a sweetheart she is. Carey's arrival convinced Dorothy and me we had made the right decision to return to Michigan.

The condo in Onekama, while comfortable, was not built as a year around residence. It was more of a cottage than a home. Besides its location next to the marina, it offered a beautiful setting overlooking Portage Lake and had been our summer home since 1984. It has been the longest continuous residence Dorothy and I have had during our married life. The condo has served as a full-time residence, summer home and where we go just to relax for the weekend. While small in size, approximately twelve-hundred square feet, the condo has served as a hotel and re-sort for countless events ranging from weekend guests to family reunions and weddings with people sleeping on couches and on the floor. Dorothy and I have more friends and memories of our life together in Onekama than of any other place we have lived. Perhaps not as exciting as some of our more exotic overseas assignments and fishing adventures, but Onekama provides a feeling of home much like my early years growing up on the farm.

Dorothy and I agreed, Onekama reflects our values and who we are, we made the decision to continue with the condo in Onekama as our summer base of operation for the charter business and buy a second home inland to be closer to our son and his family. We found a condominium at the Landings at Rayner Ponds, in Mason, Michigan, five miles from East Lansing, home to my alma mater, Michigan State University and a few blocks from where, my son, Dennis, was planning to build a new home. We put a deposit on a condo pending the sale of our home in Florida, convinced that God was directing our return to Michigan.

In September, we headed back to Riverwood and put our house up from sale. I had booked a few trips not knowing when the house would sell. It seemed strange not being on the water every day. I was already missing it. Don Beck was deer hunting at home in Wisconsin and was not scheduled to arrive in Florida until after the holidays. Houses were still selling at a rapid pace in Florida but signs of a slowdown were evident. A few months previously, a house would sell in a few days after being placed on the market; now it was few weeks. We listed the house with a broker at a sizeable increase over what we paid for it in 1993. By Christmas 2005 we had several inquiries but no offers.

On January 15, 2006, Dorothy met a couple at

the golf club who were looking to move to Riverwood. They came to see our house that very afternoon. They liked what they saw and made an offer. We agreed on a price including the golf membership and golf cart with a clause allowing us to rent the house from them until our departure for Michigan in April. I arranged for Palmer Moving and Storage to move and store our belongings in Dearborn, Michigan until our condo in Rayner Ponds was complete. Yes, they were still in business! Dorothy and I had used Palmer Moving and Storage numerous times during the 1960s, '70s and '80s when we were moving around the world with Ford.

In February 2006, Jim Mrozinski and I went to the Miami Boat Show to launch the new marketing program for Rampage Yachts on the Great Lakes. There were several three-by-four foot color posters on pedestals featuring Captain Denny Blue at the Rampage display booth and similar advertisements placed in major boating and fishing magazines. Tred Barta, host of the popular NBC television program, *The Best and Worst of Tred Barta*, was also there. He would be using a Rampage 33 just like mine for salt water fishing episodes on his TV program. Jim and I discussed with Tred his coming to Onekama to film a salmon tournament for one of his shows but it never materialized due to Tred's work schedule.

Chuck and Nancy May sold their home in Riverwood just as Dorothy and I were leaving for Michigan in April. We both sold just in time; by summer there were sixty homes for sale in Riverwood, and the market was in free fall and so were the prices. Dorothy was busy getting ready to move our household again.

She was an expert at overseeing packing what we wanted to keep and selling items we didn't want. I called Rayner Ponds in Michigan to confirm our need for a condo and was told our new home would be ready by July 2006.

It was April 16 when the realization we were leaving Florida really hit me. It was the day I sold my Hell's Bay flats boat. When the gentleman who purchased the boat came to pick her up, for a moment, I hesitated to take his certified check. Sensing it was a difficult decision for me, he graciously said, "Don't worry. I'll take good care of her." I don't want to be melancholy, but as the new owner drove away with my boat in tow, I had tears in my eyes.

Driving home from Florida, Dorothy and I looked back on the almost fourteen years in Florida. What a wonderful "assignment" the Lord had given us! Just as with our other relocations around the world with Ford, we were now leaving fond memories and friends behind. A little longer than our previous "assignments" and perhaps our last relocation. When I said this to Dorothy, she laughed. "We said that last time." As we drove north, we were eagerly anticipating learning what the Lord had in store for us back in Michigan.

Looking back over the past two-years, it was apparent to Dorothy and me the move back to Michigan was not by chance. The enjoyable but unsuccessful attempt to start a business in the Bahamas was the first I realized God had other plans for us and they were not in the Bahamas. Then, in rapid succession, the purchase of a Rampage, sponsorship on Tournament Trail, rotator cup surgery, the knowledge of a new granddaughter, the realization that guiding in Florida was taking its toll on me physically and the housing market boom making it attractive to sell our home in Florida before the market crashed. God was preparing Dorothy and me for another phase of our life and ministry, one that wasn't so physically demanding.

We arrived in Onekama the end of April, after a stop to visit with Donna, Dennis and our new granddaughter. Any doubt we had moving from Florida was erased when we held Carey for the first time.

CHAPTER 8
BACK TO MICHIGAN

From May through July, Dorothy and I were busy with visits to Mason to check on the construction of our condo at Rayner Ponds and to buy furniture to replace what Dorothy had sold before leaving Florida. With all of our previous moves around the world and to Florida, we were excited to think this might be our last move. Dorothy and I agreed we had reached a season in life where a simpler lifestyle was in order.

Rayner Ponds is comprised of sixty individual units. Our condo, one of three joined together in the same building, is located on the end of a road and overlooks a pond and a wooded park. At just over two-thousand square feet, the main floor consists of a kitchen, living/dining room, den, master bedroom and bath with a deck overlooking the pond. The walk-out lower level has a utility room with furnace and laundry, a recreation room and a bedroom with bath. Each condo has a garage placed between units as a contiguous part of the building. The common grounds are expansive and its lawns, shrubs and trees well maintained by the condo association.

Our condo, Rayner Ponds, 2017

It was Dennis and Donna who had introduced us to the Rayner Ponds development. Because Dennis lived about thirty miles from where he worked at Jackson National Life Insurance Company, six miles north of Mason, he and Donna had purchased a wooded lot a few blocks from Rayner Ponds as a future site for a new house. When they learned we were moving back to Michigan, they thought it would be nice to have Grandpa and Grandma close by at Rayner Ponds.

We couldn't have chosen a better location. Mason, a city of approximately eight thousand residents, is the county seat of Ingham County and ten miles south of Lansing, the capital city of Michigan. A little-known fact, Michigan is the only state in the US with a capital that is not also a county seat. That distinction belongs to Mason. Surrounded by thousands of acres of farmland, Mason has the charm of a small town, yet is only twenty minutes from my old alma mater, Michigan State University, and the state capital in Lansing.

We hadn't realized the benefits of living near a University. There are unlimited activities to suit the young and old alike: sports activities, Broadway plays, medical facilities, continuing education programs and walks on the beautiful campus. Current enrollment at Michigan State University is over fifty thousand; when I started school there in September 1951 on a baseball scholarship, there were approximately thirteen thousand students. Times have changed.

Palmer Moving delivered our household goods to our condo on July 26, 2006. I was busy with charters and tournaments in Onekama which once again left Dorothy with the primary responsibility of moving into a new house. This would be our eleventh move since our marriage in 1963. Would it be our last? I offered to come to Mason whenever I had a free day to help Dorothy, but she wouldn't hear of it as she wanted to handle details on her own. Like I have said many times before, we couldn't have had the life we lived overseas without Dorothy's support and strong will.

The joy of moving back to Michigan and into our new condo was tempered somewhat as Dorothy and I were committed to living in Onekama until after my charter season ended in the fall. The fact we had a lovely brand-new condo in Mason that we were unable to move into until October was not lost on Dorothy, so every other week she visited Mason to make sure everything was in order at our condo to live in full-time.

In July, we had to put our Labrador, Daisy, to sleep. She was twelve years old and could no longer get around on her own. When I called our veterinarian in Onekama to make an appointment, he could

Dennis and Daisy, 2004

tell I was distressed and asked me to bring her in right away. I hesitated but said I would. Pat and Luanne were visiting us in Onekama at the time, so Pat went with me to the veterinarian's office. I was holding Daisy when she went to sleep. I cried all the way home.

I said to Dorothy, "That was our last Labrador. I can't do that again!" Daisy was the fifth Labrador we had parted with since Dorothy and I married in 1963. I seem to recall saying the same thing to Dorothy each time we had to put one of our Labradors to sleep. History has a way of repeating itself as, the following September, Dorothy and I travelled to Goshen, Indiana, one hundred and forty miles south of Mason, to pick up an eight-week-old female yellow Labrador from a breeder who was referred to me by a friend. We decided to name her Daisy, as a tribute to our last Daisy. I found out later that my daughter, Luanne, had been telling Dorothy to encourage me to buy another Labrador. Luanne said to Dorothy, "I have never known Dad to not have a Labrador. He can't stop now."

On Labor Day, September 4, I cruised *True Blue* from Onekama to Bay Harbor, one-hundred miles north on Lake Michigan, to fish the Tournament Trail 333 Championship Series season finale the following week-end. The 333 Championship is a separate tournament from the port tournaments. Participants in each of the fifteen individual port tournaments can also weigh their three biggest fish caught in the port tournament in the 333 Championship tournament. Points are awarded to the top ten finishers in the 333 Championship tournament and the boat with the most accumulated points from each tournament at the end of the season was to be the overall champion.

True Blue was leading the 333 Championship with victory in sight. George Peplinski, his son Chris, my first mate Frank and Dennis made up my tournament fishing team, and they had done a great job getting us in a position to win the championship.

I wanted to have *True Blue* at Bay Harbor several days ahead of the tournament to pre-fish and make sure everything was ready to give us our best chance of winning the championship. My fishing team would travel to Bay Harbor by car the next day, and we would all stay until after the tournament on Sunday. With the cabin of the boat filled with fishing tackle and clothes, as was my practice when fishing a tournament away from Onekama, I rented a motel room where my team and I could spend the night and shower.

Not wanting to interrupt a holiday weekend for my team, I decided to make the four-hour trip to Bay Harbor by myself. The weather was perfect, warm and sunny with Lake Michigan flat calm. Content with life and listening to the drone of the engines, I had plenty of time to reflect on the past tournament season and the unique circumstances that had enabled *True Blue* to be fishing for the 333 Championship.

True Blue's first Tournament Trail event of the season had been the Onekama Marine Shake Down on the 2006 Memorial Day weekend. The reporting format for the Shake Down tournament was to weigh your five-largest fish each day with the combined two-day total weight declared the winner. The 333 Championship tournament, in which you weigh your three biggest fish, was held simultaneously with the Shake Down, and the same fish could be weighed for both tournaments.

Since Onekama was my home port and fishing grounds, I felt I could place well in this tournament. George Peplinski, who was also docked at Onekama Marine, and I agreed we would both enter our boats in the Memorial Day tournament to support Onekama Marine. My friends Chuck May and Gary Adeska and my new first-mate, Frank Baker, made up my team. Dennis couldn't fish that weekend due to work commitments. Chuck, Gary and Frank were good fishermen and I felt comfortable fishing with them in our home waters. I was fortunate to have hired Frank Baker as my first mate just the previous month. A junior in high school, he was a fine young man in need of summer work. Frank loved to fish and would become my right-hand man on *True Blue* in the coming years.

Saturday, the first day of the tournament, we fished a place called the "Barrel", two-miles north of Onekama. Over the years, I have caught dozens of large salmon in the Barrel, a deep circular depression in the bottom of the lake, a mile in diameter and one-hundred and forty feet deep. Based on earlier reports of good fishing, all of the thirty boats in the tournament fished south of Onekama, leaving us alone in the Barrel. We were marking fish in the Barrel on the fish finder (sonar) but couldn't get them to bite. Just the day before on a charter, I caught several large salmon in the Barrel using the same lures. My frustration grew as the hours passed. I changed lures, boat speed, depth of the lures and everything else I could think of but we didn't catch a fish that first day.

Back at Onekama Marine for the weigh in, there were numerous boats that weighed well for their five-fish limit. *True Blue* didn't have a fish to weigh in the first day. We were in last place, sixty-five pounds behind the leader! There was a little disbelief at the weigh in from some of the captains and spectators who were surprised that *True Blue* "got skunked", a dreaded word to any charter captain.

I was obviously embarrassed and didn't sleep well that night thinking of what I could have done differently to get the fish to bite. The next morning, my crew and I decided we would give it our best to have a respectable catch on day two, and so we agreed to head south to fish. At the six-a.m. shot-gun start from the Onekama pier head, I began to follow the majority of boats running south toward Manistee, but after a few minutes, I had a feeling—yes, like many times before, I know it as the gentle nudge of the Holy Spirit. I made a sudden one-hundred and eighty-degree turn and headed north toward the

Barrel. Chuck, Gary and Frank looked at me in surprise. "

"I thought we were going to fish by Manistee," Chuck said.

"That's where all the fish were caught yesterday."

"I know," I said, "but we also know there are fish in the Barrel. We just couldn't get them to bite. We need some big fish to win, and I have a feeling they will bite today."

The team was skeptical, but I was the captain and had the decision-making role, so we headed for the Barrel.

We were just setting the second fishing line, when the first rod had a bite. A big salmon was peeling line off the reel. We all shouted with excitement, as Chuck and I continued to set the other six lines while Frank netted the twenty-pound chinook salmon. By noon, we had four large salmon—all around twenty pounds. Tournament boats had to be inside the Portage Lake pier head by one p.m. Just as we were pulling lines to head home, another fish bit. Gary Adeska took the rod and after a ten-minute fight had the fish to the boat. Frank was attempting to net the fish when it darted under the boat. Gary instinctively backed away from the transom to put more pressure on the fish.

WRONG!

When a fish charges under the boat, you need to be at the back of the boat and thrust the rod tip into the water to keep the fishing line clear of the props and rudders that can cut the line.

I shouted, "Gary, go to the back of the boat, get the rod tip into the water." Gary rushed to the back of the boat, forgetting to reel in the slack line as it went limp into the water. I again shouted even loader, "REEL! REEL!" We all stood breathless as Gary furiously reeled taking up the slack in the line as fast as he could. Suddenly the line came tight—the fish was still on. Gary eased the salmon to the surface as Frank leaned over the transom netting the largest fish of the day, over twenty pounds. The emotional roller coaster of the last few minutes drained us all, yet there were shouts and high fives.

There was excitement at the weigh in as the participants waited in anticipation for their fish to be placed on the scale. As Frank put each of our fish on the scale, there were shouts of glee and groans of despair from the on-lookers. Some couldn't believe it! How could *True Blue* catch five big fish in the Barrel that day when

l-r, Son Dennis, Dennis, John, George and Chris, won Bud-Pro Am, Manistee, 2006

they got skunked the day before? Captain Kevin Hughes, my friend and dock mate, said to me, "When we saw you turn back north to the Barrel, one of my crew said, 'Denny is a brute for punishment going back to the Barrel after yesterday.' I replied, 'Don't count Denny out until it's over.'"

When the final results were tallied that Memorial Day, *True Blue* ended up in second place in the

Onekama Shake Down tournament, but we won the 333 Championship event and won the biggest fish of both tournaments. Tournament chairman, Fred MacDonald, said to me after the tournament, "I don't think I have ever seen a comeback like that in all the tournaments we have held."

Two weeks later, *True Blue* had another 333 Championship tournament win at the Budweiser Pro-Am tournament in Manistee which gave us a fighting chance at winning the overall 333 Championship. The money wasn't bad either with prize money and side bets from those two tournaments at over four thousand dollars.

In June and July, we had fished tournaments in Grand Haven and Ludington, two beautiful Michigan ports one hundred miles and thirty miles south of Onekama. In early August, we had taken *True Blue* sixty-five miles across Lake Michigan to Green Bay, Wisconsin, for a tournament. We didn't win in either the Michigan nor in the Wisconsin tournaments but we placed in the top ten finishers at each of these three tournaments. With five tournaments completed that summer, *True Blue* was in first place in the season-long 333 Championship. The two remaining tournaments at the ports of Frankfort and Bay Harbor, thirty and one hundred miles north of Onekama respectively, would determine the overall champion for 2006.

I was feeling good about our chances for the championship when an unexpected—and unfortunate— incident at the Frankfort tournament occurred. Dennis was removing the hooks from the first salmon of the morning, when he buried a treble hook into the palm of his left hand. I cut the hook from the lure with wire cutters which I carry for exactly that purpose. Dennis was in pain and bleeding from the wound, the hook was too deep to remove with pliers or to cut out with a knife. My first thought was to return the twenty miles back to Frankfort and a hospital, BUT—we were leading the season's 333 Championship

l-r, Dennis and son, Dennis,
won 333 Onekama Shake Down, 2006

with the finale at Bay Harbor in two weeks. We needed to place well that day in Frankfort to remain in contention for the 333 Championship. Going back could cost us this tournament and perhaps the championship. In a quandary, I asked Dennis what he wanted to do, and he showed us his Blue grit when he replied, "Keep fishing."

We put ice from the cooler in a freezer bag for Dennis to place on the wound to stop the bleeding and keep the pain in check. Dennis couldn't fish, of course, but he helped the best he could with one hand and he cheered us on. After eight grueling hours, we arrived back in Frankfort. George and Chris took the cooler to the weigh-in as I rushed Dennis to the hospital where the hook was surgically removed. While I was waiting for Dennis at the hospital, George called to tell me we had finished third in the Frankfort tournament with enough points to keeping us in the lead for the overall 333 Championship. I was proud of Dennis who was "a chip off the old block." As I have mentioned before, tournament fishing takes a different mind-set: play by the rules but engage in your best effort on the field or in our case, the water.

That had been the summer and now it was Sunday, September 10, the last day of the 333 Championship for the 2006 season at the prestigious Bay Harbor Resort in Petoskey, Michigan. Points were awarded to the top ten finishers in the tournament, ten-points for first place and one-point for tenth place, based on the total pounds of your three biggest fish weighed over the two-day tournament. The boat with the most accumulated points from each tournament at the end of the season was to be the overall champion.

After weighing in two fish the first day and one fish on the second and final day of the Bay Harbor tournament, I felt good about our chance to win. George, Chris, Dennis (who had recovered well), Frank and I crowded around the weigh-in station, nervously waiting for the other competitors to weigh their fish. With the final boat weighed in, we held our breath, but the 333 Championship victory which we had been pursuing all summer was not meant to be ours as the last boat to weigh-in finished just ahead of us in the standings. In the end, we lost the overall 333 Championship by two points. We were disappointed but gratified. George, Chris, Frank, Dennis and I had given it our best, and we were proud of our effort. As I have long said, it's not the fish that count—it's the fishing.

We did, however, win three thousand dollars for second place in the 333 Championship (five thousand went to first place) and seven thousand dollars for winning the season-long side bet, "Best Overall Big Fat$$$ Jack-pot" (each boat pays one-hundred dollars to enter at the beginning of the season and the winner takes all). Lucky for us, the first-place boat

George, son Dennis, Dennis and Fred, Bay Harbor, won Best Overall Jackpot, 2006

had not participated in the side bet! This was a case of *True Blue* losing but still winning. Rampage Yachts was happy, Onekama Marine was happy, we were happy, everyone was happy. What a great way to start my transition from backcountry fishing in Florida to tournament fishing in Michigan!

The 2006 summer was a busy and rewarding season: our move from Florida back to Michigan, charters, tournaments and training my new puppy, Daisy. That fall, I was elected to the board of the Manistee County Sport Fishing Association, the Portage Lake Harbor Commission and the Michigan

Port Collaborative. All three organizations are involved with fishery conservation and protecting our water resources. Apart from the benefit I have derived from our natural resources, I also knew I was responsible to be a good steward of God's creation.

In October, after putting *True Blue* in storage for the winter, Dorothy and I spent much of our time enjoying our new condo at Rayner Ponds in Mason. We could see more of Dennis, Donna and our granddaughter, Carey, who were still living thirty miles away in Pinchney but planning to build a home on the land they owned near us. We also visited with Pat, Luanne and our three grandchildren who lived a four-hour drive south in Lebanon, Ohio.

Pat, who was a pilot before he and Luanne were married, had built and flown remote-control model airplanes for years and was very good at it. After moving to Lebanon, Pat started rebuilding vintage single engine aircraft, such as an Aeronca Champ, piece by piece, re-covering the wings and fuselage and rebuilding the engine. He flew one of his rebuilt aircraft to Onekama one summer and gave everyone a ride. Pat also built several experimental aircraft which he taught himself to fly. He took me for a ride on several occasions. It was fun if you liked flying "by the seat of your pants." This reminded me of my flight in a Fathom F-4 jet in 1988 when I was working at Ford Aerospace, but Pat's rides were, of course, on a smaller scale.

We got to know the neighbors in the other two condos of our unit and the other condo owners at Rayner Ponds. Once again, we were blessed with great neighbors, many of whom soon became friends.

After visiting several churches in the area, we started attending an Assembly of God Church in Lansing about fifteen miles from Mason. The church was the same denomination that we had attended in Florida, and we felt comfortable with its beliefs as well as with the pastor and the congregation.

When Donna and Dennis told us they were expecting another baby the following June, Dorothy and I were even more convinced moving to Michigan was the right thing to do. The timing was perfect. We could be nearby to help out as the baby's arrival grew closer. An added bonus of our return to Michigan came over the holidays when the entire Blue and Hacker families spent Christmas together for the first time since Dorothy and I went to live in Venezuela in 1969. I said to Dorothy, "You and God were right again, moving back to Michigan was the right thing to do."

The winter of 2007 was our first in Michigan since we moved to Florida in 1993. At times, I missed the backcountry fishing and my friends in Florida, but finally accepted, at age seventy-four, poling a boat in the hot sun every day was for the younger guides. The excellent tournament season with *True Blue* the previous summer and attending the winter boat shows marketing Rampage made the transition from Florida easier and I was enjoying this new phase of my fishing life.

In the spring Dennis, Donna and Carey moved to their new house just a few blocks from our condo in Rayner Ponds. It was great having them close and seeing them almost every day. Dennis was still working for Jackson National Life Insurance Company headquarters in Okemos, just six miles north of Mason and doing well in his new position as director of facilities. We were all excited about the arrival of the new baby.

On June 10, 2007, Dennis and Donna had their second child, Amanda. We were so happy for them and for us that we lived so close by. Dorothy spent much of her time in Mason that summer while I was busy with salmon charters and tournaments in Onekama.

Following our successful 2006 tournament season, George and I agreed it was time for him and his son, Chris, to further their own fishing career and start fishing tournaments in their boat in 2007. I missed fishing with them as they were excellent fisherman and good friends. Dennis was so busy at work he didn't have time to fish, so Frank, an occasional charter with friends and family, made up my tournament team from then on. It is difficult to be competitive with the professional tournament teams with lesser skilled charter customers, but Frank and I still had fun fishing the tournaments.

With Frank and me on the boat, we were still competitive and frequently placed in the money in the tournaments we fished. *True Blue* was to finish again in the top ten of the 333 Championship Series but never again was I to come as close to winning the overall championship as my crew and I did in 2006. Without George, Chris and my son as my crew, it was hard to repeat the success we achieved in that first season. I recall when I first started chartering at age fifty-five. I could conquer the world then and a first mate was simply an extra pair of hands. I could run charters on my own if necessary. As time went by and my physical capabilities declined with age, I counted on my first mate and crew to do more of the chores that had always been my duty.

Luanne and Emilee fished several tournaments with Frank and me in 2007. It was like old times fishing together again. After a successful tournament, winning the biggest fish and some money in Grand Haven, Luanne and Emilee returned home to Lebanon, Ohio, while Frank and I took *True Blue* back to Onekama, a little over one hundred miles north of Grand Haven.

We left after the award ceremony at four p.m. thinking we could make the four-hour trip home by dark. Unfortunately, about an hour after we left Grand Haven, the fog set in reducing visibility to less than a quarter of a mile. I reduced speed from twenty-five to ten miles per hour and with the radar and GPS felt comfortable we could safely make our way home. During the next hour, the visibility continued to drop to less than two hundred feet as we continued to reduce speed to five miles per hour, slow going but appropriate for the weather conditions. Fog is not uncommon on Lake Michigan, and with the proper electronics and caution can be navigated safely. My years of flying in fog and making instrument landings was a big help in learning to understand and trust my instruments in the fog. In a boat you can always slow down or stop to assess the situation, not so in flying, but there are still similarities.

Frank was my lookout and I was at the helm keeping an eye on the radar and chart plotter. Another uneventful hour went by when I picked up a large image on the radar a mile directly in front of us. It appeared to be moving slowly at less than five miles per hour as we were still closing the distance. I was puzzled: I had the radar on a three-mile range, where did such a large object come from without us seeing it a greater distance?

The target on the radar screen seemed to be stationary as we closed to less than one-quarter of a mile. In accordance with USCG regulations, I sounded the fog horn one prolonger blast every two-minutes to alert other boats of my presence. I put the boat in neutral to determine the movement of the target on our screen. It moved very slowly away from us. The target appeared to be about one hundred feet across and low in the water, a barge I thought, but where was the tugboat? I started forward again and could barely make out a large dark object on the water, Frank shouted, "Canadian Geese!" It was a large flock of geese setting on the water. It was too foggy to fly we guessed. As we got too close or sounded the fog horn, these geese would swim away from the boat, keeping their distance. Frank and I laughed and breathed a sigh of relief. The fog eventually cleared somewhat, but It took over seven hours to arrive back in Onekama at almost midnight. Frank and I were, as they say, "dog tired," after being up since four a.m. that morning. The life of a charter captain!

The winter of 2008 I was busy representing Rampage at the fishing shows and working on the boat. Owning and maintaining a charter boat is physically demanding, even in the winter. Starting in February,

Frank and I spent many hours in the heated storage building at Onekama Marine getting *True Blue* ready for spring. Even with a new boat there was polishing, painting the bottom and repairing equipment that was broken. Checking and replacing fishing gear, fire extinguishers, life jackets, toilet, downriggers and pumps and hoses was not as physically difficult but tedious and time-consuming work.

One of the first signs that you are aware of your reduced physical capabilities is the willingness to let someone else do it for you. Every once in a while, I would have a twinge of guilt and regret watching Frank do things that were once my responsibility. Mentally, I didn't feel old and thought I could still conquer the world; physically I realized I had to ad-just to what I was able to do with the strength I had left and let Frank do the rest.

Fishing tournaments for Rampage reduced my charters to about thirty trips during the summers of 2007 to 2010. However, when added to the tourna-ment days we fished, Frank and I were fishing over fifty days a summer. Financially, with the income from charters, my stipend from Rampage and Onekama Marine and tournament prize money, the fishing was very rewarding. Physically, it was de-manding but I was still enjoying it.

Most of my customers were old friends who had fished with me before, and I wasn't adding any new customers unless referred by an existing customer. The highlight of my 2008 charter season was when Don Beck called to let me know he, his wife Ann, and Larry Schantz and his wife were coming to charter with me right after Labor Day. We all had a great time reminiscing about old times, and Dorothy and I enjoyed showing them around Onekama. It turned out to be an annual affair, with the Becks and Schantzes coming each September for the next several years.

I started another annual affair in 2009 with a group of friends known as the Romeos (Really Old Men Eating Out). The group of about forty, started by my friend and retired pharmacist, George Punches, consisted mostly of retirees in the Onekama area who gathered once a month to eat at different restaurants. The Onekama Marine Shoot Out tournament, held on Memorial Day weekend, was the first tournament I fished each spring. I suggested to my fellow Romeos we enter *True Blue* as a Romeo team. We had such a good time that the Shoot Out became an annual event with the Romeos, Frank and I fishing the Shoot Out together every year. We won a few non-cash prizes but most of all we enjoyed the camaraderie.

By 2009, Frank was basically running *True Blue*. I had taught him how to dock the boat, rig the lures, set lines, net fish, clean the boat and the fish. I was still the captain, however, and responsible for the safe and successful outcome of our charters. I made the key decisions, booked charters, drove the boat and conversed with customers, many of whom were old friends. I was grateful to have Frank as a first mate; had it not been for his help I would have stopped chartering a few years sooner. I wasn't about to break in another first mate, and anyhow where would I find another one like Frank?

An interesting aspect of representing Rampage was the boats shows I did with Onekama Marine.

The Bay Harbor In-Water Boat Show in Petoskey, Michigan, was one of the premier boat shows on Lake Michigan. Held in June for three days, it drew boat dealers and approximately two hundred boats, from runabouts to yachts over one hundred feet, from around the Great Lakes. Everything about Bay Harbor was first class, the retail shops, hotels, restaurants and marina. Lake Michigan Yacht Sales, a subsidiary of Onekama Marine located at Bay Harbor, had six to seven boats on display, including several Rampages. My role was to represent Rampage to potential customers with on-board presentations and demo boat rides. My having just missed winning the 333 Championship at Bay Harbor in 2006 gave Onekama Marine and Rampage some free publicity at the show.

My granddaughter, Emilee, started at Michigan State University in the fall of 2009 with both a swimming and a United States Army Reserve Officer Training Program scholarship. I don't know who enjoyed it more, Emilee or Dorothy and me. Being only twenty minutes from MSU, Emilee came to visit us for a home-cooked meal or to spend the night every chance she had.

The highlight of the 2010 fishing season was Tight Lines for Troops. Fellow charter captain Bob Guenthardt, a former Ogema (Chief) of the Little River Band of Ottawa Indians and Army veteran, conceived the idea in the fall of 2009. With the help of the Little River Casino in Manistee and a host of volunteers, the first charity salmon fishing tournament for Michigan veterans took place on May 15, 2010, with sixty boats and over two hundred and fifty veterans participating. It was an honor to host these deserving veterans, some from World War II.

The most memorable time of the tournament was a brief ceremony held outside the Manistee pier heads prior to the 6:30 a.m. shotgun start. A United States Coast

True Blue at Tight Lines for Troops Tournament

Guard Cutter floated at rest in the water alongside sixty tournament boats, all flying American flags. The fishing crafts had gathered closely around the Cutter. All engines were turned off and marine radios were tuned to VHF channel 68. The orange hue of the sunrise peaked over the shoreline behind us. There was not a sound except for the solemn notes of "Amazing Grace" played by a Scottish Guardsman aboard the Cutter. Afterwards, there followed a prayer to honor the fallen. There wasn't a dry eye in the fleet. The tournament proved so popular it has continued on to this day.

The downturn in the US economy that had begun several years earlier negatively impacted boat manufacturers across the country. The new state-of-the-art Rampage plant that I visited in 2005 at Wilmington, North Carolina, closed in 2008 and the manufacturing equipment was transferred to the original Rampage plant in Oconto, Wisconsin. Participation in the tournaments declined by thirty percent. Rampage Yachts and Onekama Marine ended their sponsorship of *True Blue* the summer of 2010.

Onekama Marine, Rampage and I were disappointed to see our relationship end, but we agreed we all benefited from our almost five years together. Onekama Marine sold numerous Rampage boats from thirty to thirty-eight feet, a new Rampage dealer was added on Lake Erie in 2006, I had five years of financial support that had included a generous discount on the beautiful Rampage 33 that I owned. Jim, the owner of Onekama Marine and I agreed, they were five great years as business partners and friends.

Most importantly, I had five years of unforgettable memories fishing with family and friends at ports around Lake Michigan. I couldn't have planned a better transition from Florida to Michigan. During the past five years, I went from two businesses with one-hundred and fifty charters a year, plus international fishing expeditions and ventures in the Bahamas to approximately thirty salmon charters and six tournaments a year in Michigan.

Now that's the way to ease into retirement!

Through the Eyes of a Fisherman

CHAPTER 9
EASING INTO
RETIREMENT

2010 was a time of sadness and joy for the Blue families. Tom and Joann were blessed with six children, Tommy, Michael, David, Danny, Mary Ann and Kathy. All had successful careers and families of their own and were settled close to Tom and Joann in Frederick, Maryland.

In February, Kathy (Blue) Shores, Tom and Joann's youngest daughter was diagnosed with multiple sclerosis. As her condition worsened, she gave up her career as a dental hygienist and was confined to a wheelchair. Her husband, Dave, and two young children, Olivia and Christopher, have shown remarkable support and love caring for her. Kathy and my daughter Luanne look like sisters and have always been close, so her illness resonates even more with me when I see Kathy. We continue to pray for her healing and trust God for the future.

Dennis and Donna gave us some good news in March when they announced they were expecting another baby in November. Dorothy and I were excited, we may be grandparenting the rest of our lives!

On July 19, 2010, Dorothy and I got a call from Tom that their oldest son, Tommy, had been killed in a car accident. We were devastated. Tommy was fifty-two years of age, divorced, and had four grown daughters. He retired two years before the accident after thirty years of service at Eastalco, where his dad worked, to pursue his passion for the outdoors. Tommy was one of a kind—born one-hundred years too late, a mountain man would best describe him.

When Tommy was six to eight years old, he would spend his time in the fields catching small animals, birds and snakes with his bare hands. One day, when Tom and the family were still living in Trenton, Michigan, Dorothy and I went to visit, and as we got out of the car, Tommy ran up to show us a bouquet of five or six live snakes in his hand. His mom, Joann, would get upset when he would lose one in the house! Tommy loved all kind of animals and had many as pets.

Tommy didn't care for school and dropped out of high school. He wasn't lazy just not academically inclined. He went to work at Eastalco where his dad, Tom, worked and was a valued employee for thirty years. Tommy and his dad came fishing with me in Onekama several times, and while Tommy enjoyed it, he liked hunting better. "The ground is more stable than a boat," he said. Tommy acted and dressed like someone out of the Daniel Boone era. A big man with a bushy beard, he would greet me with a bear hug, beard and all. He often dressed in a large brim felt hat, Levi's, flannel shirt and hunting boots. Being tied down just wasn't Tommy's way. He will be missed.

The sadness we felt with the loss of Tommy was turned to joy on November 13, 2010, when Dennis and Donna called to announce the birth of their son, Dennis Michael Blue. Dennis Michael is the fifth of six generations of the Blue family to be named Dennis. I was proud to have a grandson to carry on the Blue family name. Luanne told me that when her son, John, was born in 1994, she had thought of naming him Dennis but deferred to her brother, Dennis, who was not married at the time, to carry on the name. No matter the name, I love them all. I can recall Dorothy and me agreeing one day, "It's a good thing we came home when we did. How would Dennis and Donna have managed three young children without us!"

In June 2011, my son, Dennis, took me to Deep Creek Lodge in Alaska. Dennis was now a vice president of Jackson Na-

Dennis and son Dennis, Alaska

tional Life Insurance Company and he wanted to reciprocate for when I took him to Alaska a few years earlier. We flew from Detroit to Anchorage where we stayed the night, and the next day, took a local flight to the fishing lodge on the Kenai Peninsula. It was first class all the way, food, accommodations, guides and equipment. We fished three days for salmon and halibut, shipping home sixty pounds of frozen halibut fillets. The biggest halibut was one hundred forty-five pounds—caught by Dennis, of course.

The highlight of the trip, however, was not the fishing. Each night, we gathered for dinner around a large round table that seated fourteen. The owner of the lodge, his wife and twelve other guests socialized and chatted about the fishing. The first evening, we learned one of the guests, John we will call him, had arrhythmia, which is an irregular heartbeat, and his medication wasn't helping. He appeared weak and pale yet he didn't want his health to interfere with the long-planned fishing trip for himself and the three friends that accompanied him. Everyone at the table wished him well and hoped he would be feeling better in the morning.

The second night at dinner, I asked John how he was feeling and he replied, "Not good." He was still having a problem with his heartbeat, and if it didn't improve by morning, he had decided he would seek medical help in Anchorage. There was obvious concern by others at the table, and the owner said he would arrange air transportation to Anchorage in the morning if requested. I made eye contact with John and said, "Dennis and I will pray that you feel better in the morning." He smiled and said, "Thank you," while others at the table nodded their agreement or just looked on. When we got back to the room that night Dennis and I prayed for John, not only to heal his irregular heartbeat, but to provide a witness for the others of the power of prayer.

Dennis and I didn't see John the next morning and wondered how he was doing. I inquired about him from some of the other guests and was told he had gone fishing. That night at dinner, John looked better, the color had returned to his face and his voice was strong. After we were all seated, John wanted to make an announcement, he looked at Dennis and me and said, "Thank you for your prayers. I went back to my room last night and was in bed by ten p.m. At around two a.m., I awoke and realized my heartbeat was normal." Everyone at the table applauded and lifted their glasses in celebration. I said, "Don't thank us. Thank the Lord for answered prayer." A few of the others at the table said, "Amen."

The summer of 2012 was the first time I seriously considered retiring from the charter business. I still had the passion for fishing but at age seventy-nine was physically slowing down. I vividly recall when I lost my passion for flying after I left Venezuela in 1972. It took me a year to realize it was never about the flying. My plane was only a vehicle for me to fulfill God's purpose. In like manner, Ford provided me the vehicle, no pun intended, to travel and witness to others in different countries around the world. Following my retirement from Ford in 1988, my charter boat *True Blue* became the vehicle to witness to people about Christ. My boat had now served God's purpose, and He was telling me it was time to look for another ministry commensurate with my age and ability.

Joann called in early January to tell Dorothy and me that my brother, Tom, had been admitted to the hospital due to breathing problems but that he seemed to be doing well. Tom was seventy-eight, a year and four months younger than I and had been suffering from heart problems for the past few years. Joann was concerned but was told by the doctor that Tom should be alright after adjusting his medications. The next day, Tom called me from the hospital to say he was doing fine and expected to be released in a day or two. He sounded tired but seemed in good spirits. We talked for a while, and I asked if we should come to visit. Tom replied, "No, that's not necessary, I will be home in a few days." After we hung up, I had an uneasy feeling. Something told me all was not well; the timing and tone of our conversation sounded like Tom was impelled to call to say goodbye.

Two days later, Joann called to tell us Tom was in intensive care and not doing well. She would keep us informed and let us know if we should come to Frederick. The next morning, January 7, 2013, Joann called to tell us Tom had passed away. His condition had deteriorated rapidly overnight, and before she could make any calls, Tom was gone. Tom was buried in Frederick next to his son Tommy. All of the Blue families were there to bid farewell to Tom, my brother and best friend. He is missed.

In the mid-1990s, Tom started a tradition of having Thanksgiving at his house every other year. It was anticipated by both families and rarely did anyone not attend. In the earlier days when the kids were young, running and playing as kids do, all the movement and noise would get disconcerting to the adults, but Tom, being mild mannered like my dad, didn't seem to mind the nearly fifty people in attendance. Joann and her family have continued to host the gathering since Tom passed away. In 2014, to reciprocate and to encourage all the nieces and nephews to get together, Dorothy and I started a summer gathering at our condo in Onekama during alternate years to the Thanksgiving gathering. The attendance for our summer reunions was not as large as Thanksgiving at Tom's, maybe twenty people, but everyone had a great time fishing, swimming and enjoying each other's company. As often happens with families, when the children marry and start their own families and careers, it gets increasingly difficult to get everyone together. Joann and Dorothy and I have agreed to continue our get togethers as long as possible, even though they are less well attended. My daughter Luanne and my nephew David keep in close touch and will hopefully continue our reunions into the future.

After several years at the Assembly of God church in Lansing, Dorothy and I came to realize the fifteen-mile drive from Mason could be difficult, if not impossible, during the winter months, and it was time to explore a church closer to home. We enjoyed the fellowship and the pastor at our Lansing church but we missed not being more involved with church activities due to distance and the occasional inclement weather. We visited several churches in the Mason area and liked the Mason First Church of the

Nazarene, located a mile from our Rayner Ponds condo. From our first visit, we knew that community was where God wanted us to attend. Dorothy and I learned over our years of moving and attending numerous churches that, as Christians, we are all part of the body of Christ but that it is important to have the fellowship of a church home.

We got to know the pastor, Gerhard Weigelt, a charismatic man in his early forties, in a personal way when Dennis was diagnosed with a tumor on his adrenal gland and underwent surgery at University of Michigan Hospital in Ann Arbor in March 2013. Part of the adrenal gland was successfully removed and Dennis made a complete recovery. Pastor Gerhart spent the day with us at the hospital during the surgery, and we felt blessed to have him there. The pastor's dad and mom, Morris and Eula-Adine, who have a condo near Dorothy and me in Rayner Ponds, also became good friends.

On June 18, 2013, Dennis and I returned for a third time to Deep Creek Lodge in Alaska. We each paid our own way this time. The big surprise was, when we deplaned in Anchorage, there was a sign advising fishermen that the chinook salmon season had been closed due to low returns of chinook salmon to the rivers. "Just another little bump in the road," I said to Dennis. "We can still fish for halibut. Who knows but there may be other options."

At the lodge, the owner apologized for the change in the fishing regulations by the Alaska Department of Fish and Game and said he would arrange a discounted day trip by helicopter to fish sockeye salmon, which were not affected by the change in regulations. Dennis and I decided we had come this far so "Why not?" The other ten guests at the lodge declined the offer and fished for halibut which they were soon to regret after hearing of our adventure at dinner that night.

The helicopter picked Dennis and me up at the lodge and flew us west across Cook Inlet to a remote glacier lake region that was part of the Aleutian mountain chain. The scenery was gorgeous, the green tundra surrounding Cook Inlet was capped by the snow-covered mountains in the distance. We saw a brown bear with cubs, and the pilot hovered near the ground with the helicopter to let Dennis get pictures of them.

Flying low over the rivers, the pilot/guide soon spotted fish and landed next to a river where Dennis and I caught sockeye salmon one after another. We kept to a limit of five sockeye each, and then we flew to the base of a nearby glacier where the guide landed and prepared a lunch of grilled sockeye salmon, asparagus and corn bread. Being surrounded by the beauty of God's creation with Dennis was priceless. The early closing of the Chinook salmon season

Son Dennis with rainbow trout, Alaska

resulted in an extraordinary experience and once

again affirmed that behind every cloud there is a silver lining.

I was now eighty years old and had been looking for a new ministry. I hadn't realized it at the time, but God had been preparing me for a new ministry since I purchased my new Rampage and moved back to Michigan in 2006. My role as a charter captain had changed over the past several years as my first mate, Frank, increasingly took over the physically demanding activities. I was the captain, but Frank did the heavy work of fishing. Each year the number of charters diminished. I was no longer booking new customers. I had never thought of it quite this way before, but my charter business was slowing dying off. Literally, many of my original customers had passed away or were no longer physically able to go fishing. It was time I listed *True Blue* for sale in the winter of 2013-2014.

In August of 2013, I learned from a long-time customer, Lou Tegtmeyer, while on a salmon charter, that Larry Schantz had passed away. Lou, a physician, was relating to me how Larry had passed away at a hospital in Garden City, Michigan, the previous week and that he was the attending physician during the last days of Larry's life. Lou wanted me to hear the story of how this friend had been a mentor to him in medical school and during his residency training. Lou said neither he nor Larry knew of their mutual friendship with me until the week before Larry passed away at the hospital. Larry told him of our trip to Venezuela, and salmon fishing together with Don Beck in Onekama where I had last seen him in 2011, He asked Lou to let me know how much he enjoyed our friendship and the time together. I was saddened to hear of Larry's loss and as surprised as Lou and Larry had been that we three had been mutually friends for years without knowing it. Lou and I both had tears in our eyes.

During the previous year, when Frank was not working for me, he had been working part-time at a sporting goods store in Manistee that was part of a national chain. We had run only twenty charters the past summer,

l-r, Larry Schantz and Don Beck, with salmon, 2005

and I encouraged Frank to look for other employment that had a career potential. Based on his excellent work performance and knowledge of fishing, Frank was offered a full-time position as head of the fishing department at the store in September 2013. I knew Frank would do well, and he subsequently was promoted to store manager with a bright future ahead.

By the spring of 2014, I had had no offers to buy my boat so, as not to let an opportunity go by, I fished the Tight Lines for Troops veteran's tournament in May. During the summer, I ran a few charters with old customers, using a first mate that was a friend of Frank's, while I was continuing to look for a buyer for *True Blue*. I sent a letter to customers to let them know this would be my last season of charter fishing. Some of my customers emailed or called to wish me well and tell me how much they had enjoyed our time fishing together over the years. Several customers sent copies of old photos taken on previous charters with me and a note of thanks.

I know fishermen like to tell "fish tales," but the summer of 2014 produced one I will not forget. I was fishing a charter with a father and his fourteen-year-old son who had fished with me several times before. It had been a slow morning with only four fish caught when we had a bite. The fishing line was accelerating off the reel at a rapid rate as the son took the rod. After ten minutes, with the fish no closer to the boat than when he started working the fish, the exhausted young man passed the fishing rod to his dad. Another fifteen minutes went by before the dad grew tired and handed the rod to my first-mate Josh Metiva. Josh, six-feet-four-inches tall and over two-hundred pounds was also working hard to get the fish close to the boat! A few more minutes went by and Josh had the fish close enough to the boat for me to reach out and net it.

At first, I thought the net was snagged on the back of the boat as I was having trouble lifting the fish out of the water. I had netted hundreds of fish over the years and could tell this one was big. As I lifted the fish over the transom, everyone shouted at the size of the fish, including Josh and me, as we exchanged high-fives. Back at the dock, the fish weighed 31.4 pounds on a certified scale, the biggest chinook salmon I have caught on my charter boat. I even have a picture to prove it. That evening, I said to Dorothy, "Do you think it was providential that I caught the biggest salmon of my fishing career on my last summer of charter-ing?" Dorothy answered, matter of factually, "Yes, of course."

That fall, I asked Fred MacDonald if I could place a "For Sale" advertisement in his 2015 Tournament Trail magazine to be re-leased at the Grand Rapids Boating and Fishing Show in February. As always, Fred was happy to accom-modate me. The show, one of the largest in the mid-west, would reach thou-sands of potential buyers

Dennis with 31.4-lb chinook

for my boat. Dorothy and I were vacationing in Florida when Fred called me from the fishing show with a potential buyer. I immediately called the gen-tlemen, and within a week, we agreed on a sale price contingent on a sea trial that would be conducted as soon as the ice cleared on Portage Lake in April.

On May 5, 2015, following a successful sea trial, *True Blue* was sold. It was a bittersweet day seeing the new owner pull away from Onekama Marine in HIS new boat. When I left Florida in 2006 and sold my flats boat I still had my charter business and *True Blue* in Onekama. Now, selling *True Blue* was the end of an era, the end of my charter fishing career. After our many moves overseas, Dorothy and I were familiar with the difficulty of saying goodbye to the old and embracing the new but it didn't make it any easier. There is a saying among boaters that the two happiest days in a boater's life are when you buy your boat and when you sell your boat. For me the saying was only half right as I had a lump in my throat watching *True Blue* depart from Onekama Marine for the last time. On the other hand, I had a feeling of satisfaction that comes when you know you have completed the assignment and given it your best. "Thank you, Lord, for allowing me to have the opportunity to use my charter business to serve you." And yes, thank you Fred for listing my boat for sale in your magazine. For the record, my "for sale" notice was the first and last placed in the Tournament Trail magazine.

The sale of my boat didn't totally end my fishing, I still occasionally first-mated for George Peplinski or Kevin Hughes on their charters and indulged in fun fishing with other friends who had a boat docked in the marina.

During the summer, I occasionally stopped by the slip where *True Blue* had been docked for twenty-eight years. I have to admit there are times when I wished I was still chartering. I missed my boat and the camaraderie of my fellow captains. I think back to March 1, 1988 when I left Ford on faith and began a transformation to a new career and ministry. My boat, *True Blue*, replaced my corporate career as a means to witness to people about Christ. Being on a charter with customers when the fish are not biting gave me many opportunities to be a good witness.

When I think of the thousands of hours I spent on boats with people over the past twenty-eight years, most of whom I would have never met, I couldn't image a better mission field. It confirmed what I have always believed that people are more important than the fishing.

I was excited to see what God had next in store for Dorothy and me. There would be no change of career as was the case when I left Ford or sold *True Blue*. Or would there? My daughter Luanne had been encouraging me to write a book about my life, and I would tell her, "I will think about it."

Which reminds me of one last shark story that took place in April 2015. Doug and Jane Cermak have been friends with Dorothy and me for years in Manistee. Both are retired law enforcement officers and love to fish. A few years ago, they purchased a winter home and a boat in Florida not far from Boca Grande where I had had my guide business. Over the past several years, Doug and Jane had become proficient in fishing the Gulf waters for snapper and grouper but they had never fished tarpon. April is early for tarpon fishing, but Doug, Jane and I decided to go anyway so I could show them the technique I use to catch tarpon. It was a beautiful morning idling along the beach near Boca Grande in their twenty- foot Mako. Jane saw something in the distance, a large school of fish, perhaps dolphin. As we got closer, much to our surprise, they were tarpon, hundreds of them.

We had purchased a dozen live blue crabs for bait. "Just in case," Doug had said. At two-dollars apiece, they were expensive insurance if we didn't see any tarpon. The preferred tackle was a spinning reel with eighty-pound braided line. Doug didn't have a trolling motor on his twenty- foot Mako so we moved up wind and drifted back onto the tarpon as they milled about on the surface. We cast several times, and Jane caught a bite but lost her fish. I didn't want to start the outboard motor and spook the fish so we continued to drift a few hundred yards past the tarpon before starting the motor and moving back up-wind for another drift. Being so early in the season, there were only two or three other boats in sight, which made it possible for us to fish the school of tarpon unmolested by other boats.

On our second drift, Jane had another bite and I

was rigging a blue crab for her when Doug shouted, "I've got one." The tarpon jumped several times and took about fifty yards of line off the reel before it stopped. As Doug was working the tarpon back to the boat, the line went slack. "I think we lost him," Doug said. I replied instinctively, "Reel hard." It was not unusual for a fish to run toward the boat causing slack line and this gave the impression it had gotten off the hook.

Doug, releasing tarpon with shark bite, 2015

As Doug was reeling, the line suddenly came tight and simultaneously the water roiled. A shark was after our tarpon! At first, I

304

thought the shark had taken the tarpon, but Doug shouted, "The tarpon is still on." He continued to fight the tarpon another ten minutes before getting the fish to the boat with no further sign of the shark. I took the fishing leader and guided the tarpon alongside the boat for Doug to take the hook out and release the fish. You could see the wound on the side of the tarpon where the shark had taken a bite.

With the tarpon still in the water alongside the boat, Jane took some photos and Doug released the fish. As the tarpon swam slowly away from the boat, the shark re-appeared from nowhere and the tarpon charged back under the boat with the shark in pursuit. Twenty feet on the opposite side of the boat, the water roiled and blood stained the water where the shark caught up with our tarpon for the last time. All we could say was WOW. We were excited for Doug's first tarpon but we were disappointed it couldn't have ended in a better way for the tarpon. A lesson in the survival of the fittest.

Going back to Florida for a few weeks each winter keeps Dorothy and me in touch with friends. Dorothy plays golf at Riverwood, and I fish with Ben Kittrell who graciously invites me to go fishing with him several times a week. Don Beck and Tom Balisteri and families come to Florida every winter so we continue to see them. Unfortunately, Don Volk, Bob Voell and Larry Schantz have passed away.

OK, I will admit that I have no will power and I couldn't resist buying a new boat. In January 2016, I bought a seventeen-foot boat with a 75 horsepower outboard engine, much like the flats boat I used in Florida. I rationalized to myself and Dorothy that I could trailer the boat to Florida in the winter and bring it back to Onekama to use on Portage Lake in the summer. Most of all I could take the grandkids and teach them to fish.

Having more free time with the grandkids, walking my Labrador, Daisy, and community volunteer projects were enjoyable, but I still needed a new ministry. By nature, I don't like to sit around, and Dorothy could tell I was getting edgy. Just as she had done so many times in the past when I was interfering with her golf, she said, "Don't you think it's time for you to go fishing again!" Just as with my Ford career, flying and chartering, I now needed a new vehicle to spread God's word. I still hadn't identified a new ministry but truly believed God strategically

l-r, Grace, John and Emilee, ROTC graduation, 2017

places each Christian to serve Him, but for now I just had to be patient.

My new boat worked out great during the summer of 2016. I loved fishing for bass and taking friends and the grandkids fishing. I even caught a couple of salmon that summer on Lake Michigan. Not recommended with a small boat like mine unless the lake is calm and you stay close to shore but really fun.

October 23, 2016, after thirty-years as a USCG Captain, I let my United

States Coast Guard License expire. It was hard to believe I had been a charter captain for as long as I worked for Ford.

By November, my new ministry emerged. Following Luanne's much expressed suggestion, I embarked on writing a book of my life and how God has guided Dorothy and me and our family over the years. At first, struggling for words to pen, recalling events, searching through old photos and family records was slow work. I contacted an editor, Denis Ledoux, to help me turn my thoughts into words and then a book. Slowly the passion I once had for flying and fishing emerged again, I had found a new ministry that would consume me in the coming months and years.

This story would not be complete without a word about grandparenting. We were blessed with six wonderful grandchildren who have added so much joy to our lives. Fortunately, Pat and Luanne's children, Emilee (twenty-six), John (twenty-three) and Grace (eighteen) and Dennis and Donna's children, Carey (twelve), Amanda (ten) and Dennis (seven) are far enough apart in age to provide us the joy of grandparenting for years to come. Each occupies a special place and time in our lives.

Dennis, Amanda and Carey

Emilee, a graduate of Michigan State University and the Army Reserve Officer Training Corps (ROTC) scholarship program, is now a nurse and first lieutenant in the Army and is stationed in San Antonio, Texas. John, who graduated from Michigan State University in chemical engineering in December 2017, was also on the ROTC scholarship program and is now working for a large corporation. Grace graduated from Lebanon High School in the spring of 2017 and is pursuing a career as a dental assistant. What a pleasure to see them mature as individuals and Christians and find a purpose in life.

Carey, an accomplished dancer with numerous awards and an excellent student, is now in the eighth grade at Mason Middle School. Amanda, with her independent spirit, is everyone's sweetheart and also excels in the sixth-grade at Mason public school. Dennis, the youngest and as he says, the smartest, started first grade last year and loves it. He loves sports and life in general as any seven-year-old should. As noted previously, Dennis is the fifth of six generations in the Blue family with the first name of Dennis. In naming my dad Leland, my grandparents broke the continuum, for which I have no reasonable answer.

Dorothy and I returned from our winter in Florida on May 4, 2017, just in time for the Manistee County Sport Fishing Association Annual Spring Banquet. The MCSFA was formed in the 1980s to promote fishing and conservation in Manistee County and has grown into a strong advocacy for fishery policies in Michigan. I have been a member since its inception serving in various capacities and on the board.

The Spring Banquet is our annual fund raiser and well attended with over a hundred members and guests in attendance. It is always good to see old friends and meet new members. Kevin Hughes, who had been so helpful to me in the early days when I was establishing myself in Onekama, has been our president for the past twenty years and is doing a great job growing the organization.

Following dinner and a speaker, the program turned to announcing the award for "Unprecedented Commitment to the Manistee County Sport Fishing Association." The award, given periodically to recognize outstanding service to MCSFA, was an honor to receive. No one, other than the nominating committee, knew the name of the person who was about to receive the award. Kevin, the master of ceremonies, read through the list of achievements of this year's beneficiary. Catching large salmon, fishing internationally, catching peacock bass in Venezuela—wait a minute, that sounded too familiar. I looked around the room, all eyes were turned on me, as Kevin completed the list of achievements and then looked at me and said, "Congratulations, Denny, you are the recipient of the Unprecedented Commitment Award." I was totally surprised and humbled as I gave a few extemporaneous remarks of how grateful and blessed I have been to be part of the MCSFA and to have met so many fine people over the years.

On the way home from the banquet, I asked Dorothy, "How did Kevin get so much information on my fishing background?" She replied, "You gave it to Luanne. Don't you remember when she called a couple of months ago and asked you to send information about your fishing experiences so Grace could write a class report?" Yes, I remembered and had to admit I had been had by my own clever daughter and "scheming" wife!

On August 5, 2017 our first granddaughter, Emilee, chose to be married in Onekama. Emilee spent two years of her early childhood at our condo in Onekama after her parents Pat and Luanne and brother, John, moved to Michigan from California. Emilee's first two years of school were at the Onekama Consolidated School. (John was not of school age). After Pat, Luanne, Emilee and John moved to Lebanon, Ohio, where Pat was working for Ford, Emilee, John and Grace continued to spend their summers with Dorothy and me at the condo in Onekama. All the grandkids helped cleaning my charter boat and fished tournaments with me throughout their early years in Onekama.

Now at age twenty-five Emilee chose to return to Onekama for her formal wedding. John Shea and Emilee had been married by a justice of the peace two months previously and wanted a formal wedding ceremony with friends and family. Her husband, Jon Shea Johnson, a former US Coast Guardsman from Georgia, and she decided to have the wedding ceremony on the beach at Lake Michigan with the reception at Onekama Marine. Graciously, they asked me to perform the marriage vows. Although I have no ministerial credentials, I was thrilled to do so, knowing it was God who was ordaining their marriage. It was a time I will never forget, reading I Corinthians 13. It is the same chapter I read at Luanne's wedding twenty-eight years previously. The weather and reception were perfect with approximately one hundred in attendance, made up mostly of the Blue, Letarte and Johnson families.

Dorothy and I try to stay out of the role of being parents again. Occasionally, we venture an opinion which is generally ignored, but for the most part, we let the parents be parents and grandparents be grandparents.

Standing l-r, in back;
Donna, Carey and Dennis
Front row l-r, Amanda and Dennis

What we notice most is that the things which seemed so important to us at the time we were raising our own children really weren't that important after all. We made our share of mistakes like most parents but our kids seemed to have survived it all in good shape. We are so proud of our sons and daughters, which of course include spouses, and the grandchildren. Watching the children and grandchildren grow up reminded me of how things change. Cultures, music, lifestyles all impact how future generations view the world. There is one constant, however, and that is the infallible Word of God. It is the same yesterday, today and forever. The greatest legacy Dorothy and I will leave behind are not fame and fortune but families that love the Lord.

Writing my first book had become a mission with five to ten-hour days spent at the computer or on the phone with my editor Denis Ledoux. I realize now, more than even, no matter our status in life, God has a ministry for each of us. The passion I had for flying, working at Ford and running my charter business had returned, the only difference is my computer is now the means to witness to others. No sooner had *Running the Good Race* been released on December 5, 2017 that I started on my second book, *Through the Eyes of a Fisherman.* My editor Denis commented several times that most books take months if not years to complete, to which I replied, "Maybe so, Denis, but at my age, I don't have the luxury of years, months maybe, but not years, let's get the book done as soon as we can."

Blessed beyond words. Writing my life story, I was repeatedly reminded of how God has directed my path over the years. In good times and in bad times, He has been there. My faith is not embedded in a religion or a doctrine: it is a personal relationship. If you don't already know Jesus, I encourage you to ask Him into your life. You won't regret it. One advantage of growing older is that you can witness your faith become reality. You have lived it. I often tell people, "We are just passing through. Make the most of it."

The best part, the story that began on January 20, 1933 hasn't ended yet. The Christian life is a marathon, not a sprint, "We are cheered on by a host of witnesses that have gone before us" Heb 12:1. Stop along the way to help those that have stumbled just as others have helped us along the way so that we may all finish the race and receive the crown awaiting us in heaven. I can't wait to get up tomorrow morning to see what the Lord has in store for me. I have a feeling the best is yet to come. I wonder if there is a need for a fly fishing instructor in Heaven?

So, there you have it, folks.

l-r, Emilee, John, Pat, Luanne, and Grace Letarte

Made in the USA
Middletown, DE
06 September 2021